Exploring the Basic Income Guarantee

Series Editor
Karl Widerquist, Georgetown University in Qatar
Doha, Qatar

Basic income is one of the most innovative, powerful, straightforward, and controversial proposals for addressing poverty and growing inequalities. A Basic Income Guarantee (BIG) is designed to be an unconditional, government-insured guarantee that all citizens will have enough income to meet their basic needs. The concept of basic, or guaranteed, income is a form of social provision and this series examines the arguments for and against it from an interdisciplinary perspective with special focus on the economic and social factors. By systematically connecting abstract philosophical debates over competing principles of BIG to the empirical analysis of concrete policy proposals, this series contributes to the fields of economics, politics, social policy, and philosophy and establishes a theoretical framework for interdisciplinary research. It will bring together international and national scholars and activists to provide a comparative look at the main efforts to date to pass unconditional BIG legislation across regions of the globe and will identify commonalities and differences across countries drawing lessons for advancing social policies in general and BIG policies in particular.

More information about this series at
http://www.palgrave.com/gp/series/14981

Brent Ranalli

Common Wealth Dividends

History and Theory

palgrave
macmillan

Brent Ranalli
The Cadmus Group
Waltham, MA, USA

ISSN 2662-3803 ISSN 2662-3811 (electronic)
Exploring the Basic Income Guarantee
ISBN 978-3-030-72415-3 ISBN 978-3-030-72416-0 (eBook)
https://doi.org/10.1007/978-3-030-72416-0

This Palgrave Macmillan imprint is published by the registered company Springer Nature Switzerland AG
The registered company address is: Gewerbestrasse 11, 6330 Cham, Switzerland

To Vera, Benjamin, Alexander, and Oliver

Acknowledgments

It was my accidental discovery of the writings of Alfred and Dorothy Andersen during student days, and the correspondence and friendship that followed, that set me on the path to write this book. I remain grateful to Al and Dorothy.

I want to thank all those who reviewed part or all of the manuscript, or pointed me toward resources, or otherwise provided assistance and encouragement, including Peter Barnes first and foremost, and also Laura Bannister, Rahul Basu, Mitchell Beer, Nancy Birdsall, Joseph Blasi, Julie Blue, Nolan Bowie, James Boyce, Gregory Claeys, Maurie Cohen, Robert Costanza, Michael Crowder, Sofia Echegaray, David Ellerman, James Engell, Gregg Erickson, Gary Flomenhoft, Gwendolyn Hallsmith, Heidi Hammond, James Hansen, Paul Harnett, Annabelle Harris, Oliver Heydorn, Robert Hockett, Michael Howard, Steve Kahn, Peter Kalmus, Richard Krop, Sharon Kunde, Chris Mackin, Alison McIntyre, Christopher Michael, Emily Monosson, Jack Moriarty, Todd Moss, Jason Murphy, Paul Raskin, Sheila Regehr, Sarah Reibstein, Malan Rietveld, Mike Sandler, Nora Slonimsky, Larry Smith, John Stutz, Caroline Whyte, Michele Wick, Karl Widerquist, Sara Patton Zarrelli, and Alma Zelleke. Christopher Michael organized a session on the book-in-progress at the 2021 Rutgers University Kelso Workshop (recording at www.kelsoworkshop.org) in which Peter Barnes, Maurie Cohen, David Ellerman, and Sarah Reibstein graciously served as panelists.

Houghton Library provided access to the first edition of Paine's *Agrarian Justice* pamphlet, published in Paris in English. The Cadmus Group, Feasta, and the Ronin Institute provided encouragement and support.

I want to give special thanks to Karl Widerquist, whose guidance was pivotal in turning this research project into a book, and to Elizabeth Graber, Wyndham Hacket Pain, Uma Vinesh, and the rest of the team at Palgrave Macmillan for welcoming this title to the Exploring the Basic Income Guarantee series.

Finally, I thank my family, who endured my preoccupation and the stacks of books piled high and deep.

Praise for *Common Wealth Dividends*

"This book blazes a new frontier in economic thinking: the potential use of co-inherited wealth to pay lifelong dividends to everyone. It is must-reading for heterodox economists — and anyone else seeking ways to share the fruits of markets more equitably."

—Peter Barnes, *author of* Who Owns the Sky?, Capitalism 3.0, *and* With Liberty and Dividends for All

"This outstanding work by Brent Ranalli delves deeply into the morality, history, and practicality of the needed reform of dividends from our shared common wealth."

—Gary Flomenhoft, *Sustainable Minerals Institute, University of Queensland*

"A tour de force of the history of wealth sharing and a welcome addition to the literature exploring ways to mitigate the harmful effects of concentrated natural resources. Ranalli helps to keep alive the spirit of Alaska's pioneering Governor Jay Hammond."

—Todd Moss, *author of* Oil to Cash: Fighting the Resource Curse Through Cash Transfers *and* The Governor's Solution: Alaska's Oil Dividend *and* Iraq's Last Window

"This is a book I've been waiting for."

—Gregg Erickson, *economist, former director of research for the Alaska Legislature, trustee of the Robert Schalkenbach Foundation*

"Brent Ranalli's book *Common Wealth Dividends* represents a real advance in the literature on the idea of a universal basic income.... Too often the UBI is argued for as a streamlined welfare state redistribution program or as a pacification program for the AI-unemployed without realizing that there is a stronger rights-based argument .... This book fills in that gap in the literature."

—David Ellerman, *University of California at Riverside, author of* Property and Contract in Economics: The Case for Economic Democracy

"Much of [today's] inequality in wealth arises, directly or indirectly, from the appropriation of revenues associated with the ownership or control of land and natural resources by a small minority. In his important new book Brent Ranalli challenges this appropriation. Drawing on theoretical positions first articulated more than 200 years ago as well as actual current arrangements, he argues for broad sharing of the revenues arising from our common wealth, in land and natural resources and in other areas as well."

—John Stutz, *Tellus Institute*

"Brent Ranalli has been thinking about common wealth and dividends for a long time, and the result is this superb, concise book that covers the history and theory of common wealth dividends, from Thomas Paine's proposal for a tax on land to fund a lump sum payment and a pension, through Alaska's Permanent Fund Dividend, to current proposals for carbon dividends.... Particularly distinctive and illuminating is Ranalli's rich historical narrative of the origins of this idea and its practical realizations.... For anyone interested in common wealth dividends, and their relevance to current debates about inequality, poverty, and sustainability, this book should be considered essential reading."

—Michael Howard, *University of Maine, co-editor of the journal* Basic Income Studies

Contents

1 Introduction 1

2 Thomas Paine Solves the Perennial Problem of Land Reform 7

3 Natural Resources and the Alaska Model 31

4 Ecosystem Services and Carbon Dividends 57

5 Common Wealth Dividends, Generalized 101

Index 165

Abbreviations

APF	Alaska Permanent Fund
AUD	Australian Dollars
B.C.E.	Before the Common Era
C	Celsius
CAD	Canadian Dollars
Calif.	California
CBRS	Citizens Broadband Radio Service
CCL	Citizens Climate Lobby
C.E.	Common Era
CHM	Common Heritage of Mankind
CLC	Climate Leadership Council
CLEAR	Carbon Limits and Energy for America's Renewal
CO_2	Carbon Dioxide
Conn.	Connecticut
COP	Conference of the Parties (to the UNFCCC)
D	Democrat
D.C.	District of Columbia
Del.	Delaware
ESOP	Employee Stock Ownership Plan
ETS	Emissions Trading Scheme
FCC	U.S. Federal Communications Commission
FDIC	U.S. Federal Deposit Insurance Corporation
Fed	U.S. Federal Reserve
FIRE	Finance, Insurance, and Real Estate
Fla.	Florida
GDP	Gross Domestic Product

GWP	Global Warming Potential
ICANN	Internet Corporation for Assigned Names and Numbers
IMF	International Monetary Fund
IPCC	Intergovernmental Panel on Climate Change
ISA	International Seabed Authority
ITU	International Telecommunication Union
LTP	Labor Theory of Property
LTV	Labor Theory of Value
Md.	Maryland
MRV	Monitoring, Reporting, and Verification
NSI	Network Solutions Inc.
PFD	Permanent Fund Dividend
ppm	Parts Per Million
QE	Quantitative Easing
R	Republican
RGGI	Regional Greenhouse Gas Initiative
ROI	Return on Investment
S.C.	South Carolina
UHF	Ultra High Frequency
U.K.	United Kingdom
UNCLOS	United Nations Convention on the Law of the Sea
UNFCCC	United Nations Framework Convention on Climate Change
U.S.	United States
USD	United States Dollars
Va.	Virginia
Wash.	Washington
WBI	World Basic Income

List of Figures

Fig. 3.1	The five principles of fair extraction (*Source* The Future We Need. Courtesy Rahul Basu)	51
Fig. 5.1	Producer surplus	121

List of Tables

Table 4.1	Carbon pricing programs that recycle revenue	73
Table 5.1	Applicability of common wealth dividend concept to renewable and non-renewable resources	110

CHAPTER 1

Introduction

The subject of this book is a moral intuition: the idea that *there are some things in this world, like land and natural resources, that ought to be considered our common heritage, and that those who own or control these common-heritage resources owe some compensation to the rest of us who are excluded from their use*. This insight has struck many individuals separately over the years. In at least three significant cases, as we will see, it was discovered and fleshed out independently in different domains. Thomas Paine, hero of the American and French revolutions, applied the principle to the distribution of land in a 1797 pamphlet. Alaska Governor Jay Hammond applied it to oil in the 1970s, after an abortive attempt to apply it to fisheries. And entrepreneur Peter Barnes applied it to the atmosphere as a sink for greenhouse gases at the turn of the twenty-first century, inventing the concept of the carbon dividend.

As a work of history, this book tells the story of the discovery and rediscovery of this moral insight: how it has been put into action in some cases (like Alaska's Permanent Fund Dividend), and how there have been near-misses in others (like a similar proposal to ensure that all residents of Maine benefit from big bottlers' exploitation of Maine groundwater), and how at times the idea was buried (like the astonishingly long neglect of Paine's original proposal), and how we may be on the cusp of implementing it on a wide scale (in the case of carbon dividends). We are

B. Ranalli, *Common Wealth Dividends*,
Exploring the Basic Income Guarantee,
https://doi.org/10.1007/978-3-030-72416-0_1

interested in the question of why this moral intuition appears to belong only to the modern era. In fact, as we will see, it is a distinctly modern solution to a universal problem, a problem that societies around the world in every era have contended with. The problem, simply put, is *how to allocate land and natural resources*. Hunter-gatherers wrestle with it, and so did the ancient Greeks and Romans. It was Roman terminology (the *lex agraria*) that Paine used and adapted when explaining the problem and describing his solution. A fair allocation leads to harmony and stability; a grossly unfair allocation leads to revolution and the toppling of kingdoms and empires. In the modern era, a robust money economy makes possible the solution discovered by Paine and rediscovered by others: *control* of land and natural resources can readily be separated from the *financial benefit* that flows from the resources, and the latter can easily be shared equitably.

As a work of theory, this book seeks to generalize from the particular cases discussed and explore the possibility of articulating a general theory of common wealth dividends. We will seek to give the moral intuition as precise and universal a statement as possible. We will want to know: How far beyond land and natural resources can be it generalized? Does it apply, for example, to man-made commons? And we will want to know in what respects actual (and proposed) implementations of the principle differ from the ideal. (For example: Should the wealth that flows from Alaska's North Slope benefit only Alaskans, or should it benefit all Americans, or all global citizens? Or, on the other hand, do local communities in the vicinity of the North Slope have a greater claim than other Alaskans that should be respected?) We will not necessarily answer all of these questions definitively, but we will scope them out.

The topic of common wealth dividends is of particular interest at this moment because of the rising interest in the closely related topic of a *basic income guarantee*. Common wealth dividends are frequently viewed as one among several types of basic income variants, and proponents of basic income frequently point to the Alaska Permanent Fund Dividend as an example of a partial basic income in action. Champions of basic income, like 2019 U.S. presidential contender Andrew Yang, advocate for carbon dividends as well as more traditional forms of basic income.

As typically envisioned, a common wealth dividend program involves imposing a tax or fee on resource use. The revenue is placed in a trust, from which it is redistributed in equal amounts across an entire population. A traditional basic income program, on the other hand, is typically envisioned as a government program that makes universal payments to all citizens in an amount that ensures freedom from poverty. The funding can come from general taxation or other sources. Clearly, the two visions have much in common. The benefits are comparable. Even if a common wealth dividend program does not distribute sufficient wealth to *eliminate* poverty, it can make a significant difference (like what is termed a "partial" basic income) in reducing poverty and giving people more economic freedom and more options for managing their time and arranging their life—e.g., financing education, being able to take entrepreneurial risks, or being able to take time off from paid work to do volunteer work or to care for children or elders. And it is subject to some of the same sorts of criticisms and concerns as basic income. Critics and skeptics frequently ask: "will giving people unearned income make them lazy, will it undermine their work ethic?"

There are also critical differences, though, between common wealth dividends and a traditional basic income. Two differences are key. First, with common wealth dividends, the source of revenue is baked right into the plan. Common wealth dividends are dividends paid out from some definite source of common heritage wealth. So a common wealth dividend scheme is never subject to one of the objections frequently raised against traditional basic income: "where will the money come from; how can we possibly pay for it?" Second, with common wealth dividends, the redistribution of wealth is not just a nice idea, not just a piece of social engineering, it is a *right*. There are many ways to respond to the other objection already stated in the previous paragraph—the idea that giving people unearned income will somehow spoil them. One can cite the findings of studies from around the world showing that, as a rule, receiving additional money does not ruin people's lives but improves them in measurable ways. One can also point to the ready example of the wealthy, who live off of unearned income (interest and dividends) and on the whole appear to suffer no ill effects. But even if a critic is convinced that unearned income is bad for people, there is no arguing against giving people money that they have a *right* to. Common wealth dividends are a species of income that is a *right*.

Implementing a common wealth dividend program, therefore, ought to be less technically challenging and politically fraught than implementing a traditional basic income. It is quite possible that successful implementation of common wealth dividend programs, by demonstrating clear social and personal benefits and alleviating some of the fears of skeptics, will clear the ground for more ambitious traditional basic income programs.

But regardless of how one feels about a basic income guarantee, I hope that readers of this book will come away with a clearer appreciation of the compelling moral logic behind common wealth dividends.

Chapters 2 through 4 of this book tell the history of the discovery and (successful and attempted) implementation of the moral logic of common wealth dividends in three different domains. They are ordered chronologically. Chapter 2 is focused on land. It tells the story of Thomas Paine's discovery of a compelling modern solution to the perennial problem of maldistribution of land, and how his ideas went largely unheeded, even as others in Europe and North America continued to wrestle with the problem throughout the nineteenth century, and sometimes partially adopted or reconstructed his solution. The most prolific and influential of these successors, as many readers will know, was Henry George, who proposed taxing land values but using the revenue to fund government rather than distributing it as dividends.

Chapter 3 focuses on natural resources. The central story is the genesis and implementation of the Alaska Permanent Fund and the Permanent Fund Dividend. The APF and PFD, in due time, have been recognized as models worth emulating, and there have been many proposals, some successfully implemented, to replicate the PFD in other natural resource domains. This chapter delves even more deeply into the question *"why issue dividends?"* that separates the approach of Paine from that of George. Alaska Governor Jay Hammond and his allies had specific and compelling reasons to keep at least some of the resource revenue out of the state coffers and put it in the hands of people instead. We explore in this chapter the problem of the *resource curse*, and the function of dividends as an antidote to the curse.

The topic of Chapter 4 is ecosystem services, and the chapter is taken up almost exclusively with a single example, that of carbon dividends. The idea of charging those who pollute the atmosphere with greenhouse gases is a little bit more abstract than the idea of charging those who make private use of land or oil fields, but the underlying logic is the same. After Barnes articulated the idea of a dividend-issuing "Sky Trust" in a 2001 book, it was taken up by climate scientist James Hansen and others. Carbon dividends are currently the centerpiece of the two most energetic climate change mitigation lobbying movements in the United States, and will therefore almost certainly be on the agenda the next time the U.S. Congress takes up climate policy. In the meantime, over a dozen other countries and subnational jurisdictions have chosen to return some or all of their carbon pricing revenues to their citizens as tax rebates and in other forms. None of these programs have all the elements of a "Sky Trust" as envisioned by Barnes, but some come close—notably, the programs in British Columbia and Switzerland. This chapter takes a deep dive into the design of carbon pricing programs (which may take the form of either a carbon tax or a cap-and-permit system) and seeks to show that dividends will be an essential part of any successful, ambitious carbon pricing program.

Chapter 5 seeks to synthesize the insights of the preceding chapters into a general theory of common wealth dividends. We first integrate the idea of common wealth dividends from Nature into a general framework of natural resource governance and sustainability. Next we explore three candidate principles that can, perhaps, explain the moral imperative behind common wealth dividends and help generalize it beyond Nature to man-made sources of common wealth. One principle, from the domain of political theory, is the public trust doctrine. Another, from property theory, is the labor theory of property. A third, from microeconomics, is the concept of economic rent. This chapter also delves into several specific examples of man-made wealth that could be considered candidate sources of common wealth dividends. Finally, we examine some of the practical questions that arise in the design of common wealth dividend programs.

The book is global in outlook, but it also has somewhat of a U.S. focus, reflecting the author's knowledge and experience.

Those who write about common wealth dividends sometimes like to calculate the size of payments that could be expected if various resources were monetized. Since the bases for making such calculations change rapidly, and since the focus of this book is on history and theory rather than practice, we will not be performing such calculations. But we hope this book will be a useful grounding resource for those who do seek to put the idea into practice by tweaking existing institutions and creating new ones.

CHAPTER 2

Thomas Paine Solves the Perennial Problem of Land Reform

The winter of 1795–1796 was severe in France, and it came on the heels a record poor harvest. Inflation was rampant. With grave shortages of necessities, the death toll was appalling (McPhee 2006, 195; cf. Conway 1895, 4368; Keane 1995, 426; LeFebvre 1977).

Thomas Paine, hero of the American and French Revolutions, was nearly among the victims of that cruel winter. Living as a guest at the Paris home of U.S. Minister to France James Monroe, Paine was recovering from maladies acquired in a French prison, including typhus and a suppurating wound that doctors attributed to a "decaying rib." In September of 1795, Monroe wrote that he feared that Paine might not survive the year. In November, a visitor found him suffering "incurably." Rumors flew abroad that he had already expired (Hawke 1974, 315–316).

But Paine survived, and his health improved. In fact, over the course of that winter, the author of *Common Sense*, *The Rights of Man*, and *The Age of Reason* found the strength to take up his pen again and compose the last of his major works, the treatise that some scholars consider his neglected masterpiece: *Agrarian Justice* (Claeys 1989, 196).

Agrarian Justice was short and to the point. It was an antidote to the suffering of the masses. In brief, Paine argued that the Earth was given to all to enjoy, and therefore, if some few (the landowning classes) monopolized it, they owed compensation to the rest. Paine proposed taxing

B. Ranalli, *Common Wealth Dividends*,
Exploring the Basic Income Guarantee,
https://doi.org/10.1007/978-3-030-72416-0_2

bequests of land and distributing the funds among all citizens in the form of a pension for the aged and disabled, plus seed capital for every young man and woman on reaching the age of 21. This would not be charity, but a just compensation for forgoing a birthright.

"There are two kinds of property," Paine argued. "Firstly, natural property, or that which comes to us from the Creator of the universe—such as the earth, air, water. Secondly, artificial or acquired property—the invention of men." Equality in the second category is neither possible nor a legitimate goal, for people have different gifts and they put forth different levels of effort. But "equality of natural property … or its equivalent" is both possible and just (Paine [1797] 1945, I/606-607). "Every proprietor, therefore, of cultivated lands, owes to the community a *ground-rent* … for the land which he holds" (Paine [1797] 1945, I/611). He proposed that there should be "paid to every person, when arrived at the age of twenty-one years, the sum of fifteen pounds sterling, as a compensation in part, for the loss of his or her natural inheritance … : And also, the sum of ten pounds per annum, during life to every person now living, of the age of fifty years, and to all others as they shall arrive at that age."

This was a novel argument. It was, in fact, the first statement of the case for common wealth dividends, and it is frequently cited by advocates of basic income as a significant precedent. But although Paine's argument was novel, it grew out of longstanding debates among European thinkers on property, land, and political equality. Before we inquire about the legacy of *Agrarian Justice*, we ask: where does Paine's proposal fit in those earlier debates, what made it unique, and how did Paine come by it?

Natural Law and Property: A Question of Justice

The starting point of Paine's argument, that the Earth was given to all mankind in common, was a premise with which many previous property theorists agreed. In the Christian world, it commonly took the form of an argument from Genesis that the Earth had been bequeathed to Adam and Eve.[1] The "primitive communism" of Eden held fascination and appeal as an ideal state, while actual (unequal) property arrangements could

[1] On pre-Christian precedents, see Claeys (1987, 5–6).

be explained as a consequence of the original couple's fall from grace. Thomas Aquinas, the great systematic theologian of the High Middle Ages, captured this ambivalence. He argued that natural and divine law decreed that "all things are to be held in common and that there is to be no private possession" (as cited in Claeys 1987, 6). But in practice, communal living, "the apex of perfection," was an appropriate goal only for the most disciplined followers of Christ. For ordinary sinners, private property was an acceptable compromise arrangement. Holding a piece of mankind's common inheritance as private property, though, brought with it some obligations. "Men should not hold material things as their own but to the common benefit: each readily sharing them with others in their necessity." In other words, landowners had an obligation to aid the poor. Writes historian Gregory Claeys (1987, 7), quoting Aquinas: "In case the duties of property were neglected, this natural right [of the poor to sustenance] was so clear and strong.... that when the poor were in danger of starvation and had no other means of satisfying their need, they might 'take what is necessary from another's goods, either openly or by stealth,' and that this was not, 'strictly speaking, fraud or robbery.'"

Even as the basis for reasoning about property became more secular, the intuition that property holders had an obligation to the community persisted. Early "natural law" theorist Hugo Grotius postulated that the common ownership mankind originally enjoyed was not a positive community of goods, which requires active sharing, but a negative community of goods, in which the Earth and its fruits belonged to no one exclusively but were available for the taking. Grotius borrowed a metaphor from Cicero to explain the negative community of goods: "Although the theater is a public place, yet it is correct to say that the seat a man has taken belongs to him" (Salter 2001, 540). When mankind started cultivating the land, mixing his labor with God-given materials and storing produced items for future use, the concept of private property became necessary. Land became private property "by a kind of agreement," either explicitly by dividing it up or implicitly by occupying it (Salter 2001, 546). Against "Adamites" who argued that private property rights were granted to Adam and his descendants by God (and so were inviolable), Grotius viewed private property as a human convention, an agreement among people that had no divine sanction. And he retained the sense of communal obligation. "We must, in fact, consider what the intention was of those who first introduced private ownership; and we are forced to believe that it was their intention to depart as little as possible from natural equity.... Hence it follows, first, that in direst need the primitive right of use revives, as if community ownership had remained" (Salter 2001 549). In other words, the poor have a right to sustenance that trumps property rights.

Another seventeenth-century thinker whose views have had a lasting influence on modern conceptions of property is John Locke. Like Grotius and other natural law theorists, Locke believed that God granted the Earth to mankind as a negative community of goods, in which sharing was not required but individuals were free to take what was unclaimed. Unlike Grotius, Locke did not think that any consent, explicit or implicit, was necessary for a private individual to appropriate common property (Claeys 1987, 11). All that was necessary to justly claim a piece of the commons, since one had a natural right to the work of one's hands, was to mix one's labor with it: to till the field.

In his doctrine, Locke drew tight boundaries on the extent of private property that an individual could justifiably take and hold. First, Locke believed a person could take only as much as he could legitimately "enjoy," or make good use of: "As much as any one can make use of to any advantage of life before it spoils; so much he may by his labour fix a Property in. Whatever is beyond this, is more than his share" (Locke [1690] 2017, 290; cf. Salter 2001, 549). Second, Locke believed that an individual can fence off a piece of the commons as private property only when "enough, and as good" remains for others (Locke [1690] 2017, 288).

Like Aquinas and Grotius, Locke believed the propertied have an obligation not to allow the poor to starve. He labels this not justice but charity. "*Justice* gives every Man a Title to the product of his honest Industry," he writes, while "*Charity* gives every Man a Title to so much out of another's Plenty, as will keep him from extream want, where he has no means to subsist otherwise" (Locke [1690] 2017, 170, orthography as in original; cf. Salter 2001, 549).

Locke's restrictions on private property, if taken seriously, would quite seriously curtail the hoarding of land. The first restriction (that one may take only as much as one can "enjoy") would limit the size of estates. The second (that "enough, and as good" must remain for others) might prevent any new enclosures at all. But there is no indication that Locke took his own criteria seriously. He argued that one's property includes not only the land that one personally cultivates, but also that cultivated by *one's servant*—a loophole that great aristocratic estates can pass through

(Locke [1690] 2017, 289). And he took it as an article of faith that he lived in a world that was far from full, with prime land free for the taking. Like many of his countrymen, he turned a willfully blind eye to the land management practices of the American Indians, for example, to preserve the illusion that land in the New World was "unoccupied" and consequently free for taking by Europeans. In Locke, we see the schizophrenia of a thinker attempting to be logically and morally rigorous, but also committed to justifying the status quo.

In fact, each of the "mainstream" figures we have briefly looked at can be seen as attempting the same sort of balancing act, with greater or lesser success: attempting to reconcile an ethical ideal, that of equal rights to a divine gift of common land, with a practical reality, an inequitable distribution of land. There were other voices that made no such attempt at balance. On one hand were "Adamites" like the arch-conservative Robert Filmer, who justified the privileges of landowning classes and heaped scorn on the notion of equality (Tully 1982 55ff; Horne 1990 23ff). On the other side were radical egalitarians who sought to overturn the status quo. In the Christian world, there had long been communes and monastic orders and minor sects that sought to hold property in common. The Reformation saw a flowering of new experiments: e.g., the revolutionary Anabaptist commune of Thomas Müntzer and attempts by English "Diggers" to camp out on common land in defiance of gentry who would enclose it for private use. In Paine's own day, advocates of "agrarian law"—pooling land and holding it in common, or re-dividing it equitably—included Thomas Spence in England and François-Noël Babeuf in France.

The full title of Paine's pamphlet described agrarian justice as "opposed to agrarian law: and to agrarian monopoly." Like Aquinas, Grotius, and Locke, Paine can be seen as treading a middle course, attempting to reconcile actual property arrangements and an egalitarian ethical ideal. The "agrarian law" he rejects is the impractical collectivist or redistributist program of a Spence or Babeuf. The "agrarian monopoly" is the unjust status quo.

The middle course traced out by Paine is in some ways more satisfying than those of Aquinas, Grotius, and Locke. It is more militant than the others about the rights of the dispossessed. Not satisfied with mere sentiment, it specifies in concrete terms what the dispossessed are owed by the landowning classes. The compensation is articulated in terms of right, not charity. It applies universally, at all times, not just in times of famine and hardship. It promises to lift the dispossessed out of abject poverty, not merely to preserve them in poverty. And unlike Aquinas's solution, it does not demand breaches of law and ethics (theft and fraud) on the part of the poor.

On the other side as well, strangely enough, Paine's solution can be seen as the most reassuring to possessors of property. The demands that Paine places on property owners (or rather inheritors) are well-defined. There is no open-ended obligation to compromise property rights in times of hardship. There is no justification for fraud and theft (as in Aquinas) or implicit threat to break apart large estates (as in Locke).

The point is not that Paine was necessarily cleverer than Aquinas, Grotius, and Locke. In a sense, Paine's proposal was a product of its times. Paine's proposal could not have been conceived except in a robust money economy, where land parcels of every size could easily be valued in cash and where the financial system was capable of distributing paper money to every corner of a nation. Paine's proposal would have been inconceivable in Aquinas's day. It would have been a technical challenge even in Paine's own day. Our own twenty-first century commercial and financial infrastructure is well suited to it, as we will see illustrated in later chapters. But first we turn from the justice of Paine's proposal to other considerations that also recommend it.

Additional Considerations: Humanity and Sustainability

Paine takes pains to emphasize that his proposal is first and foremost a matter of justice, not charity or expediency. But he does make those other appeals as well.

He tugs at the heart-strings, asking his audience to look favorably on a plan that would relieve the misery of the poor. Civilization ought to be a blessing, he says. That the poor in civilized nations are actually worse off than were their ancestors who lived in a state of nature, worse off than the contemporary "savages" of North America, is a scandal that demands redress.

Furthermore, he argues that the reform he proposes will put modern European civilization on a more sustainable footing—sustainable in the sense of political stability. By eliminating abject poverty (the appeal to humanity) and reconciling the landowning and landless classes (the appeal to justice), it will stabilize the social order, forestalling further revolutionary conflict. "It is necessary as well for the protection of property as for the sake of justice and humanity," he writes, "to form a system that, while it preserves one part of society from wretchedness, shall secure the other from depredation" (Paine [1797] 1945, I/620). Europe is in a revolutionary mood, he reminds his readers. "When, instead of drawing forth admiration, [affluence] is beheld as an insult upon wretchedness;... it is only in a system of justice that the possessor can contemplate security.... When the more riches a man acquires, the better it shall be for the general mass; it is then that antipathies will cease, and property be placed on the permanent basis of national interest and protection" (Paine [1797] 1945, I/620-21).

Here too, Paine is echoing a theme that resounds in both ancient and modern history. Inequitable distribution of land creates political instability. In the twentieth and twenty-first centuries, land reform has been a cause championed by radicals and revolutionaries, and also embraced by conservative regimes to forestall revolutionary challengers (e.g., Tai 1974, Lipton 2009, Powelson 1988, and the extensive literature on land reform in specific countries and regions). Land reform was a live issue in ancient Greece and Rome. The constitution given by Lycurgus to the Spartans required farmland to be divided into equal plots, assigned to individuals by the state, and this arguably gave the constitution durability (Plutarch [c. 100 C.E.] 1914, 228–229). The reforms of Solon in Athens fell short of breaking up the large estates, and the resulting instability threw the polis into continued turmoil that ended (at least for a time) with the ascendency of the party of the smallholders and landless (Plutarch [c. 100 C.E.] 1914, 443–450; Tuma 1965; Powelson 1988, 27–28). Historian Elias H. Tuma reports that the land reforms introduced by the famous Gracchi brothers in Rome in the second century B.C.E. "used methods and responded to situations of disequilibrium and tension similar to those found in modern times, and similarly it was intended to prevent a revolution or political upheaval" (1965, 28).

Land reform has been a perennial issue because, as anthropologist David Graeber makes clear in his magisterial *Debt: The First 5,000 Years* (2011), equal distribution of land is unstable in a money economy. If farmers are obliged to incur debt, some proportion inevitably default, forfeiting their property and their liberty. Over time those with more resources at their disposal tend to swallow up those with fewer, leading to the creation of an owning class and an underclass—and political instability.

There is more than one way to relieve the problem of politically destabilizing land consolidation. The solution that evolved in ancient Mesopotamia, the region that pioneered both settled agriculture and a money economy, was for each new king on assuming the throne to declare a general amnesty. Debt-slaves were freed, and all property was returned to its original owner. And then conditions were permitted to deteriorate again. The ancient Israelites borrowed the practice in the form of regular "Jubilees." Every fifty years, slaves were released and property ownership was reset.

Lycurgus, in addition to dictating equal plots for the Spartans, excluded market transactions in agricultural land. Solon and his successors in Athens, in addition to destroying the *horoi* (the mortgage stones that marked indebted property), forbade citizens to lend to each other with liberty as collateral. Those in need of financing could borrow from the state; those with surplus capital had to direct their investments elsewhere: e.g., in trade and in setting up new colonies (Tuma 1965, 23, 26). Colonial expansion served as a safety valve for the Athenians, as it would for others as well like the Phoenicians and the Romans. It was not only an outlet for surplus capital, it also provided careers and new land for younger sons. But colonial expansion was, of course, not really a sustainable strategy. Even when pursued successfully, it only lasted until diminishing returns on the size of empire set in (Tainter 1990). And conquered populations only added to the dispossessed underclass. The practice of rewarding soldiers by settling them on the land of the conquered was a common one in the ancient world. Lycurgus's Spartans were settlers in hostile and enslaved territory. As Alexander the Great marched through Asia, he left in his wake a string of settlements populated by retired Macedonian soldiers. In the modern world, too, spoils went to victors. Paine's own landholding, a small farm on Long Island, was the confiscated property of a British loyalist, granted to Paine by the State of New York for his service in the struggle with Britain.

The "agrarian law" to which Paine referred in the title of his pamphlet derives from *lex agraria*, the term given to the Gracchi brothers' reforms in Rome. The program of Tiberius and Gaius Gracchus was to ease revolutionary discontent by capping the amount of public (conquered) land wealthy Romans could hold and distributing the excess in small plots to Rome's poor (Plutarch [c. 100 C.E.] 1921, 165; Tuma 1965 31ff; Powelson 1988, 37–38). In time, the expression "agrarian law" carried connotations of either redistribution in individual plots (as the Gracchi proposed) or holding land in common (like the Spartans).

What about non-agricultural societies? Are they subject to the same dynamic? In describing "what the state of society ought to be," Paine holds up the North American Indians as representative of the "natural and primitive state of man." In the natural state, according to Paine, "every man [is] born to property. He [is] a joint life proprietor with the rest in the property of the soil, and in all its natural productions, vegetable and animal" (Paine [1797] 1945, I/610-11). Here, Paine (like many other Europeans had done and would continue to do) idealizes Native American societies for his own rhetorical purposes. In fact, Native American societies too recognized rights to land use and had to deal with issues of apportionment. The Penobscots of the Maine coast, to take one concrete example, periodically redistributed the rights of member families to forage and hunt in different areas to reflect demographic shifts (NPS 2007, 34–36). And demographic pressure—demand for more and better land—was one reason why hunting, gathering, and horticultural societies went to war.

But there were important differences as well between foraging and farming societies. First, land had multiple uses in pre-agricultural societies, so the right to forage and the right to hunt game (for example) on one and the same parcel of land could be held by two different groups. Certain uses might be restricted to particular families or lineages, other uses open to all members of the tribe, and still others (such as rights of free passage) to all non-hostile comers. It would be fair to say that such customs persisted because they were "sustainable" in the sense that they promoted survival and minimized conflict. Second, with comparatively little effort spent "improving" (as Europeans would say) the land, it was relatively easy for Native American societies like the Penobscots to carry out periodic reapportionment. Third, most pre-agricultural societies were mobile and did not store surpluses, so there was not much "stuff" to quarrel over, not much opportunity for invidious distinctions between groups or classes to take hold. Those who held leadership roles generally did so by virtue of talent and charisma and exertion. Europeans who encountered such leaders often thought of them as aristocrats or royalty, but really they were what anthropologists call "big men." Big men lead by persuasion and example and gift-giving; they have no power to compel obedience. In fact, one common feature of pre-agricultural societies is what anthropologists call "counter-dominance." People resent being dominated, so they use tactics ranging from ridicule to ostracism and violence to rid themselves of self-proclaimed "leaders" who become domineering (Erdal and Whiten 1996; cf. Boehm 2009). Whereas oppressed agriculturalists are chained to a plot of land, hunters and gatherers can easily pick up stakes and leave an obnoxious "leader" behind. Not uncommonly, disagreements in foraging societies are resolved by fission rather than violence: groups split up and go their separate ways. So, in this sense, Paine is correct. It is ready access to the Earth and its fruits that enables pre-agricultural peoples to avoid the problems of economic inequality and political domination and revolutionary reaction that plague civilization.

What about "post-agricultural" society, our own industrial and post-industrial civilization? Already in Paine's day, England had begun to organize itself in ways that effectively disconnected economic security from landholding, and other so-called advanced societies were following close behind. In the discussion above, we have used the terms "land" and "property" practically interchangeably, because before the modern era land was the most salient type of property, the most important source of wealth and security. With the Industrial Revolution, and the advances in agricultural production and finance that went along with it, the nature of economic security changed. Now, large segments of the population could enjoy economic security from ownership and employment in sectors of the economy that had once been niches: commerce, manufacturing, finance, the professions, civil and military service. One result has been consolidation of arable land on a scale virtually unprecedented in history. To take the United States as perhaps the most dramatic example, the proportion of the workforce that engaged in farming fell from 41% in 1900 to less than 2% in 2000 (Dimitri et al. 2005). Since those who have left the land in the United States are on the whole much better off than the sans-culottes in Louis XVI's Paris, is Paine's argument (and that of Aquinas and the others) moot? Does unequal access to the Earth and its fruits no longer matter? Later chapters will take up the question of distribution of common wealth in domains other than land.

Paine's warning in *Agrarian Justice* that depriving the landless of their share of the common wealth would lead to political instability—no peace without (agrarian) justice—was prescient. In the same miserable winter of 1795–1796 that Paine was composing the pamphlet, the agitator François-Noël Babeuf—who had adopted the nom de plume "Gracchus" Babeuf—was leading a party of discontented radicals, organized as a "Committee for Public Safety," to secretly plot the overthrow of the new bourgeois republican regime and replace it with one built on agrarian law (on the Spartan model, with property held in common). By May 1796, the plot was discovered and the conspirators were arrested. Babeuf was executed a year later. When Paine finally published the pamphlet in 1797, he added a preface addressed to the French government, urging the new regime to adopt his plan as a way of preventing such revolts as Babeuf's from occurring again in the future.

Paine's Backstory

To understand how Paine reached that point, let us turn back the clock and trace Paine's career following the American War of Independence. The celebrated author of *Common Sense,* as we already noted, was granted a small farm after the war by New York State as a thank you for his services. There Paine turned to gentlemanly pursuits in science and civil engineering. Intent on spanning the Schuylkill River at Philadelphia with an iron bridge of his own design, in 1787 he travelled to Europe to obtain financial backing. As he commuted between Britain and France he was drawn into the politics of both countries. With the outbreak of the French Revolution, he took a lead role in propagandizing for the founding of a republic in France rather than a constitutional monarchy. In England, he countered the influential *Reflections on the Revolution in France,* written by his one-time ally Edmund Burke, with *The Rights of Man*, which justified the French Revolution and commented scathingly on the British aristocracy and monarchy. When Paine had a cheap edition of *Rights* published for consumption by the lower classes, the government's agents chased him out of the country, tried him in absentia, and sentenced him to hang.

Exiled to France, Paine immediately accepted a nomination to serve as a deputy in the French National Convention, where (with the help of translators) he took a prominent role, including serving on a constitution-drafting committee and urging the Convention to spare the life of King Louis XVI, who had been apprehended while attempting to flee the country. Louis was condemned to death by the narrowest of margins and executed. By this time, the Assembly had devolved into two implacable factions. The Jacobins, in combination with the Parisian mobs, got the upper hand and began arresting, trying, and executing members of the Girondin faction, with which Paine was associated. Paine retired to a hotel outside the city, wrote a treatise on his Deist faith, *The Age of*

Reason, and waited for his inevitable arrest, which came on December 28, 1793. The U.S. Minister to France, Gouverneur Morris, who was not an admirer of Paine, made only feeble attempts to help him. Paine was shut in the Luxembourg prison for ten months.

During the height of the Jacobins' Reign of Terror, dozens of people were carted off daily from the prison to the guillotine. "No man could count upon life for twenty-four hours," Paine later wrote (Hawke 300). Paine developed a fever and was moved to a larger cell where he was nursed by three Belgian prisoners. Whether through luck, or their own wits, or the cooperation of the prison guards, the four of them narrowly escaped execution. On the morning of July 25, 1794, a "4" was chalked on the cell door to indicate that all four occupants were to be executed. But the mark was placed on the in-facing side of the door, since the Belgians had prevailed upon the guards to leave the door open during the day to give the semi-conscious Paine some fresh air. In the evening, the door was closed and the mark hidden from the execution party, which passed them by. Within a few days, before the error had been discovered by the authorities, the Jacobin party had been overthrown and the executions ceased. Shortly after, Monroe arrived in Paris to relieve Morris as U.S. Minister, and before the end of the year he had sought and received Paine's freedom. As Monroe explained in a letter to James Madison, he had found Paine "in extreme ill health, without resources, & (affairs being unsettled) not without apprehension of personal danger.... From motives that will readily occur to you I invited him to take a room in my house" (Monroe 1898, 440).

Although Paine was reinstated in the Convention and given back pay, he did not make a habit of attending. He remained at Monroe's residence, and when his health permitted he continued to write. He did, however, make one more notable contribution to the work of the Convention. He was asked to comment on a new draft Constitution, and he appeared in person with an interpreter to present his views. On the whole, he approved the new document. But he strongly objected to the limitation on the franchise. Only former soldiers and those who were wealthy enough to pay direct taxes would be permitted to vote. "To deprive half the people in a nation of their rights as citizens" Paine considered a gross violation of republican principles and "a most dangerous experiment" (Paine [1797] 1945, II/590). We saw above the prescience of this remark: within a year the new regime faced a revolt by the disenfranchised under Babeuf.

When he composed *Agrarian Justice* in the winter of 1795–1796, after his bout with a recurrence of "jail fever" (typhus), he might still have had the defect in the French constitution on his mind. The franchise, he may have reasoned, ought to be universal. If a minimum of wealth is a prerequisite for the franchise, why then should not every person in the nation be endowed with a minimum of wealth? A commitment to political equality could have tugged Paine to invent and articulate the argument for economic justice in *Agrarian Justice* (Keane 1995, 427). The connection is not drawn explicitly in the essay itself, but it is in the dedication. Referring to the flaw in the new French constitution, he writes in the dedication that "the right of voting... is inherent in the word liberty, and constitutes the equality of personal rights. But even if that right (of voting) were inherent in property, which I deny, the right of suffrage would still belong to all equally, because... *all individuals have legitimate birthrights in a certain species of property*" (Paine [1797] 1945, I/607; emphasis added).

To be sure, *Agrarian Justice* was not the first time Paine had written on economic justice. The second part of *The Rights of Man*, written only a few years earlier, includes some of the same elements, but without the same forceful, compact argument. There, Paine argues a soak-the-rich policy of progressive taxation on large British estates, justified by the government's own logic of taxing luxuries. "If they or their champion, Mr. Burke,... can prove that an estate of twenty, thirty, or forty thousand pounds is not a luxury, I will give up the argument," he writes (Paine [1797] 1945, I/434). The tax will provide an incentive for landed families to distribute their wealth more equitably among younger sons and poor relations, of which "every aristocratic family has an appendage" (Paine [1797] 1945, I/439). It will also generate an enormous amount of public revenue. This revenue, in combination with savings from cessation of the wasteful, unnecessary war with revolutionary France, could be spent on a wide range of socially useful items, Paine argues, and he provides a list: not only pensions for the elderly and seed money for young adults (upon marriage, in this case), but also tax relief for the poor and middle classes, employment for the able-bodied poor, education for poor children, and funeral expenses for "persons traveling for work, or dying at a distance from their friends" (Paine [1797] 1945, I/440). There is no priority order or logical progression in this list; it appears to be off the top of his head. Land reform arguments do not make an appearance. What changed between *Rights of Man* and *Agrarian Justice*? Maybe simply a few years of reflection and reading. Maybe the prospect of death in the Luxembourg prison concentrated his mind wonderfully. Certainly the defect in the French constitution prompted him to think about the question of property in a new light, as we have seen. In any case, *Agrarian Justice* reflects a certain maturity in Paine's thinking. It takes elements of his earlier writing and compresses them into a unified, self-contained, and (it would seem) quite compelling argument.

The Reception of *Agrarian Justice*

Paine sat on the essay for over a year. He had considered deferring publication until the war between France and England should end, according to the preface he wrote for it in 1797—perhaps thinking that his proposals would get a more attentive hearing in peacetime. But he finally had it published in March of 1797, while making abortive plans to leave for America. (In the end, he judged it too risky for a fugitive from British justice to cross the Atlantic, and he returned from Le Havre to Paris.) The pamphlet was published in Paris and London, and soon editions appeared as well in Edinburgh, Dublin, Cork, New York City, Philadelphia, Baltimore, and Albany, as well as in German translation in Neustrelitz (Ranalli 2020).

Agrarian Justice reached a wide audience, but no government lifted a finger to put the proposal into effect. In France, Paine no longer had any official role once the Constitution of 1795 was established and a government (the Directory) was elected. Political and military developments continued at a frantic pace. Napoleon Bonaparte, whose phenomenal rise to power began around the time the pamphlet was written, consulted Paine on the best way to land an amphibious invasion of Britain, but Paine no longer had influence among the nation's legislators. When the war between Britain and France concluded in 1802 and it was safe for him to travel by sea, he departed for America.

In the United States, Paine was no longer a national hero. In the mind of the public, he had been tainted by French radicalism and atheism. A bitter open letter denouncing George Washington, who Paine believed had deliberately allowed him to languish in prison in France, did not win him sympathy. Paine was shunned by some: stagecoach drivers refused him service; mobs jeered and threw rocks (Nelson 2007, 312). Further, the defeat of the conservative Federalist party and the ascendency of the Democratic-Republicans in the 1800 election took some wind out of the sails of radicalism in the U.S. (Cotlar 2011, 158–159; Ranalli 2020). This was not fertile ground for new writings like *Agrarian Justice*, even if his handful of remaining friends, including President Thomas Jefferson, held sympathetic views.

British authorities continued to treat "Tom Paine" (as they called him derisively) and his ideas as dangerous and subversive. The war with Republican and Napoleonic France made British society more conservative on the whole. What radicals remained were divided on Paine's legacy. The bookseller John Bone wrote to a friend that the pamphlet "met the Approbation of those I have conversed with about it, and think it does win them to our Cause." Thomas Spence, on the other hand, denounced Paine's proposal as wholly inadequate to address the urgent needs of the poor. In *The Rights of Infants,* Spence proposed instead putting land in the hands of communities, to be administered for the benefit of all (i.e., "agrarian law" along the lines of Sparta and the late Babeuf).

After Paine

Although Paine's idea of issuing financial dividends based on common ownership of common resources was not revived as a serious policy proposal until the 1970s (in Alaska, as described in Chapter 3), others continued to explore the natural law principle of common inheritance, the principle that Spence attributed to "The Psalmist [and] Mr. Locke" as well as "Mr. Paine": that "God hath given the earth to the children of men, given it to mankind in common" (Spence 1797, Preface).

In addition to political radicals like Spence and Babeuf who would forcibly appropriate private lands and assign them to the community, there were reformers who sought to reach similar ends by more moderate means. One of the best-known of these was Robert Owen, the Welsh businessman and philanthropist who had demonstrated to a skeptical British public that it could be profitable to look after the basic needs of factory workers and their families. He built schools and a community center, phased out child labor, and established a sick fund for his employees. Dreaming even bigger, he envisioned entire townships managed as co-operative enterprises with land held in common. He travelled to the United States to establish a model planned community in Indiana that he dubbed "New Harmony." Like most utopian communal experiments of the era, this one was short-lived (Cole 1953).

When Owen passed through New York City on his way to Indiana, he was interrogated by the leader of the local land reform party, George H. Evans. Evans challenged Owen to explain how he proposed to obtain the land for the community. Owen replied, Evans reports, "that as he had always seen the land bought and sold, he expected to buy it." Evans was not satisfied. This method might work as a one-off for a wealthy dilettante, but it did not solve the more general problem of how the "hireling, landless tenant" would get his fair share of the soil. Evans's party had other ideas. They believed that "the land should never [be] bought or sold, any more than the bodies of men" (Masquerier 1877, 97).

According to Evans and other members of the New-York-based National Land Reform Association, the principle that the Earth belongs equally to all implies that each person ought to have an equal share of its surface. In practice, they thought that unoccupied land in the United States ought to be divided into parcels of no smaller than 40 acres, and that these should be assigned to landless households. There would be no buying and selling of land, no hoarding and speculation, and no taxation. Large estates would not be forcibly appropriated but would be divided among heirs until they reached the appropriate size. The land reform party put pressure on candidates for political office to endorse their principles. Their lobbying met with some success. Several states passed homestead exemption laws, protecting smallholders from forced sale due to debt. In 1862, the federal government passed a Homestead Law granting settlers in the Western territories the ownership of plots of limited size if they occupied and cultivated them. Despite these impressive achievements, Evans's friend Lewis Masquerier considered it a disappointment that the party never secured a law "limiting the quantity of land any man may purchase as their own" (Masquerier 1877, 96–97).

Evans was an admirer of Thomas Paine and *Agrarian Justice*. A printer by trade, in 1835 he published an edition of the complete political works of Thomas Paine, including *Agrarian Justice*. Despite his affinity for Paine, he claimed that he had formed his own views on land reform independently (Zahler 1941, 22).

In fact, Evans's practical program was more in line with the views of Thomas Jefferson than those of Thomas Paine. Jefferson had written that "the earth is given as a common stock for man to labor and live on. If for the encouragement of industry we allow it to be appropriated, we must take care that other employment be provided for those excluded from the appropriation. If we do not, the fundamental right to labor the earth returns to the unemployed." Jefferson had drafted a bill in 1778 for the Virginia legislature that would have granted 75 acres of Commonwealth land to (freeborn) landless married couples. And "the abolition of primogeniture, and equal partition of inheritances" Jefferson considered "the best of all Agrarian laws" (Katz 1977, 15–17).

Another approach to the problem of sharing the Earth as a common inheritance would be to levy a tax on land and have the government spend the money for the benefit of the community rather than (as Paine had proposed) distribute it as dividends. In Scotland, Patrick Edward Dove advocated this view. "This the true... theory of a *Nation*—that the soil belongs to it in perpetuity, and never can be alienated from it; and that he who gives the greatest rent for the soil becomes its cultivator, and pays the rent to the nation for the benefit of the whole community" (Dove 1854, 330). Like Paine's ground-rent, Dove's "rent" here is really a tax. (He proposes "to tax the rents of the soil" [Dove 1854, 329].) The London-based Irish reformer James Bronterre O'Brien offered a slightly different vision: the state should buy up land piecemeal as it becomes available on the open market and then charge an actual rent (Turner 2012, 15). But the most influential proponent of this type of solution was an American, an individual who became one of the most celebrated writers and reformers of the second half of the nineteenth century: Henry George.

George, like Evans and Paine, worked in the printing trade. He was haunted by the poverty he experienced in his own early adulthood and the poverty he witnessed all around him in the rapidly modernizing cities of Philadelphia, San Francisco, and New York. His major piece of writing, *Progress and Poverty*, sought to explain the connection between those two phenomena. How was it possible that progress in civilization—growth in population, advances in construction, manufacture, commerce, arts and sciences, etc.—was not ameliorating poverty, but (as he saw it) exacerbating it? The answer, he explains, came to him in an epiphany one afternoon while riding on horseback in the hills overlooking San Francisco Bay.

> Stopping for breath, I asked a passing teamster, for want of something better to say, what land was worth there. He pointed to some cows grazing off so far that they looked like mice and said: "I don't know exactly, but there is a man over there who will sell some land for a thousand dollars an acre." Like a flash it came upon me that there was the reason of advancing

> poverty with advancing wealth. With the growth of population, land grows in value, and the men who work it must pay more for the privilege. I turned back, amidst quiet thought, to the perception that then came to me and has been with me ever since. (George, Jr. 1900, 210)

Whereas John Locke thought so much land was available in the New World that "enough, and as good" would always be available for new comers, George stood face to face with the abyss of the Pacific Ocean. There was (or soon would be) no new land for the taking. With every step in the direction of "progress," the value of land would rise, deepening the economic disadvantage of the landless. And since, despite the best efforts of Evans and company, there was no cap on the amount a person could own and no restriction on buying and selling, land was ripe for speculation. An investor could make a killing by simply purchasing land like those hills around San Francisco, leaving it empty, and waiting for the value to rise. While speculation rewards the investor, it punishes those who would make productive use of the land if they could access it at a reasonable price—the farmer and the manufacturer and the skilled and unskilled laborers they would employ.

George's *Progress and Poverty* explained this dilemma and proposed a solution: a tax on land. The tax should be high enough to capture the full market value of the rent that a landlord could collect at that location. This would have several effects. First, it would eliminate the incentive to hoard and speculate in land. Holding land would be expensive, so people would only hold on to as much as they intend to use. Second, the tax would ensure that land is put to its most efficient, profitable use. This would dramatically expand economic activity. Third, the tax would raise revenue for the government. It would raise revenue so effectively that government would require for its support no other taxes or fees or customs or quotas. For this reason, George called his proposed land tax the "single tax."[2]

George was so focused on the benefits of siphoning rent out of the economy that the question of what to do with the tax money was secondary. He recognized that the funds raised via the Single Tax

[2] There is a vast literature on George and his legacy. Gaffney (1982) maps out the fault lines within the discipline of economics over George's central insight. The first articulation of the insight (possibly) may have been a 1782 pamphlet by the Scotsman William Ogilvie: "If the original value of the soil be the joint property of the community, no scheme of taxation can be so equitable as a land-tax, by which alone the expenses of the state ought to be supported until the whole amount of that original value be exhausted" (1782, 206).

belonged to the community and accepted that government should spend or manage it for the benefit of the community. But as contemporary critics pointed out, the tax would raise far more money than a nineteenth century government required. (Later critics, in the twentieth century, would make the reverse argument, that a "single tax" on land would not provide enough revenue to support the emerging welfare state [Cord 1965]. For all that, official statistics systematically undervalue land, so a land tax could generate much more revenue than is commonly acknowledged [Gaffney 2009].)

Why not distribute some of the money to members of the community as dividends? This was not on the top of George's mind when he wrote *Progress and Poverty*. George was a firm believer in the Protestant work ethic. Like many Americans, he thought work instilled virtues like discipline and frugality and self-respect. George considered land speculators degenerate in their idle accumulation of wealth, much as Paine and others had inveighed against the moral degeneracy of the European landed aristocracy. George was convinced that the Single Tax, by changing the incentives for landholding, would create economic conditions in which anyone with initiative would find work and opportunities for entrepreneurship.

Nevertheless, he did endorse Paine's concept of direct payment to individuals. In an April 1885 speech, he spoke of using Single Tax revenue to support widows, orphans, and the elderly. "Out of the fund..., we might, without degradation to anybody, provide enough to actually secure from want all who were deprived of their natural protectors or met with accident, or any man who should grow so old that he could not work." And he directly addressed the work-ethic objection. "All prating that is heard from some quarters about its hurting the common people to give them what they do not work for is humbug. The truth is, that anything that injures self-respect, degrades, does harm; but if you give it as a right, as something to which every citizen is entitled..., it does not degrade. Charity schools do degrade children that are sent to them, but public schools do not" (George [1885] 1901a, 217–218). A few months later, in July 1885, George repeated this argument: "I think a payment might well be made to the citizen when he came to the age at which active powers decline that would enable him to feed and clothe himself for the remainder of his life" (George [1885] 1901b, 228).

While there is no direct evidence that George read Paine, he left a hint in the April 1885 speech that some auditor or correspondent may have clued him in about Paine's pamphlet, or at least nudged him in the direction of Paine's thinking. "As an English friend of mine puts it: '*No taxes and a pension for everybody*;' and why should it not be?" (George [1885] 1901a, 217–218, emphasis added).

In fact, in the July 1885 publication, George goes even a step further. Pressed by an interlocutor to say what should be done with revenue in excess of what government requires, he answers: "If it were to appear that further extension of the functions of government would involve demoralization, then the surplus revenue might be ***divided per capita***" (George [1885] 1901b, 233, emphasis added). Here, George goes beyond Paine (who proposed only pensions and seed capital), right to the idea of universal dividends. This remark by George puts him directly in line with modern thinkers who will be discussed in the coming chapters. George's thinking, we must conclude, was more flexible than he has often been given credit for (see even this author's evaluation in Ranalli [2020]). Nevertheless, because George envisioned the tax being used first and foremost to fund government and Paine viewed payments to individuals as the primary purpose of the revenue, it still makes sense to maintain the conventional distinction between those two approaches as "Georgist" and "Paineite."[3]

George's land-tax proposal was enormously influential. Though he was ridiculed as a one-trick pony and a practitioner of an outmoded form of economics (viz., the classical economics of Adam Smith and David Ricardo) by the new guild of academic economists, whose math-heavy re-invention of the discipline would be dubbed "neo-classical," George heaped scorn on them in return as pedantic and out of touch with real-world problems. And he reached a much wider reading public than any academic economist. From the 1879 publication of *Progress and Poverty*

[3] Social conditions might have made the idea of direct payment to individuals a harder sell in George's time and milieu than Paine's. Paine's proposal that English and French nobles and gentry share a portion of their financial security with their poor tenants and neighbors would have run up against class-based prejudices, but *noblesse oblige* was a well-established principle. George's post-bellum United States was much less homogenous; it was a land of immigrants and a former slave society. It is likely that the idea of universal dividends, if George had pressed it, would have been met with race prejudice and xenophobia as well as class prejudice. Over a century later, although the United States has made progress in living up to its egalitarian ideals (and conversely, as European nations have become more ethnically diverse), racism and ambivalence about immigrants still present a stumbling block for basic income advocacy.

until his death in 1897, George was much in demand as a writer and speaker, both in the U.S. and abroad. He lent his weight to many pressing issues of the day, including free trade, women's suffrage, and the secret ballot. He ran twice for mayor of New York City.

George left behind a movement committed to studying and promoting his land tax, including perceptive readers who recognized the resemblance between George's proposal and Paine's (e.g., Ingersoll 1920, 94; Murray 1910). Some enthusiastic adherents gathered to found new townships expressly on Georgist principles, such as Fairhope, Alabama and Arden, Delaware. More broadly, Georgist principles have influenced tax codes on several continents. Denmark, Australia, New Zealand, and the "Asian Tigers" have made good use of them. Some cities in the U.S., like Pittsburgh, Allentown, and Harrisburg in Pennsylvania, have experimented with hybrid real estate taxes, levying a higher tax rate on land than on buildings and other improvements. Commentators generally agree that such policies encourage denser development and create more walkable neighborhoods, among other benefits (Andelson 2001). Contemporary Georgists acknowledge the trade-offs that may occur between land-tax-induced dense development and community preferences for extensive uses of urban land such as green-space and gardens (Hartzok 2010).

While Paine's proposal to distribute dividends from land rents made little headway for nearly two centuries and was largely overshadowed by the land-tax solution of Henry George, the principle was independently resurrected and applied to oil wealth in Alaska in the 1970s. The Alaska Permanent Fund and Permanent Fund Dividend, discussed in the next chapter, have become models, much-studied and imitated, of Paine-style common wealth dividends in action.

References

Andelson, Robert V., ed. 2001. *Land-Value Taxation Around the World: Studies in Economic Reform and Social Justice*, 3rd ed. Hoboken, NJ: Wiley-Blackwell.

Boehm, Christopher. 2009. *Hierarchy in the Forest: The Evolution of Egalitarian Behavior*. Cambridge, MA.: Harvard University Press.

Claeys, Gregory. 1987. *Machinery, Money and the Millennium: From Moral Economy to Socialism, 1815–1860*. Princeton, NJ: Princeton University Press.

Claeys, Gregory. 1989. *Thomas Paine: Social and Political Thought*. London: Unwin Hyman.

Cole, Margaret. 1953. *Robert Owen of New Lanark*. New York: A. M. Kelley.

Conway, Moncure D. 1895. The First French Socialist. *The Open Court* 387 (January 24): 4367–4369.

Cord, Steven B. 1965. *Henry George, Dreamer or Realist?* Philadelphia: University of Pennsylvania Press.

Cotlar, Seth. 2011. *Tom Paine's America: The Rise and Fall of Transatlantic Republicanism in the Early Republic.* Charlottesville: University of Virginia Press.

Dimitri, Carolyn, Ann Effland, and Neilson Conklin. 2005. *The 20th Century Transformation of U.S. Agriculture and Farm Policy.* USDA Economic Research Service. Economic Information Bulletin No. (EIB-3). https://www.ers.usda.gov/publications/pub-details/?pubid=44198.

Dove, Patrick Edward. 1854. *The Elements of Political Science...* Edinburgh: Johnstone & Hunter.

Erdal, David, and Andrew Whiten. 1996. Egalitarianism and Machiavellian Intelligence in Human Evolution. In *Modelling the Early Human Mind*, ed. Paul Mellars and Kathleen Gibson, 139–150. Cambridge, UK: McDonald Institute for Archeological Research.

Gaffney, Mason. 1982. Two Centuries of Economic Thought on Taxation of Land Rents. In *Land Value Taxation in Thought and Practice*, ed. Richard Lindholm and Arthur Lynn, Jr. Madison, WI: University of Wisconsin Press.

Gaffney, Mason. 2009. The Hidden Taxable Capacity of Land: Enough and to Spare. *International Journal of Social Economics* 36 (4, March): 328–411.

George, Henry. [1885] 1901a. The Crime of Poverty. In *The Complete Works of Henry George [Volume 8]: Our Land and Land Policy: Speeches, Lectures, and Miscellaneous Writings*, ed. Henry George Jr., 185–218. New York : Doubleday and McClure.

George, Henry. [1885] 1901b. "Land and Taxation: A Conversation between David Dudley Field and Henry George." In: *The Complete Works of Henry George [Volume 8]: Our Land and Land Policy: Speeches, Lectures, and Miscellaneous Writings*, ed. Henry George Jr., 219–240. New York : Doubleday and McClure.

George, Henry, Jr. 1900. *The Life of Henry George.* New York: Doubleday & McClure.

Graeber, David. 2011. *Debt: The First 5,000 Years.* New York: Melville House Publishing.

Hartzok, Alanna. 2010. Land Value Taxation: Panacea or Placebo. *The Land* (Winter 2009/10). Reprinted online at: https://commonground-usa.net/hartzok-alanna_land-value-taxation-panacea-or-placebo-2010.htm.

Hawke, David Freeman. 1974. *Paine.* New York: Harper & Row.

Horne, Thomas A. 1990. *Property Rights and Poverty: Political Argument in Britain, 1605–1834.* Chapel Hill: University of North Carolina Press.

Ingersoll, Chas H. 1920. Extract from Speech at the Thomas Paine Dinner, January 29, 1920. *The Single Tax Review* 20 (1, January–February): 94.

Katz, Stanley N. 1977. Republicanism and the Law of Inheritance in the American Revolutionary Era. *Michigan Law Review* 76 (1): 1–29.

Keane, John. 1995. *Tom Paine: A Political Life*. New York: Little, Brown and Company.

LeFebvre, Georges. 1977. *La France Sous le Directoire, 1795–1799*. Paris: Éditions Sociales.

Lipton, Michael. 2009. *Land Reform in Developing Countries: Property Rights and Property Wrongs*. London: Routledge.

Locke, John. [1690] 2017. *Two Treatises of Government*, ed. Peter Laslett. Cambridge, UK: Cambridge University Press.

Masquerier, Lewis. 1877. *Sociology: Or, the Reconstruction of Society, Government, and Property, Upon the Principles of the Equality, the Perpetuity, and the Individuality of the Private Ownership of Life, Person, Government, Homestead and the Whole Product of Labor*. New York: Published by the Author.

McPhee, Peter. 2006. *Living the French Revolution, 1789–1799*. New York: Palgrave Macmillan.

Monroe, James. 1898. *Writings of James Monroe*, vol. 2, ed. Stanislaus Murray Hamilton. New York: G. P. Putnam's Sons.

Murray, Ella M. 1910. Thomas Paine and the Land Question. *Twentieth Century Magazine* 2 (12, September): 522–525.

National Park Service (NPS). 2007. *Asticou's Island Domain: Wabanaki Peoples at Mount Desert Island 1500–2000*. Two Volumes. Prepared by Harald E. L. Prins and Bunny McBride. Boston, Massachusetts: National Park Service, Northeast Region Ethnography Program. Available at: https://www.nps.gov/acad/learn/historyculture/wabanaki.htm.

Nelson, Craig. 2007. *Thomas Paine: Enlightenment, Revolution, and the Birth of Modern Nations*. New York: Penguin.

Ogilvie, William. 1782. *An Essay on the Right of Property in Land*.... London: Printed for J Walter, Charing Cross.

Paine, Thomas. [1797] 1945. Agrarian Justice. In *Complete Writings of Thomas Paine*, two volumes, ed. Philip Foner. Citadel Press.

Plutarch. [c. 100 C.E.] 1914. *Lives, vol. I [Loeb Classical Library vol. 46]*, trans. Bernadotte Perrin. Cambridge, MA: Harvard University Press.

Plutarch. [c. 100 C.E.] 1921. *Lives, vol. X [Loeb Classical Library vol. 102]*, trans. Bernadotte Perrin. Cambridge, MA: Harvard University Press.

Powelson, John P. 1988. *The Story of Land: A World History of Land Tenure and Agrarian Reform*. Cambridge, MA: Lincoln Institute of Land Policy.

Ranalli, Brent. 2020. Thomas Paine's 'Neglected' Pamphlet: *Agrarian Justice*. *Journal for the Study of Radicalism* 14 (1, Spring): 167–190.

Salter, John. 2001. Hugo Grotius: Property and Consent. *Political Theory* 29 (4): 537–555.
Spence, Thomas. 1797. *The Rights of Infants* ... London: Printed for the Author, at No. 9, Oxford Street.
Tai, Hung-chao. 1974. *Land Reform and Politics: A Comparative Analysis*. Berkeley: University of California Press.
Tainter, Joseph. 1990. *Collapse of Complex Societies*. Cambridge, UK: Cambridge University Press.
Tully, James. 1982. *A Discourse on Property: John Locke and his Adversaries*. Cambridge, UK: Cambridge University Press.
Tuma, Elias H. 1965. *Twenty-Six Centuries of Agrarian Reform: A Comparative Analysis*. Berkeley: University of California Press.
Turner, Michael J. 2012. Chartism, Bronterre O'Brien and the 'Luminous Political Example of America.' *History* 97 (325): 43–69.
Zahler, Helene Sara. 1941. *Eastern Workingmen and National Land Policy, 1829–1862*. (Columbia University Studies in the History of American Agriculture, No. 7.) New York: Columbia University Press.

CHAPTER 3

Natural Resources and the Alaska Model

Since Paine's time, and since George's, economic security has come to depend less and less on landholding. As agriculture's role in the total economy has diminished, that of industry has grown. But the question of fair sharing of common wealth remains relevant, because common wealth includes the raw materials of industry as well as farmland.

Gifford Pinchot (1947, 324–325), the pioneering head of the U.S. Forest Service under Theodore Roosevelt, expressed this insight particularly well. "It is not easy for us moderns to realize our dependence on the Earth," he wrote. "As civilization progresses, as cities grow, as the mechanical aids to human life increase, we are more and more removed from the raw materials of human existence, and we forget more easily that natural resources must be about us from our infancy or we cannot live at all." But:

> What do you eat, morning, noon, and night? Natural resources, transformed and processed for your use. What do you wear, day in and day out—your coat, your hat, your shoes, your watch, the penny in your pocket, the filling in your tooth? Natural resources changed and adapted to your necessity.... What do you live in and work in, but in natural resources made into dwellings and shops and offices? Wood, iron, rock, clay, sand, in a thousand different shapes, but always natural resources. What are the

B. Ranalli, *Common Wealth Dividends*,
Exploring the Basic Income Guarantee,
https://doi.org/10.1007/978-3-030-72416-0_3

> living you earn, the medicine you take, the movie you watch, but things derived from nature?

The moral intuition expressed by thinkers from Aquinas through Paine and George is easily extended from arable land to other natural resources. Since natural resources are (to the religious thinker) a gift of God or (to the secular thinker) "found" rather than made, no one has a right to monopolize them. To hold them, yes. But all members of the community have a claim to benefit from them. (We will work toward a more precise expression of this moral intuition in Chapter 5.)

How should the community benefit from natural resources? Again, arguments can be imported from the land reform debates. Monopolizers of natural resources could be said to have a duty of charity (Locke). The dispossessed could have a right to take what they require in times of need (Aquinas). In theory at least, every individual could be given a plot of forest land or a vein of ore for his or her own use (Evans). The resource rent could be taxed away and used to fund government services (George). Or, along the lines proposed by Paine, the extracted resource rents could be distributed to members of the community as dividends.

The first working example of Paine-style dividends in action involved not land but petroleum. In the 1960s, it became clear that large oil reserves were present beneath state land in Alaska. Over the course of the 1970s, politicians and the public debated what to do with the expected windfall. In 1976, the legislature proposed and voters approved an amendment to the state constitution that established a Permanent Fund (the Alaska Permanent Fund or APF) in which a percentage of the oil wealth would be placed and invested. In the early 1980s, the legislature determined that a portion of the fund's annual earnings should be distributed to Alaska residents as a dividend. Since 1982, the Permanent Fund Dividend (PFD) distributed each October to residents has ranged in value from several hundred USD to over two thousand USD per person.

Here we ask: How did this dividend program come about? How well does it conform to the principles articulated by Thomas Paine? And how has it served as a model for other common wealth dividend programs?

As we will see, the creation of the APF and PFD was quite haphazard. (A "strange and bumpy ride," writes one insider, who asserts that "no one envisioned the final product until it was nearly complete" [Rose 2008, 205, 115].) That the APF and PFD were created at all was partly due to the fact that the programs meant different things to different people. The "Thomas Paine" interpretation is only one of several ways of looking at the PFD. But, it is an interpretation that fits quite comfortably. And we will see that in recent decades a wide range of other common wealth dividend programs have been established or proposed based on petroleum and other natural resources. Some have been directly inspired by the Alaska program. Others have come about, like the APF and PFD, as strange and happy accidents. All are motived at least in part by the concern for distributional justice articulated by Paine: that the common inheritance of a nation or community should equitably benefit the whole nation or community.

Origins of the Alaska Permanent Fund and the Permanent Fund Dividend

That oil should have been discovered under state land was not entirely a surprise. In the 1958 Alaska Statehood Act, Congress allowed the new state government to select and claim 103 million acres of federal land in the territory, on the condition that the state retain the mineral rights under those lands. (If the state tried to privatize mineral rights, the affected lands would be forfeited back to the federal government.) Among the lands selected by Alaska's first governor, on the advice of a savvy geologist, was a strip of Alaska's North Slope that included Prudhoe Bay on the Arctic Ocean. Until that point, oil companies had not shown interest in the area. But in 1968 it was confirmed that Prudhoe Bay lay atop the largest oil field in North America (Hammond 1994, 222; Rose 2008, 206).

Before the oil began flowing through the Trans-Alaska pipeline, Alaskans had more than a decade to debate what to do with the coming windfall. Some favored state spending to make up the deficiencies in services and infrastructure that Alaska suffered in comparison to other states. Others wanted to use the money to subsidize private-sector development in the state. Still others favored saving the money to cover future state budget shortfalls. The colorful Jay Hammond, a former fighter pilot, trapper, and wildlife biologist who served as Governor during the critical period of 1974–1982, envisioned a profit-sharing arrangement he called "Alaska, Inc." that would receive and invest 50% of state oil revenues and issue dividends to citizens, each of whom would be assigned one share for every year they have lived in the state. The APF and PFD, as they took shape, can be considered a distorted reflection of Hammond's original vision.

A critical consensus developed by the mid-1970s that the anticipated oil revenue should be saved rather than spent. This was in part a reaction to recent experience. In 1969, the state coffers had received a first infusion of 900 million USD from the sale of the oil leases. Some of the funds went to build schools and subsidize student loans. Some was spent on other types of infrastructure, including water and sewer, roads, and airports. It would be difficult to argue that the initial 900 million USD was not, on the whole, well spent. It served as an investment in the young state's infrastructure and human capital. Nevertheless, the public mood in the early and mid-1970s was chagrin that such an enormous sum could have been spent so quickly and completely. As Hammond (1994, 247) put it, the "nest egg" had been "scrambled." Therefore, the legislature had little trouble passing a bill, loosely modeled on Hammond's Alaska, Inc. proposal, to create a "Permanent Fund" into which a portion of annual oil revenues would be deposited for purposes of investment.

To the surprise of many, Hammond vetoed the bill. He put his weight behind a constitutional amendment instead. In public, he argued that the constitutional amendment was necessary because the legislature's Permanent Fund would likely be struck down by the courts as a violation of the existing state Constitution's prohibition of "dedicated funds." Later, he frankly admitted that his uppermost concern was not the courts but the legislature itself. Unless the Fund was enshrined in the Constitution, any future session of the legislature could change the law and divert the funds (Rose 2008, 128; Hammond 1994, 248).

The legislature placed the Permanent Fund on the ballot, and in 1976 Alaskan voters approved it. As noted above, its passage was eased by remorse over the spending of the initial 900 million USD from the lease. ("There are, of course, several other reasons to support the Permanent Fund," Hammond urged before the election, "but off the top of my head, at the moment, I can only think of 900 million!") The vagueness of the amendment language helped as well. The amendment did not specify how the money in the Permanent Fund was to be invested and how the earnings were to be used. Those who saw in the Fund a savings account, a development bank, a source of dividends, or simply a way of keeping the oil wealth out of the hands of spendthrift politicians all supported it (Groh and Erikson 2012, 21–22; Rose 2008, 130–131).

In 1977, battle lines were drawn. As recounted by Dave Rose (2008, 141ff), who went on to manage the APF in the 1980s, there were three main factions. The state Senate leadership, with the support of many in the business community, wished to use the APF as a development bank to finance in-state private-sector development. The House leadership, which considered a development bank little better than a slush fund, wanted to invest the oil money conservatively and professionally, to maximize financial returns. Governor Hammond continued to press for dividends to ordinary Alaskans.

Hammond was able to make common cause with the advocates of conservative investment. At the outset of his second term he put his full weight behind the resulting bill, and with the help of threats and logrolling it moved through the legislature quickly (in Hammond's words, "like a buttered watermelon") (Hammond 1994, 251; cf. Groh and Erikson 2012, 28–29; Rose 2008, 150ff). The 1978 law required the Fund to be invested prudently under the professional management of an independent body, the Alaska Permanent Fund Corporation. Fifty percent of each year's investment earnings would be distributed to state residents as a dividend. Dividends would be allocated according to the number of years of residence in the state (Rose 2008, 154).

The allocation of dividends by years of residence was almost immediately challenged in court. As the case wound its way to the Supreme Court of the United States, Hammond and his allies pushed through another version of the bill as a backstop, to take effect if the original plan was ruled unconstitutional (as it eventually was). The second version, which is the basis for the PFD that Alaska enjoys today, provided for annual dividends in equal amounts for all residents (i.e., all who have resided in the state for at least one year—with special provisions for students, military personnel, and others). It also included some other new provisions: It required that the fund be "inflation-proofed" by depositing a portion of each year's earnings in the fund's principal. And it made the amount of the dividend more predictable by basing it on a five-year average of the fund's performance rather than the current year's performance alone. Hammond was less enthusiastic about the second version of the bill. (With the plaintiffs of the court challenge in mind—the Zobels—he suggested with dark humor that the dividend checks should be mailed very slowly in alphabetical order [Hammond 1994 253].) But he again used the full weight of his office (he refers to "cajoling, compromise, prayer, and downright blackmail") to ensure its passage (Hammond 2001, 138). In time, he writes, he made his peace with the equal-dividends provision. It made new residents, who were a large proportion of the state's total population, enthusiastic defenders of the APF against politicians who tried to raid the funds in the early 1980s (Hammond 1994, 253; Rose 2008, 165; Groh and Erikson 2012, 33).

Interpretations of the APF and the PFD

In some respects, the ambiguity of the APF's purpose has never been resolved. Dave Rose (2008, 185) puts the matter starkly:

> One universally accepted goal was to prevent wasteful expenditure of a portion of Alaska's oil wealth. Yet … that was a negative goal: It told what the fund was *against*, but not what it was *for*. Years of legislative debate had considered and discarded a series of other potential goals, such as in-state lending, economic development, or community projects, but that process of elimination had left no single positive objective remaining.

One obvious candidate for a Fund objective, suggested early on, would have been to provide recurring income for state government when the state's oil fields were depleted (Rose 2008, 185). That would conform to textbook prescriptions for sustainably managing a non-renewable resource: transform it into a sustainable flow of investment revenue. (Sustainability will be discussed further in Chapter 5.) Such an objective would have enabled fund managers to establish clear goals and benchmarks for investment and savings. But it was never adopted. In Rose's words, "To this day, the fund's income is mandated for dividends, inflation-proofing, and whatever else the Legislature chooses to spend it on—it has no clear objective" (2008, 185).

In the minds of many state residents, there is no ambiguity about the APF's objective: it is simply a vehicle for generating dividends. The popularity of the dividend made the APF the "third rail" of Alaska politics. For decades, politicians understood that to propose raiding the Fund would be political suicide. But in the absence of an income tax (which was abolished in 1980), as oil revenues decline and the state's finances become increasingly dire it becomes more and more likely that the APF will eventually be tapped for the state's operating expenses. Since the APF has not been managed with that eventuality in mind, it is quite possible that the result will be either a drawing down of the principal, or elimination of the dividend, or both.

The purpose of the PFD itself is similarly ambiguous. The 1980 legislation creating the PFD cited three distinct purposes: to provide for equitable distribution of oil wealth, to reduce the rapid turnover in Alaska's population, and to encourage residents' interest in the management and expenditure of the fund (Rose 2008, 160).

The third named purpose is the one emphasized by hard-nosed insiders like Rose. Grassroots enthusiasm for the PFD is part of a many-layered defense that protects the APF from being raided by politicians. (Other defenses include the Fund's carefully cultivated transparency and its independent, non-partisan status, and a protective ring of other state agencies that deflect mischief by providing alternative financing options for public- and private-sector projects [Rose 2008, 146–149].)

The second named purpose—to reduce "turnover" in the state's population—is a peculiar one, given that the state was in no danger of losing residents in the late 1970s and early 1980s (in fact immigration was accelerating), and that the danger of attracting freeloaders to the state was a commonly heard argument *against* the idea of a dividend. This stated purpose may have been code for "rewarding old-timers," and also for "rewarding permanent residents" (reflecting ambivalence toward the transient labor force that built much of the state's oil and other infrastructure). The high cost of living that long-time residents had so long endured (Hammond 1994, 251), and the contributions many of them had made to building up the state (at the very least by paying income tax, before the tax was abolished), were all arguments to favor old-timers.

The first named purpose—providing for equitable distribution of the state's oil wealth among its citizens—was championed by Hammond and is widely accepted today as *the* purpose of the PFD (Cummine 2016, 169). Hammond and others frequently point to the State Constitution as justification for it. "The dividend concept," Hammond wrote, "is based on Alaska's Constitution, which holds Alaska's natural resources are owned, not by the state, but by the Alaskan people themselves" (1994, 251).

Actually, this is hyperbole. The Alaska Constitution does not say that the people *own* the state's resources. It speaks of management of natural resources "*belonging to* the State... *for the maximum benefit of* its people" (Article VIII, Section 2, emphasis added). A court case in the 1980s reinforced this point, flatly rejecting the argument (reminiscent of George H.

Evans) that each Alaskan "owns" a share of the state's oil and timber and fish and water and air (Rose 2008, 168–169).

Does it actually matter who owns the resource? In most nations, ownership of subsurface mineral rights is reserved for the government. The U.S. is a significant outlier: in many jurisdictions, whoever owns a piece of land owns any minerals that lie beneath it. In Alaska, it was simply one geologist's savvy intuition that placed Prudhoe Bay, and the rich oil deposit beneath it, in the hands of the state rather than the federal government or a private party.

The revenue that the State of Alaska receives from the oil companies that are contracted to do the actual drilling includes a combination of taxes, fees, and royalties. Some of those payments (e.g., royalties) are due to the state as the owner of the resource. But others are due to the state as a public trust. A severance tax, for example, represents compensation to the public for the irrevocable loss of the resource. The severance tax is paid to the state regardless of who holds title to the resource, and in this respect it reflects the same natural law principle that was applied deftly by Paine to the problem of land.

To answer the question, then: As a matter of principle, it does *not* matter who owns the resource. In theory, if Prudhoe Bay had been owned by private citizens or the federal government or even Alaska Native tribes, an Alaska Permanent Fund could still have been established on the basis of severance taxes and related revenue streams. It simply would have been a smaller fund.

This raises a related question: how much compensation should the public actually receive from private exploiters of common resources? Paine proposed an estate tax of 10%, a number he seems to have plucked out of the air. The amount of oil revenue that goes into the APF too is fairly arbitrary, and arguably too low. We will explore principled approaches to this question in Chapter 5.

In addition to the three justifications for the PFD enshrined in law, others have currency as well. Hammond, for example, saw Alaska, Inc. and the APF not only as a way to reward old-timers, but also as a way to support the poorest Alaskans, especially rural residents, including Alaska Natives (Rose 2008, 166).

Long before Hammond dreamed up "Alaska, Inc.," he had another vision: "Bristol Bay, Inc." Since 1950 or so, he had lived in the fishing community of Naknek on Bristol Bay. When he took on the part-time job of managing Bristol Bay Borough in 1965, he began scheming to improve local economic conditions. As he tells the story, "shortly after taking that job a cursory study showed almost ninety-seven percent of the payday from fish caught within our borough's boundaries left in the pockets of folks who lived elsewhere—mostly outside Alaska" (Hammond 1994, 152–153; cf. Hammond 2012a, 9). Outsiders, mostly commercial concerns based in Seattle, were harvesting the community's marine wealth, while residents lived in poverty. "We had no high schools, sewer or water systems, health care facilities, fire, police, or ambulance services. Garbage was dumped over the riverbank in hopes it would flush out with the ice during high spring tides" (Hammond 2012a, 9). Hammond's inspiration was to slap a use tax on fish. This would raise 97 USD for the borough from outsiders for every 3 USD paid by locals. Then, in order that the locals would be able to share in the bounty generated by the tax, he proposed that the revenue be assigned to a dividend-issuing investment corporation, Bristol Bay, Inc., of which every borough resident would own shares in proportion to their length of residence (Hammond 1994, 152–153).

Recalling the episode later, Hammond lamented that he must be a terrible salesman (Hammond 2012a, 12). Neither the prospect of righting an injustice against themselves nor the prospect of net financial gain could overcome residents' knee-jerk opposition to taxes.

Eventually, the borough's voters did approve the fish tax (when Hammond sweetened it by linking it to a simultaneous repeal of another tax) but not the investment corporation. The result was that the borough was deluged with new revenue and had no way to share it with residents except by providing services. As Hammond tells it, "our 'rural slum' had become what a *Fortune* magazine study called '*the richest municipality in the nation*,' in terms of borough income per person'" (Hammond 1994, 153, emphasis in original).

"Parkinson's Law," he continues, "asserts that government will always expand to spend every available dollar. The Bristol Bay Borough proved no exception." As the revenue grew, the Borough found ways to spend it, not necessarily wisely. Hammond the part-time manager and his full-time secretary, together, had once cost the borough only 20,000 USD per year. A couple of decades later, he reports, the borough's manager had a salary of 80,000 USD and a staff of 21 full-time employees, and property taxes had gone up rather than down (Hammond 1994 152–153; cf. Hammond 2012a, 10–11; Hammond 2004, 22).

From Hammond's perspective, Bristol Bay was a cautionary tale for all of Alaska. Alaskans should get a fair share of the wealth their natural resources generate. And an individual's share should go right into his or her pocket, Paine-style. If it is filtered through government instead, George-style, the people will not get equivalent benefit. The benefit will be distributed unevenly, according to political access rather than need or desert. The sheer quantity of it will invite waste and corruption. And the government that metastasizes in order to digest that quantity of money will eventually become a burden on the taxpayers.

Alaska did see waste, corruption, and metastasized government when the Prudhoe Bay oil money started flowing into the state coffers in the late 1970s. Rose (2008, 149) writes of "a money-intoxicated mood in the capitol" in 1979, "with legislators behaving like children who suddenly get their hands on more candy than they can possibly eat." And it got worse. "The 1980 legislature, for all of its unprecedented spending, was a model of fiscal conservativism compared to the Legislatures that followed in the next few years... In one fiscal year, six billion USD flowed from the Legislature. The public process disintegrated as the capital budget grew. Legislative staffers were able to obtain funding for projects with a word to a finance committee aide" (Rose 2008, 153, 162). During this period, two senators were indicted for bribery and using their office for personal gain (Rose 2008, 162).

From this perspective, the APF arrived just in time to sweep at least some oil money off the table—to moderate the corrupting influence of the giant sums in hand, and to preserve some wealth for orderly distribution to ordinary Alaskans over time.

Beyond Alaska

For many years, the APF and PFD were institutions of purely local interest. Then, around 1999, Hammond recalls, he started getting inquiries. A Danish television crew wanted to interview him for a show about resource development in Greenland, thinking the concept might be applicable there. A group from British Columbia called, interested in starting a Permanent Fund of their own. The World Bank invited him to Washington, D.C. for a briefing. "They had looked at every other state and nation with oil wealth and concluded that Alaska had done by far the best job of assuring that all [citizens] receive some benefit," he recalled. The World Bank representatives were captivated by the dividend program in particular, which they considered "a stroke of genius" (Hammond 2001, 140; Hammond 2012a, 47ff).

Experienced observers understand that oil resources are a mixed blessing. Some call them a curse. "I call petroleum the devil's excrement," one Venezuelan official told *The Economist* (as cited in Hammond 2012a, 5). "It brings trouble.... waste, corruption, consumption, our public services falling apart. And debt, debt we shall have for years." The Alaskan experience was comparable to that of Venezuela and many oil-rich developing nations. The influx of oil wealth caused a relaxation of fiscal discipline. Money was spent in ways that were wasteful, in ways that could not be sustained when the boom was over, and in ways that lined the pockets of insiders. The phenomenon has a name: the resource curse. It can arise from the sudden influx of wealth to the state from any number of sources; oil is the paradigmatic example.

The team of World Bank officials who interviewed Hammond in 1999 understood what is gradually being accepted as common wisdom: issuing a portion of a nation's resource-derived wealth as dividends can neutralize the problems of corruption and mismanagement associated with the resource curse. There are at least two reasons for this.

First, distributing dividends improves transparency and accountability in the handling of resource revenues. In the absence of dividends, ordinary citizens are unlikely to be aware of the sizes of the sums involved or to be able to detect mismanagement. On the other hand, if common wealth revenue is due to be distributed as dividends, every citizen has a direct stake in following the money trail and ensuring that there is no fraud or graft. This, recall, was one of the three goals enshrined in the 1978 law that created the PFD in Alaska: that the people should take an interest in how the oil wealth is managed. In Alaska, it has worked well. Stock watchers closely monitor how the APF invests. And under the watchful eye of constituents, Alaska politicians have not only refrained from (or, in some instance, been thwarted from) touching the principal of the fund, they have regularly plowed left-over earnings back into the fund rather than spending them.

Second, dividends hold out an even greater promise: they can eliminate the resource curse at the root and promote government efficiency and accountability.

By now, the dynamics of the resource curse (the observation that nations with significant mineral wealth tend to develop inefficient, authoritarian regimes and weak economies) are fairly well understood. The phenomenon can be observed as far back as the early modern era, when South American silver fueled a mighty Spanish regime that ended up chronically bankrupt and industrially backward. As silver poured into the royal treasury, nothing was easier than to raise and outfit magnificent armies and navies, lavishly patronize the Church, and multiply offices at court. Not dependent on its subjects for tax revenue, the Spanish crown largely neglected them. When the revenue from the American silver mines dried up, Spain was left a third-rate power chronically in debt, for the unwieldy and inefficient bureaucracy remained but the tax base, the domestic Spanish economy, was in shambles. Spain's main military rivals, England and the Netherlands, on the other hand, had no such easy access to cash. When they needed to raise armies and navies, they had to conscript and tax their own citizens. That was *not* an easy process; it involved real sacrifice and negotiation. The outcome was that the English and Dutch bureaucracies were lean and efficient, and government was much more responsive to the people's needs and desires.[1]

The distinction to be drawn is between governments that rely for support on taxing their citizens and governments with independent sources of wealth. A government that is dependent on its citizens for revenue will be subject to citizens' demands for efficiency and good governance. Furthermore, that government will have incentives to make investments (in infrastructure, education, health, etc.) that will foster a strong middle-class tax base. In other words, the obligations incurred by taxation amount to a social contract (see, e.g., Moss and Young 2009).

If a resource-rich nation wants to avoid the resource curse, therefore, it should follow Paine rather than George. It should not deposit resource revenues directly in the treasury, but should distribute as much of them as possible to the public. And then it should raise public funds by *taxing* the citizenry. The money—some of it—will end up in the nation's treasury,

[1] An entirely separate dynamic that is also sometimes discussed in the literature under the heading of the resource curse, a dynamic commonly known as the "Dutch disease," involves natural resource extraction affecting exchange rates and depressing other sectors of the economy. As introductions to the literature on the resource curse, see Humphreys et al. (2007) and Deacon (2011). See Landes (1999, 168ff) for an account of the early modern Spanish experience.

as before, but it will have reached that point by a route that obliges the government to be frugal with it and give a good account of it. Hammond understood that well. One of his greatest regrets from his time in the Governor's mansion was that he permitted Alaska's state incometax to be repealed under his watch (Creating Alaska 2004, 30). The PFD may have preserved some of the oil wealth from being squandered by government, but without an income tax the state was nevertheless in the same state of fiscal free-fall as early modern Spain—legislators were spending slush-fund money rather than their constituents' money, and were thus relatively unmoored from fiscal restraint. As oil revenues decline, legislators will undoubtedly find it necessary at some point to restore the tax, and that step will be extremely painful. It remains to be seen whether the APF will be raided, as a temporary expedient, before that happens. (As of 2020, journalists write that "Alaska [is] facing a billion-dollar budget deficit and a nearly-empty primary savings account" and anticipate painful cuts to education and Medicare spending [Herz 2020a]. In 2020, the government withdrew from the APF three billion USD, "the maximum amount that can be withdrawn sustainably" according to a formula adopted in 2018–2019 [Herz 2020b].)

Some analysts, like Sandbu (2006) and Shaxson (2007, 2008) and Pegg (2018), propose paying broad-based dividends directly out of revenue from fuel and mineral wealth, rather than investing it and distributing only the earnings as Alaska does. These authors offer perceptive accounts of the resource curse and show how broad-based dividends and taxation can cure it. But they fail to grapple with the question of sustainability, which we will take up in detail in Chapter 5. In brief, when extracting a non-renewable resource, it is in a society's long-term interest to use the revenue to capitalize some other kind of resource that can provide benefits in perpetuity, such as an APF-like investment fund. In the case of Alaska, it is easy to see that if the state had not capitalized the APF but simply dissipated the oil revenue in spending and/or dividends, it would be in far worse fiscal shape than it is today. Shaxson (2008, 13) suggests that setting up an APF-like fund would not be feasible in many third-world nations due to corruption. Corruption is a serious problem, but the objection is easily overcome. One could use of the very mechanism Shaxson proposes for distributing the resource revenue as dividends: require the companies performing the extraction to deposit the funds with an independent body (a "trusted international organization like a specialized United Nations or World Bank unit") without it ever passing through the hands of the government (2008, 17).

To date, no oil- or mineral-extracting nation has navigated a clear path out of the resource curse. Many nations do a good job of capturing resource rents for the public benefit (the Georgist path). Many, for example, have established sovereign wealth funds (SWFs) that convert non-renewable resource wealth into a stream of investment earnings along the lines of the APF (Cummine 2016). A handful of nations have done a commendable job of using resource wealth to benefit the citizenry, and even transferring a portion of the wealth directly to individuals. Norway offers socialized health care and unemployment benefits (Hammond 2012a, 48). Kuwait has fostered broad-based prosperity with generous subsidies for education and employment guarantees, as well as pensions and other types of transfer payments (El-Katiri et al. 2011). In 2008, Bolivia instituted an old-age pension system funded by 30% of natural gas revenues. The Bolivian government describes the pension scheme *Renta Dignidad* as "the concrete result of the nationalization of our natural resources" (Segal 2012a).

As APF has gained visibility, it has directly inspired some other efforts to establish common wealth dividends. For example: a portion of revenue received by Sherman County, Oregon, from commercial wind farms is paid out to landowners in the county. This dividend program was inspired directly by the example of the Alaska Permanent Fund. The dividend is intended in part to compensate residents for changing the appearance of the landscape, and in part to make the program more politically palatable by "sharing the wealth" even with landowners who do not have turbines on their property (and thus do not receive compensation directly from the wind power company). The dividend is paid to property owners, not to all residents. The amount is fixed arbitrarily at just under 600 USD annually, because more than that would require the county to prepare extra tax paperwork. Wind farm revenues not distributed as dividends go to meet other county expenses, including school programs (Barnes 2014, 128; Van Der Voo 2011).

Other efforts have not been implemented—yet. In Maine, entrepreneur and former state legislator Jim Wilfong set out on a quest in 2004 to create a Maine Water Dividend Trust, funded by a small tax on ground water extraction (Corrigan 2004). Water, he argued, is Maine's oil. Maine was, "if not a Saudi Arabia, at least a Texas or Alaska" (Wilfong 2007). The insight came to him, appropriately enough, in the shower (Tomales Bay 2006, 9). Was it right for big bottlers like Poland Springs to extract Maine groundwater for free and then sell it for large profits? As taxpayers and as homeowners, the citizens of Maine had for decades made sacrifices and incurred expenses to keep their underground treasure pristine. A household might easily spend ten or fifteen thousand USD on a septic system, and industrial wastewater management systems cost much more (Corrigan 2004). It hardly seemed right to give away that pristine water for free. On a road trip through East Texas, Wilfong had been struck by the poverty of oil-producing communities (Smith 2004). It was easy to imagine a similar future for Maine communities dominated by big out-of-state bottlers (Wilfong 2007). (In 1980, the bottled water giant Poland Springs was bought by the French company Perrier, and in 1992 Perrier was purchased by international food conglomerate Nestlé.)

Wilfong first approached his former colleagues in the legislature about implementing a surcharge on groundwater extraction (Corrigan 2004; Wilfong 2006). Finding little enthusiasm for the idea there, he then organized a referendum petition. The petition called for a surcharge of 3 cents per 20 fluid ounces (about 18 cents per gallon) on extraction by water bottlers. It would only apply to water extracted in excess of 500,000 gallons per year, so as not to place a burden on small businesses. The revenue would be placed in a special fund that would be used for a variety of purposes, including loans to small businesses, out-of-state investments, state and municipal water infrastructure maintenance, and water conservation education programs. Trustees would be permitted to issue a portion of each year's investment earnings to Maine taxpayers as dividends ("An Act to Preserve Maine's Drinking Water Supply" 2005). The dividend component of the plan was directly inspired by the Alaska PFD; Wilfong had learned of the PFD from a brother who lived in Alaska (Tomales Bay 2006, 9).

The big bottlers fought hard against the 2004 referendum petition (Wilfong 2005; Wilfong 2006). In the end, the grassroots campaign's organizers thought they had collected well more than the 51,519 signatures required to get the referendum on the ballot, but several thousand signatures were challenged and invalidated on technical grounds and the petition was denied (Quinn 2005; Wilfong 2006).

Following this defeat, Wilfong and his allies shifted tactics. In 2007 they sought a referendum to declare Maine's ground water a "public trust," which would give Maine's aquifers the same legal status that

Maine's lakes have had since colonial times. (For more on the public trust doctrine, see Chapter 5.) Ownership of Maine's lakes is assigned to the people of the state, and the government is charged with managing them for the benefit of all citizens and future generations. Declaring ground water a public trust would settle the question of who owns the water, and it would give the citizens of Maine and their representatives some leverage to say where bottlers can operate and how much they can extract (as opposed to the current system of "absolute dominion," also known in Texas as "the law of the biggest pump," which allows anyone to pump as much as they like from their own property, regardless of the effect it has on others who share the same aquifer) (Wilfong 2007). It could also be a first step toward requiring bottlers to pay market price for the water and toward issuing dividends to the water's legal owners (Wilfong 2006). The petition to place the issue on the ballot succeeded this time, but the referendum failed. Wilfong blamed the loss in part on undue influence of the big bottlers in shaping the wording that appeared on the ballot (Wilfong 2007).

Some of the most persistent and imaginative of common wealth dividend advocates have been found in nearby Vermont. In 2004, a team based at the University of Vermont led by ecological economist Gary Flomenhoft set out to prove that even a jurisdiction as resource-poor as the stony Green Mountain State could benefit from common wealth dividends (Flomenhoft 2012, 90). They drew up a long list of natural resources and other common resources that could be made to produce revenue for all citizens of Vermont, including fish and wildlife, forests, surface and ground water, minerals, wind, and land values. Based on preliminary calculations, Flomenhoft's team concluded that an aggressive state-level common wealth dividends program could provide financial benefits to Vermonters at least as generous as those currently enjoyed by Alaskans. (Of course, Alaska is working with one hand tied behind its back. If Alaska set out to fully capture in the APF the wealth that flows from the state's natural resources, annual dividends would be many times what they are today.) The team at the University of Vermont has found allies in the state legislature. A bill to create a Vermont dividend was introduced in 2007 and again in 2011 and 2012, so far without success (Flomenhoft 2012, 90; Farley et al. 2015, 72; Flomenhoft personal communication). In 2011, an attempt was made to impose a wholesale sales tax on water bottlers specifically, following an analysis that showed the bulk of the rents in Vermont's bottled water industry were being captured by the bottlers and not the well owners (Flomenhoft personal communication). The team has continued to explore and promote the idea of a Vermont Common Asset Trust (e.g., Farley et al. 2015).[2]

After the ouster of Saddam Hussein by the U.S.-led coalition in 2003, Iraq seemed to be a perfect testing ground for an oil-based dividend program on the Alaska model on a national scale. So thought journalist Steven Clemons. In a 2003 article printed in the *New York Times*, Clemons argued that setting up an oil revenue trust for the Iraqi people would be the perfect way to stabilize the country and to convince the world community of the U.S.'s high-minded motives. According to Hammond's memoirs, the former governor clipped the article and handed it to Alaska Senator Ted Stevens, who shared it with George W. Bush, who was "intrigued." Hammond recalled that "Secretary Colin Powell and members of Congress were on television advocating dividends as an Iraqi democratization effort" (Hammond 2012a, 50).

Similar calls to action were heard from the progressive think tank Foreign Policy in Focus and the conservative editorial pages of the *Wall Street Journal*, as well as the pages of the prestigious journal *Foreign Affairs* (Palley 2003; Smith 2003; Birdsall and Subramanian 2004). But however intrigued Colin Powell and President Bush may have been, the idea was not implemented either by the international occupying force or by the fledgling Iraqi government (cf. Hammond 2012b; Banai 2012).

Though the Iraq effort was stillborn, international interest in what is now called "the Alaska model" has grown. Specific concrete proposals have been made for Nigeria, Ghana, South Sudan, and India (Sala-i-Martin and Subramanian 2003; Moss and Young 2009; Hickel 2012; Basu 2018).[3] Studies have been made of the potential for run-of-the-mill oil-funded sovereign wealth funds (like those of Saudi Arabia and Kuwait and Norway and Venezuela) to be converted into dividend-issuing sovereign wealth funds like the APF (Cummine 2012, 2016). And—in the spirit of the Vermont study—other analysts have sought to measure the potential benefits of establishing common wealth funds even

[2] Flomenhoft (personal communication) notes that inspiration for the Vermont Common Asset Trust concept came not only from the Alaska Permanent Fund, but also from *Capitalism 3.0* by Peter Barnes (2006). Barnes's work will be discussed in Chapters 4 and 5.

[3] And there is one interesting early precursor: Brittan and Riley (1978) proposed distributing tradable shares in North Sea oil revenues.

in "resource-poor" third-world nations (Segal 2011; Segal 2012b; Ranalli 2016). The results are promising. Economist Paul Segal (2011) calculated that natural resource rents in developing countries, if distributed as dividends to citizens of those countries, could effectively halve global poverty rates.[4] In a 2015 paper of my own, I determined that the combined natural resource rents of the 146 countries receiving foreign aid in 2012 (1.4 trillion USD) was an order of magnitude higher than the 126.9 billion USD in official development assistance (ODA) contributed by major donor countries that year (Ranalli 2016). Currently, those 1.4 trillion dollars in resource rents, which by Paine's and Hammond's logic ought to go to the citizens of those developing nations (or, in the case of non-renewable resources, ought to be invested on their behalf), mostly go to corporations, to governments, and to elite households. If even a fraction of those resource rents were captured in dividend-issuing Permanent Funds in developing nations, the business of international development aid would be revolutionized.

> When such programs are established, financial assistance could be targeted more effectively to nations and subnational populations in most need. Funds targeted for poverty reduction could even be directed through [common wealth dividend] channels, producing gains of efficiency. Elimination of extreme poverty—item number one on the [international community's] proposed post-2015 development agenda—would become tractable. And once extreme poverty is eliminated, it is likely that other priorities will become more tractable as well. (Ranalli 2016, 11–12)

Both of these studies, in fact, understate common wealth revenue potential. They rely on World Bank resource rent figures for a discrete and by no means complete list of natural resources. And as the authors of the Vermont study understood, man-made commons could be tapped as well (to be discussed in Chapter 5).

[4] Natural resource rents are income attributable to the value of natural resources themselves, distinct from the effort that goes into extracting them. The concept of economic rent will be discussed in detail in Chapter 5. A striking illustration of the ratio of rent to total price in the case of mining is found in Basu and Pegg (2020). See also Basu (2020) for a compilation of calculations of public losses due to private confiscation of natural resource rents in nations around the world, and Warnock (2006) for an account of Canadian resource rents in global context (including their partial capture in provincial "Heritage Funds").

Recent years have seen a handful of national experiments in distributing natural resource wealth as universal dividends that have (apparently) *not* been directly inspired by the Alaska model, but have been home-grown, possibly nurtured by growing international awareness of the best practices associated with the Alaska model. One occurred in Mongolia. Mongolia has significant deposits of coal, copper, and gold. Between 2008 and 2014, Mongolia shared revenues from mining with the populace via universal dividends. The program had some bright spots (it succeeded in reducing poverty levels), but it was marred by fiscal irresponsibility and had to be discontinued. The immediate problem was that the amounts to be distributed were left up to the government to decide each year rather than determined by formula, and politicians overpromised. A deeper problem was that the Mongolian program distributed mining revenues directly, rather than investing the revenues and distributing dividends from investment earnings. This is an unsustainable proposition, as discussed above (and will be discussed in more detail in Chapter 5). Opinion polling suggests that the Mongolian people understood this. Polls showed a strong preference for the state to invest the mining revenue rather than distribute it (Yeung and Howes 2015; Angela Cummine 2016, 144–147).

Another site of experimentation has been Iran. Many oil-producing nations price fuels for domestic consumption artificially low, and this leads to market distortions. In 2010 Iran began to phase out its gasoline subsidies, which were some of the most extreme in the world, with domestic gasoline prices at around one twentieth of market rates (Guillaume et al. 2011, 6). To mitigate the resulting economic pain, the government rerouted the subsidies directly to the people. For ease of implementation, the government chose to make the program universal rather than attempting to target those most in need (Guillaume et al. 2011, 13–14). The subsidies were directed to households rather than individuals. Voluntary registration reached 80% on the eve of the launch, and within a few months fully 96% of households were registered and receiving the dividends (Tabatabai 2012, 22). Approximately 30 billion USD was distributed to households in the first year (Guillaume et al. 2011, 3), and it led to a significant reduction in poverty and income inequality (Salehi-Isfahani and Mostafavi-Dehzooei 2017, 2). Over the years since then, increases in fuel prices and increases in household subsidies have continued, not always in sync. Recent increases in household subsidies have been somewhat less universal and more targeted (Salehi-Isfahani 2019).

In recent years, an organization called The Future We Need has been pushing for global recognition of the principles discussed in this chapter. The Future We Need grew out of a campaign to reform mining in the state of Goa in India. Notable successes included Supreme Court rulings to halt illegal mining and to require mining policies to incorporate considerations of intergenerational equity, the establishment of a Goa Iron Ore Permanent Fund by state authorities, and, in 2019, the promulgation of a new National Mineral Policy for all of India that recognizes the status of minerals as a shared inheritance to which future generations have a claim (Goenchi Mati Movement [2016]; Basu 2019). The Goa Iron Ore Permanent Fund does not yet include a dividend component.

Rahul Basu, Research Director of the Goa Foundation, explains (personal communication) that it was around 2015, during litigation over mining in Goa, that he and colleagues became aware of the Alaska model (via Hammond's essay "Diapering the Devil," as reprinted in Moss [2012]). This crystalized their thinking and the recommendations they eventually presented to the Supreme Court and to the government. They have distilled the insights and the program into five easily communicated points (Fig. 3.1).

In addition to continuing to advocate in Goa and India, The Future We Need has launched several global initiatives. One, titled "Whose Mine Is It Anyway," is a campaign to reform international accounting standards so that royalties from mining will be treated in national budgets and statistics as receipts from the sale of a shared inheritance (and thus a form of capital stock) rather than windfall revenue. Another is to advocate for the Five Principles of Fair Mining (and other best practices) in the United Nations Environmental Programme's consultative meetings on mineral resource governance. A third is lobbying for a moratorium on deep sea mining and a reform of the international convention governing deep sea mining.

According to the United Nations Convention on the Law of the Sea (UNCLOS), the ocean floor in areas beyond national jurisdiction is designated a Common Heritage of Mankind (CHM). Activities that affect it are administered on mankind's behalf by an International Seabed Authority (ISA). Commercial exploration of deep seabed minerals has begun, and as of 2020 ISA is poised to authorize harvesting over a large swath of the Pacific (Hylton 2020). One problem is that ISA's mining regime is built on the conventional model of short-term private exploitation rather than intergenerational equity and rent capture for the public.

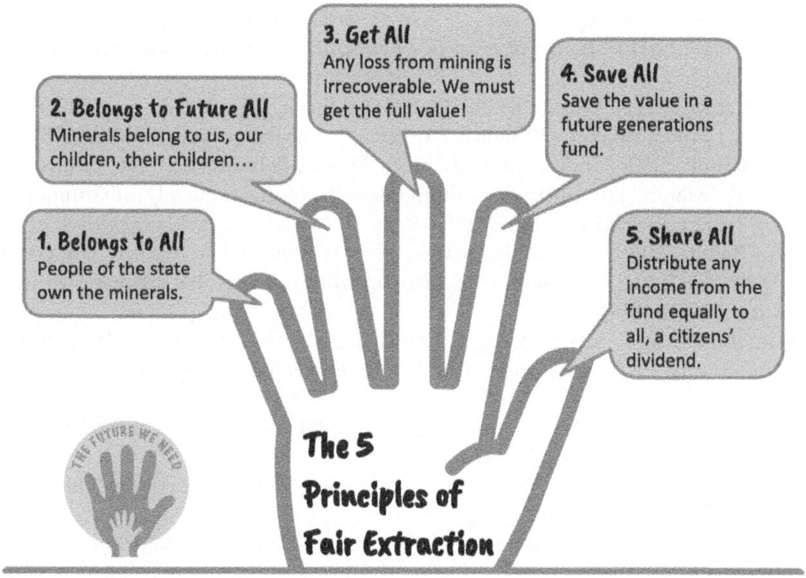

Fig. 3.1 The five principles of fair extraction (*Source* The Future We Need. Courtesy Rahul Basu)

Another is that this rush to harvest is likely to disturb ecosystems that are understudied, likely unique, and potentially of tremendous scientific and medical value. A third problem, compounding the others, is that ISA's mining regime is likely to be precedent-setting. Other resources that are formally designated as Common Heritage of Mankind or similar under international law, or are the subject of international negotiation and arguably candidates for such designation, include Antarctica, outer space, the Moon, high seas fisheries, and the human genome (Buck 1998; Buxton 2004; Buttigieg 2018).

References

An Act to Preserve Maine's Drinking Water Supply. 2005. *The Maine Woods* 8 (2, Late Summer): 4.

Banai, Ayelet. 2012 Freedom, Development, and Oil: Citizens' Capital Accounts for Iraq. In *Exporting the Alaska Model: Adapting the Permanent Fund Dividend*, ed. Karl Widerquist and Michael W. Howard, Chapter 16. New York: Palgrave Macmillan.

Barnes, Peter. 2006. *Capitalism 3.0*. San Francisco: Berrett-Koehler.
Barnes, Peter. 2014. *With Liberty and Dividends for All*. San Francisco: Berrett-Koehler.
Basu, Rahul. 2018. Will India Be First? The Future We Need. November 24. https://medium.com/@thefutureweneed/will-india-be-first-738f809d7f57.
Basu, Rahul. 2019. India: Minerals are a Shared Inheritance. The Future We Need. March 16. https://medium.com/@thefutureweneed/india-minerals-are-a-shared-inheritance-8278d98106eb.
Basu, Rahul. 2020. Global Estimates of Loss Rates. The Future We Need. April 5. https://medium.com/@thefutureweneed/global-estimates-of-loss-rates-21ae4b48b065.
Basu, Rahul, and Scott Pegg. 2020. Minerals Are a Shared Inheritance: Accounting for the Resource Curse. *The Extractive Industries and Society* 7 (4): 1369–1376.
Birdsall, Nancy, and Arvind Subramanian. 2004. Saving Iraq From Its Oil. *Foreign Affairs* 83 (4): 77–89.
Brittan, Samuel, and Barry Riley. 1978. A People's Stake in North Sea Oil. *Lloyds Bank Review* 128: 1–18.
Buck, Susan J. 1998. *The Global Commons: An Introduction*. Washington, DC: Island Press.
Buttigieg, Jean. 2018. *The Human Genome as Common Heritage of Mankind*. Stuttgart: ibidem-Verlag.
Buxton, Carol R. 2004. Property in Outer Space: The Common Heritage of Mankind Principle vs. He First in Time, First in Right, Rule of Property. *Journal of Air Law and Commerce* 69: 689.
Clemons, Steven C. 2003. Sharing, Alaska-Style. *New York Times* (April 9).
Corrigan, Mike. 2004. Wilfong Proposes Fee for Drawing Water for Large Bottling Operations. *Bridgeton News* (March 25).
Creating Alaska. 2004. Creating Alaska Oral History Interview: Jay Hammond. Interview Conducted January 24, 2004. University of Alaska. https://www.alaska.edu/creatingalaska/statehood-files/oral-history-transcripts/.
Cummine, Angela. 2012. Overcoming Dividend Skepticism: Why the World's Sovereign Wealth Funds are Not Paying Dividends. In *Exporting the Alaska Model: Adapting the Permanent Fund Dividend*, ed. Karl Widerquist and Michael W. Howard, Chapter 3. New York: Palgrave Macmillan.
Cummine, Angela. 2016. *Citizens' Wealth: Why (and How) Sovereign Funds Should be Managed by the People and for the People*. New Haven: Yale University Press.
Deacon, Robert T. 2011. The Political Economy of the Natural Resource Curse: A Survey of Theory and Evidence. *Foundations and Trends in Microeconomics* 7 (2): 111–208.

El-Katiri, Laura, Bassam Fattouh, and Paul Segal. 2011. *Anatomy of an Oil-Based Welfare State: Rent Distribution in Kuwait*. Kuwait Programme on Development, Governance and Globalisation in the Gulf States Research Papers (13). The London School of Economics and Political Science, London, UK. https://eprints.lse.ac.uk/55663/.

Farley, Joshua, Robert Costanza, Gary Flomenhoft, and Daniel Kirk. 2015. The Vermont Common Assets Trust: An Institution for Sustainable, Just and Efficient Resource Allocation. *Ecological Economics* 109 (January): 71–79.

Flomenhoft, Gary. 2012. Applying the Alaska model in a Resource-Poor State: The Example of Alaska. In *Exporting the Alaska Model: Adapting the Permanent Fund Dividend*, ed. Karl Widerquist and Michael W. Howard, Chapter 6. New York: Palgrave Macmillan.

Goenchi Mati Movement. [2016]. Intergenerational Equity Documents. https://goenchimati.org/intergenerational-equity-documents/.

Groh, Cliff, and Gregg Erickson. 2012. Chapter 2. In *Alaska's Permanent Fund Dividend: Examining Its Suitability as a Model*, ed. Karl Widerquist and Michael W. Howard. Palgrave Macmillan.

Guillaume, Dominique, Roman Zytek, and Mohammed Reza Farzin. 2011. *Iran—The Chronicles of the Subsidy Reform*. IMF Working Paper WP/11/167.

Hammond, Jay. 1994. *Tales of Alaska's Bush Rat Governor: The Extraordinary Autobiography of Jay Hammond, Wilderness Guide and Reluctant Politician*. Kenmore, WA: Epicenter Press.

Hammond, Jay. 2001. *Chips from the Chopping Block: More Tales from Alaska's Bush Rat Governor*. Kenmore, WA: Epicenter Press.

Hammond, Jay. 2004. Transcript of Creating Alaska Oral History Interview Conducted by Terrance Cole. January 24. Available at: https://www.alaska.edu/creatingalaska/statehood-files/oral-history-transcripts/.

Hammond, Jay. 2012a. Diapering the Devil: How Alaska Helped Staunch Befouling by Mismanaged Oil Wealth: A Lesson for Other Oil Rich Nations. In *The Governor's Solution: How Alaska's Oil Dividend Could Work in Iraq and Other Oil-Rich Countries: An Oil-to-Cash Reader*, ed. Todd Moss. Washington, DC: Center for Global Development.

Hammond, Jay. 2012b. The Ideal Solution: A Plan for Iraq? In *Exporting the Alaska Model: Adapting the Permanent Fund Dividend*, ed. Karl Widerquist and Michael W. Howard, Chapter 9. New York: Palgrave Macmillan.

Herz, Nathaniel. 2020a. Alaska Candidates Promise Painless Budget Cuts, But Experts Say Not so Fast. Alaska Public Media (October 8). https://www.alaskapublic.org/2020/10/08/alaska-candidates-promise-painless-budget-cuts-but-experts-say-not-so-fast/.

Herz, Nathaniel. 2020b. The Coronavirus Pandemic Is Devastating Alaska's Budget, and It Could Cost You Your PFD. Alaska's Energy Desk, KTOO

(April 2). https://www.ktoo.org/2020/04/02/the-coronavirus-pandemic-is-devastating-alaskas-budget-and-it-could-cost-you-your-pfd/.
Hickel, Jason. 2012. Constituting the Commons: Oil and Development in Postindependence South Sudan. In *Exporting the Alaska Model: Adapting the Permanent Fund Dividend*, ed. Karl Widerquist and Michael W. Howard, Chapter 8. New York: Palgrave Macmillan.
Humphreys, Macartan, Jeffrey D. Sachs, and Joseph E. Stiglitz, eds. 2007. *Escaping the Resource Curse*. New York: Columbia University Press.
Hylton, Wil S. 2020. History's Largest Mining Operation Is About to Begin. *The Atlantic* (January/February).
Landes, David S. 1999. *The Wealth and Poverty of Nations*. New York: W.W. Norton.
Moss, Todd, ed. 2012. *The Governor's Solution: How Alaska's Oil Dividend Could Work in Iraq and Other Oil-Rich Countries: An Oil-to-Cash Reader*. Washington, DC: Center for Global Development.
Moss, Todd, and Lauren Young. 2009. *Saving Ghana from Its Oil: The Case for Direct Cash Distribution. Institute of Economic Affairs*. https://www.cgdev.org/publication/saving-ghana-its-oil-case-direct-cash-distribution-working-paper-186.
Palley, T.I. 2003. *Combating the Natural Resource Curse with Citizen Revenue Distribution Funds: Oil and the Case of Iraq*. Foreign Policy in Focus Special Report, December 2003. https://www.thomaspalley.com/docs/articles/economic_development/natural_resources_curse.pdf.
Pegg, Scott. 2018. Oil to Cash in Somaliland: A Debate Whose Time Has Come. *The Journal of Modern African Studies* 56 (4): 619–643.
Pinchot, Gifford. 1947. *Breaking New Ground*. New York: Harcourt, Brace and Co.
Quinn, Francis X. 2005. Maine Ballot Initiative on Water Tax Falls Short of Signature Drive. Associated Press (December 20).
Ranalli, Brent. 2016. *Dividends for Development: A Role for Common Wealth Dividends (CWD) in the International Aid Agenda*. U.S. Basic Income Guarantee Discussion Paper No. 274. https://usbig.net/discussion-papers/.
Rose, Dave. 2008. *Saving for the Future: My Life and the Alaska Permanent Fund*. Kenmore, WA: Epicenter Press.
Sala-i-Martin, Xavier, and Arvind Subramanian. 2003. *Addressing the Natural Resource Curse: An Illustration from Nigeria*. National Bureau of Economic Research. Working Paper 9804. June. https://www.nber.org/papers/w9804.
Salehi-Isfahani, Djavad. 2019. New Cash Transfers May Lift 2 Million Iranians Out of Poverty. *Bourse & Bazaar* (December 2). https://www.bourseandbazaar.com/articles/2019/12/2/cash-transfers-increase-after-iran-protests-but-do-they-make-a-difference.

Salehi-Isfahani, Djavad, and Mohammad H. Mostafavi-Dehzooei. 2017. *Cash Transfers and Labor Supply: Evidence from a Large-Scale Program in Iran*. Economic Research Forum. Working Paper 1090. May.

Sandbu, M.E. 2006. Natural Wealth Accounts: A Proposal for Alleviating the Natural Resource Curse. *World Development* 34 (7): 1153–1170.

Segal, Paul. 2011. Resource Rents, Redistribution, and Halving Global Poverty: The Resource Dividend. *World Development* 39 (4): 475–489.

Segal, Paul. 2012a. How to Spend It: Resource Wealth and the Distribution of Resource Rents. *Energy Policy* 51: 340–348.

Segal, Paul. 2012b. Alaska's Permanent Fund Dividend as a Model for Reducing Global Poverty. In *Exporting the Alaska Model: Adapting the Permanent Fund Dividend*, ed. Karl Widerquist and Michael W. Howard, Chapter 7. New York: Palgrave Macmillan.

Shaxson, Nicholas. 2007. Oil, Corruption and the Resource Curse. *International Affairs* 83 (6, November).

Shaxson, Nicholas. 2008. Oil for the People: A Solution to the 'Resource Curse.' Paper Prepared for Association for Accountancy and Business Affairs Workshop (3–4 July). http://visar.csustan.edu/aaba/Shaxson2008.pdf.

Smith, Vernon. 2003. The Iraqi People's Fund. *Wall Street Journal* (December 22).

Smith, Taylor. 2004. Water World: Small Biz Advocate Jim Wilfong's Proposed Tax on Bottled Water Already Has Some Maine Businesses Up in Arms. *Mainebiz* (July 5).

Tabatabai, Hamid. 2012. From Price Subsidies to Basic Income: The Iran Model and Its Lessons. In *Exporting the Alaska Model: Adapting the Permanent Fund Dividend*, ed. Karl Widerquist and Michael W. Howard, Chapter 2. New York: Palgrave Macmillan.

Tomales Bay Institute. 2006. *The Commons Rising: A Report to Owners*. https://community-wealth.org/content/commons-rising.

Van Der Voo, Lee. 2011. Money Blows in to a Patch of Oregon Known for Its Unrelenting Winds. *New York Times* (May 30).

Warnock, John W. 2006. *Selling the Family Silver: Oil and Gas Royalties, Corporate Profits, and the Disregarded Public*. Parkland Institute and Canadian Centre for Policy Alternatives - Saskatchewan Office. November.

Wilfong, Jim. 2005. Nestlé Goons Disrupt Signature Collection Drive. *The Maine Woods* 8 (2, Late Summer): 7.

Wilfong, Jim. 2006. Who Owns Maine's Water? *On the Commons* (February 14).

Wilfong, Jim. 2007. Who Owns Maine's Water? *Counterpunch* (March 28).

Yeung, Ying, and Stephen Howes. 2015. *Resources-to-Cash: A Cautionary Tale from Mongolia*. Australian National University, Development Policy Centre. August.

CHAPTER 4

Ecosystem Services and Carbon Dividends

In previous chapters, we talked about dividends deriving from tangible assets: land and natural resources. In this chapter, we take a step in the direction of abstraction and talk about gifts of Nature that are less tangible: ecosystem services.

Ecosystem services are natural processes that sustain human life and well-being. They include, for example, the purification of groundwater by soil and mineral matrices, the breakdown of wastes by microbes, the fertilization of flowering food crops by insects, the protection against harmful radiation provided by stratospheric ozone, the provision of oxygen and absorption of carbon dioxide by plants, and the suppression of harmful microorganisms by communities of beneficial microbes (Daily et al. 1997). Though we call them "services" and rely on them as such, these processes do not exist for our sakes. We evolved to rely on them, or we lucked into them (Schröter et al. 2014).

In everyday life, we typically give ecosystem services little thought. It is their absence that makes their value stand out in stark relief. When we organize human activity on the International Space Station, or plan colonization of Mars, we must recreate them or find substitutes—new substrates in which to grow food, new ways to store and decompose wastes, new ways to shield our tissues from ionizing radiation, new ways to provide fresh water and maintain livable temperatures, etc. Though we

B. Ranalli, *Common Wealth Dividends*,
Exploring the Basic Income Guarantee,
https://doi.org/10.1007/978-3-030-72416-0_4

may find technological substitutes for some ecosystem services on small scales—e.g., water filtration technologies that work in a space station can also be used by households on earth—many ecosystem services on planet earth have literally no substitute—either not at scale, or not at all.

Because ecosystem services are largely invisible to us, it is all too easy to degrade them unthinkingly. For most of our species's history, our small numbers and modest technological prowess limited the extent of damage we could do. Over the course of generations we could degrade soils (e.g., the desertification of the so-called Fertile Crescent that once was a breadbasket of the ancient world [Hughes 1994, 35]), but we could not disrupt global ecosystem services. Today—roughly, since the Industrial Revolution—it is different. We can indeed disrupt ecosystem services on continental and even global scales. Examples of recent and current disruption include the decline of honeybee populations (which provide the service of plant fertilization), depletion of stratospheric ozone (which protects us from UV radiation), the general ongoing global loss of biodiversity (with many ramifications, including ecosystem instability and the impoverishment of medical research), and the climate crisis.

Mitigating ecosystem service disruption generally requires some kind of coordinated action by the public sector. This can be simple command-and-control regulation, or it can involve establishing some kind of a price signal to make the normally invisible services visible in the market economy.

We can draw a direct analogy between putting a price on water drawn from an aquifer, as discussed in the last chapter, and putting a price on the dumping of waste products into ecosystems—like, to take a concrete example, the use of a septic system to safely dispose of human waste. In the language of systems science, one is a "source" and the other is a "sink." They can both be treated as renewable resources. The aquifer will have a natural average recharge rate; drawing groundwater out of it faster than the recharge rate will deplete and degrade the aquifer. Similarly, a septic system (by which we mean not just the engineered portion of the system, but the entire system of soil and microbes and other living creatures that digest the wastes) has a maximum flow rate, above which it will be overwhelmed and fail. Establishing a price per gallon of water extracted, or per toilet flush, can help regulate the rate of extraction or injection, and by carefully adjusting the price one can ensure that the rate of extraction or injection stays below the safe threshold.

In Chapter 2, we saw that charging a tax to extract the rental value of land provides societal benefits, leaving as a secondary (but important) question what to do with the revenue raised. Similarly, if the campaign to place a modest surcharge on extraction of Maine groundwater described in Chapter 3 had succeeded, the initiative would have provided the direct social and ecological benefit of helping to ensure the sustainability of the resource, and a secondary benefit or raising revenue. So too: if we charge per toilet flush, we provide a public good—ensuring that human waste does not overwhelm the natural system that digests it—and we also have a fund of money that needs to be allocated.

Ordinarily those who maintain septic systems do not charge per flush. But the same logic of regulating waste flows with price signals can be applied in other cases, and one of those will be very salient in the twenty-first century: namely, the flow of man-made greenhouse gases into the atmosphere. This example will be the primary focus of the present chapter. The atmosphere can only absorb so much carbon dioxide (CO_2) and other greenhouse gases before dangerous levels are reached. In order to limit emissions, a price can be put on them (in dollars per ton of CO_2-equivalent), sending a market signal to encourage conservation and development of alternative energy sources. A program like this would provide societal benefits—potentially averting catastrophic warming—and would also raise revenue. And by the same logic presented in previous chapters, that revenue could be distributed as universal dividends. In fact, as we will see, there are additional reasons for distributing revenue as dividends in the case of carbon pricing.

Peter Barnes's "Sky Trust"

In 1996, entrepreneur Peter Barnes left the private sector to take up a fellowship at the San Francisco-based think tank Redefining Progress. In the 1970s, he had co-founded a company that installed solar energy systems on apartment buildings. Then, in the 1980s, he co-founded a socially screened mutual fund (Working Assets) and a phone company (Credo Mobile) that donates a portion of its revenue to progressive non-profit organizations (Barnes 2001, 5–10). By the time he stepped down as president of Working Assets, Barnes had come to believe that socially responsible companies were not enough to fix capitalism or save the planet. In Barnes's words, it was necessary to reconfigure the "operating system" of capitalism by protecting and sharing common wealth (Barnes 2006, 8ff).

Common wealth, for Barnes, includes gifts of Nature and also human-made assets like our systems of law and finance (to be discussed Chapter 5). Barnes stressed the importance of common wealth in underpinning our market economy, and noted the extent to which its privatization and overexploitation leads to ever-widening inequality and disruption of nature. The solution to both these grievous systemic flaws, it seemed to him, lay in establishing structures independent of the private and public sectors to both safeguard common wealth and share some of its economic value among everyone equally.

Barnes was aware of the work of Henry George—in 1971 he had written a review of *Progress and Poverty* for the *New Republic* (Barnes 1971)—and this may have shaped his thinking about common wealth. But Paine's *Agrarian Justice* and the Alaska PFD were not yet on his radar as he began fleshing out his ideas at Redefining Progress (personal communication). He learned about the Alaska PFD in time to discuss it in his first book from this period; both the Alaska PFD and Paine's pamphlet are discussed in the second book (Barnes 2001; Barnes 2006).

From the very beginning of Barnes's work on common wealth, he recognized that climate change was a pressing contemporary problem to which his solution was particularly well-suited. His first book from this period, *Who Owns the Sky?* (Barnes 2001), proposed what he called a "Sky Trust"—essentially what we know today as "cap-and-dividend."

Just as the United States faced a crisis at the end of the nineteenth century, Barnes wrote, when the frontier closed and "the era of free land, or at least very cheap land, came to an end," so now we face a new transition: from the era of "free sky" to an era of "scarce sky" (Barnes 2001, 30). Addressing the global warming crisis will require constraining the amount of carbon dioxide and other greenhouse gases we release into the atmosphere. And when fossil fuel users compete for the right to emit, they will bid up the price of emissions. That money will go somewhere. Where it goes will depend on how property rights are allocated.

> The Sky Trust is one of three possible kinds of [carbon cap-and-permit] systems. In one kind, the initial emission rights are given to historic polluters for free. In a second kind, the initial emission rights are sold to polluters by the government, which uses the revenue as it sees fit. In the third kind, the initial emission rights are given to a trust, which periodically sells them to polluters and distributes the revenue to all citizens equally. (Barnes 2001, 62)

Why choose the third option? First, there is the argument of collective ownership of the commons, reminiscent of Paine: a Sky Trust would return the economic value of the atmosphere's scarce waste absorption capacity "to its rightful owners—ourselves" (Barnes 2001, 64). Second, since poorer households use less energy than wealthier households, the Sky Trust would function like a progressive income recycler. And finally, the dividends would offer benefits frequently touted for basic income (though Barnes did not use that term). For example, by supporting stay-at-home parents and children it will be pro-family; it will represent an investment in children (Barnes 2001, 65).

Barnes proposed that the Sky Trust's mission be first and foremost to administer a steadily declining limit on greenhouse gas emissions and secondarily to pay dividends from the revenue (Barnes 2001, 63–64). He proposed that for the first ten years of its existence a certain percentage of the Trust's revenue be reserved for a "transition fund" that would help communities (e.g., in coal country) cope with the dislocations of the shift away from fossil fuels (65–66).

Developed independently of the proposals of Thomas Paine and Jay Hammond, Barnes's vision of a "Sky Trust" extends the logic of those proposals to a new domain. And it provided inspiration and sometimes a template for other carbon-price-and-dividend schemes that followed.

James Hansen's "Fee-and-Dividend"

In June of 1988, the U.S. Senate's Energy and Natural Resources Committee heard testimony from scientists about global warming. Against the backdrop of a record heatwave, the event made headlines. "Global Warming Has Begun, Expert Tells Senate," the *New York Times* announced on its front page (Shabecoff 1988; Block 2008). These Senate hearings are widely remembered as a landmark in national environmental policy. They "can be said to have started the public and political discussion over global warming" (Fox 2020) and "marked the date on which climate change became a national issue" (Brulle 2018). The most electrifying testimony came from Dr. James Hansen, director of NASA's Goddard Institute for Space Studies. Dr. Hansen (the "expert" singled out by the *Times* in the headline) came out with a direct and bold statement.

> The earth is warmer in 1988 than at any time in the history of instrumental measurements.... There is only a 1 percent chance of an accidental

> warming of this magnitude.... Altogether the evidence that the earth is warming by an amount which is too large to be a chance fluctuation and the similarity of the warming to that expected from the greenhouse effect represents a very strong case. [It is] my opinion, that the greenhouse effect has been detected, and it is changing our climate now. (Hansen 1988, 39–40)

By his own account, Hansen was not a natural public speaker (Hansen 2009, 60–61). But what he had learned as a scientist convinced him that he had to speak out, and he continued to do so after the famous 1988 Senate testimony. Crude attempts at censorship by political appointees over the years only raised his public profile (e.g., Hansen 2009, 112ff). As a working scientist in a prestigious post, who was willing to speak to general audiences about the practical implications of climate science, Hansen had a large soapbox. So when Hansen began plugging the idea of carbon dividends, they became part of the national conversation.

A brief introduction to climate science and policy is in order here. The basic physics of the *greenhouse effect* was discovered independently by Eunice Foote in America in 1856 and John Tyndall in Britain in 1859 and its implications for a changing climate were described by the Swedish scientist Svante Arrhenius in 1896 (Weart 2003, 3–7; Schwartz 2020). Light energy from the sun warms the earth system. The earth, in turn, radiates some energy back out into space at infrared wavelengths (so-called *radiant heat energy*). The progress of this infrared radiation is slowed by interaction with certain components of the atmosphere—*greenhouse gases*—that are composed of three or more atoms and can therefore absorb the infrared as vibrational energy. When such a vibrating molecule releases the energy again as infrared, it will be in a random direction that could just as easily be back toward the earth's surface as toward the upper atmosphere. The more greenhouse gas molecules are present in the atmosphere, the more of these interactions there will be, the longer it will take for infrared energy to escape the earth system, and the higher will be the equilibrium temperature of the atmosphere and the whole earth system. Greenhouse gases include carbon dioxide, methane, water vapor, and a variety of industrial chemicals.

For as long as our species has existed on the planet, through ice ages and interglacial periods, carbon dioxide has been present in the atmosphere within the range of about 180–280 parts per million (ppm). Since the Industrial Revolution, the burning of fossil fuels (coal, oil, and natural gas) has increased the amount of carbon dioxide in the atmosphere well beyond that range. The average concentration in 2019 was 409.8 ± 0.1 ppm, an increase of 2.5 ± 0.1 ppm over the previous year (Blunden and Arndt 2020). The underlying physics of the greenhouse effect predicts that average global atmospheric temperatures will track average global atmospheric carbon dioxide concentrations, and this is what we see in the modern era (most clearly on decadal time scales). We see it in the geological record as well. Episodes of rapid warming generally feature a positive feedback loop between these two variables: rising temperatures release deposits of organic material into the atmosphere as carbon dioxide, which generates more warming. Before humankind was around, the feedback loop was generally triggered by exogenous events: e.g., slow changes in the amount of incoming energy from the sun, due to irregularities in the earth's orbit. The current warming episode may be the first in the planet's history in which the trigger is an initial boost in carbon dioxide. (If we were not pumping greenhouse gases into the atmosphere, the natural solar energy cycle would today have us in a period of slow cooling lasting thousands of years.)

The processes that remove carbon dioxide from the atmosphere operate on timescales ranging from decades (e.g., dissolving into ocean water) to hundreds of millennia (mineral formation). According to the Intergovernmental Panel on Climate Change (IPCC), somewhere between 15% and 40% of carbon dioxide released today will likely still be in the atmosphere in a thousand years, depending on the total quantity released (since uptake by the ocean will slow down as it becomes saturated) (Ciais et al. 2013, 472, Box 6.1). The "global warming potential" (GWP) of other greenhouse gases is usually given in units of carbon dioxide equivalent. Methane, for example, is a more potent greenhouse gas than carbon dioxide. One kilogram of methane released to the atmosphere will be responsible for as much warming as about 28 kilograms of carbon dioxide over the course of a hundred years, so it can be described as having a GWP_{100} of 28 (Myhre et al. 2013, 714, Table 8.7). Since methane does not persist as long as carbon dioxide in the atmosphere, most of the warming it produces will take place over a relatively short period of time. If we consider a period of 20 years, methane has a GWP_{20} of around 84 (Myhre et al. 2013, 714, Table 8.7). (Note that most atmospheric methane degrades by oxidizing into carbon dioxide, so as it disappears it has a second life as another greenhouse gas.) Water vapor is another potent greenhouse gas. Warmer air can hold more moisture than colder air, so water vapor is likely to amplify anthropogenic warming on average, but the amount of water vapor present in the atmosphere is highly variable and depends on local conditions, making it difficult to model in detail. (Cloud formation, which in some cases will dampen and in other cases will amplify warming, poses a similar modeling challenge.)

The average global atmospheric temperature has risen about 1 degree Celsius (1.8 degrees Fahrenheit) since before the Industrial Revolution (IPCC 2018, par A.1). The international agreement forged in Paris in 2015 calls for "keeping a global temperature rise this century well below 2 degrees Celsius above pre-industrial levels and [pursuing] efforts to limit the temperature increase even further to 1.5 degrees Celsius" in order to ward off the worst effects of warming (UNFCCC, n.d.). Although emissions to date do not commit us irrevocably to warming above 1.5 °C (IPCC 2018, par A.2.1), under "baseline" or business-as-usual scenarios the IPCC projects warming well above the Paris benchmarks.[1] The voluntary commitments made at the Paris meeting are nowhere near what will be required to achieve the benchmarks.

Effects of warming, many of which are already visible, include the following:

- *Ecosystem change and loss of biodiversity*. Plants and animals migrate to higher altitudes and higher latitudes to stay in the climatic zones for which they are adapted. Many fail to migrate quickly enough or find suitable habitat.
- *Rising sea levels*. Warming releases water trapped in ice and also causes seawater to expand. This endangers island and coastal communities.
- *Changing weather patterns*: Higher average temperatures and the ability of warmer air to hold more moisture contribute to the frequency and severity of extreme weather events, including heat waves, droughts, heavy precipitation, and floods (See, e.g., Walsh et al. 2014). Regions currently well suited for agriculture become

[1] "Emissions to date" are as of 2018 (IPCC 2018, par A.2.1). The business-as-usual scenarios are those labeled RCP6.0 and RCP8.5 in IPCC's Fifth Assessment (IPCC 2014). Under these scenarios, the IPCC projects warming in the range of 1.4–3.1 °C or 2.6–4.8 °C, respectively, over current levels by the end of this century (IPCC 2014, Box 2.2 and Table 2.1). That is 2.4–4.1 °C or 3.6–5.8 °C, respectively, over pre-industrial levels, which ranges are well over the goal of no more than 1.5 or 2 °C.

less so. Some high-latitude areas may become better suited for agriculture, but conditions for growing (e.g., temperature regimes and availability of water) may be erratic.

- *Water shortages*: Mountain icepack melts, depriving some of the globe's most populous regions of reliable water supplies.
- *Ocean warming and acidification*: The world's coral reefs, once biodiversity hotspots, have already experienced severe bleaching and are in jeopardy of recurrent bleaching events and die-off under business-as-usual emission scenarios (Heron et al. 2018). Bleaching is caused by heat stress and also, increasingly, by acidification: as elevated levels of carbon dioxide migrate from the atmosphere to the oceans, they change the oceans' pH and interfere with natural processes like the ability of shellfish to take up the calcium they require to construct their shells.

As global warming continues,[2] we might reach tipping points that could greatly speed up the warming itself or its deleterious effects. For example: if melting permafrost releases carbon dioxide from deposits of organic material long locked away in ice, the result could be a warming

[2] Climate change is a complex and technical subject, but one about which all twenty-first century citizens should have some understanding. For those who want to learn more, I can do no better than to echo the recommendations offered by climate scientist Peter Kalmus in his award-winning 2017 *Being the Change: Live Well and Spark a Climate Revolution* (302):

In increasing level of reader commitment:

1. Yoram Bauman and Grady Klein's *The Cartoon Introduction to Climate Change* (Island Press, 2014).
2. The U.S. National Academy of Sciences and Royal Society's *Climate Change: Evidence and Causes* (National Academies Press, 2014), a 36-page overview available at https://www.nap.edu/catalog/18730/climate-change-evidence-and-causes.
3. David Archer's *Global Warming: Understanding the Forecast, 2nd ed.* (Wiley, 2011), a college text for non-science majors.
4. "The Princeton Primers in Climate," a series of definitive but accessible books, each written by a topical expert, available at https://press.princeton.edu/series/princeton-primers-in-climate.

Kalmus also advises readers not to rely solely on the Internet for their climate information. This is good advice not only because of uneven quality and the presence of ideologically motivated misinformation on the Internet, but also because even high-quality Internet content is often novelty-driven and therefore tends to focus on the trees (the findings in the latest specialized paper) at the expense of the forest. An aspiring well-educated citizen needs the big picture.

well beyond any of today's projections. If changing temperatures halt the circulation of the North Atlantic current (which presently conveys warm water north on the ocean surface and cold Arctic water south in the depths), climate and precipitation regimes on both sides of the Atlantic could be drastically altered on relatively quick timescales (McSweeney 2020).

Action on climate change can take three forms: ***Mitigation*** aims to slow emission of greenhouse gases and reduce the recent man-made warming trend. ***Adaptation*** involves making preparations for living in a world of higher temperatures, rising sea levels, etc. The third category is ***geoengineering***—counteracting the warming trend by taking large-scale action of some other kind, like erecting a visor of some sort in outer space to deflect some incoming solar radiation. At present, no really viable geoengineering option is available, though there will undoubtedly be more discussion in coming years. Adaptation efforts are well underway, but they are unlikely to be effective in the long run unless coupled with effective mitigation.

Mitigation involves reducing our collective usage of fossil fuels. This was the primary goal of the 1997 Kyoto Protocol and it has been the elusive goal of international climate diplomacy ever since. A number of factors make mitigation difficult. First, fossil fuels are excellent stores of energy (concentrated and reliable), and the alternatives cannot easily match them in terms of convenience. For this reason, switching automobiles from petroleum to electricity, to take one important example, involves significant engineering challenges. Second, fossil fuels are deeply embedded in our economic infrastructure. Switching to an infrastructure based on renewables and (if we go that route) nuclear energy involves cutting our losses on major investments in one kind of infrastructure and making decades-long investments in other kinds. Third, and related, the fossil fuel and allied industries are powerful lobbies. Great sums have been spent to derail action on climate change. Fourth, mitigation raises questions of distributional justice: Should all nations ramp down their use of fossil fuels at the same rate? Should poorer nations have a margin for temporarily increasing their use of fossil fuels to meet development priorities? Should the burden of mitigation fall first and foremost on nations responsible for the greatest quantities of historical emissions? These questions have vexed international negotiations (Ranalli 2012).

There are multiple ways to approach climate change mitigation. A common theme is *carbon pricing*: making it more expensive to emit greenhouse gases. Carbon pricing can be focused on carbon dioxide specifically or on multiple greenhouse gases measured in carbon dioxide equivalent. (The term "carbon" is frequently used somewhat imprecisely in discussions of climate change mitigation policy as shorthand to refer to either to carbon dioxide specifically or to multiple greenhouse gases.)

Under the United Nations Framework Convention on Climate Change (UNFCCC), international meetings are held annually to monitor progress and establish goals, including formal protocols. During the era of the Kyoto Protocol, which was negotiated in 1997 and went in effect in 2005, two primary mitigation strategies were up for discussion in policy circles. One was a carbon tax. The other was "cap-and-trade." Both were tried by different countries and regions with varying degrees of success. It was in this context that James Hansen began working the idea of carbon dividends into his writings and public talks.

In late 2007 and early 2008, Hansen was putting most of his energy as a climate advocate into calling for an end to dirty coal. He wrote letters to heads of state like Britain's Prime Minister Gordon Brown and Germany's Chancellor Angela Merkel urging a moratorium on building coal-fired power plants that do not capture and store CO_2.[3] When he was giving expert testimony and writing op-eds and attempting to buttonhole state-level decision-makers in the U.S. as well, coal remained his primary theme. It just did not make sense to be making decades-long investments in new coal plants when sound climate change mitigation policy would require shutting them down. In these talks and letters Hansen typically touched lightly on the economics of mitigation, stating that a rising price on carbon emissions would be needed, but he was fairly noncommittal about the details. "There must be a gradually increasing price on carbon emissions," he explained in one representative bit of expert testimony. "It could be a tax, but there are various options, and it does not need to increase the amount of money extracted from citizens by the government. It might include rations that could be bought and sold, cap-and-trade emission quotas for industries, and other alternatives that stimulate energy and carbon efficiencies" (Hansen 2007, 27).

But something changed in the spring of 2008. By late May of 2008, Hansen was talking about carbon pricing differently. The atmospheric scientist had found his footing on the question of climate economics.

[3] Hansen's talks, writings, mailings to his email list, etc., are archived at http://www.columbia.edu/~jeh1/

> I strongly favor a "tax and dividend" approach. The entire carbon tax should be given back to the public, an equal amount to each person. No bureaucracy is needed to figure this out. If an early carbon tax averages say $1200 per person (it can be collected in various ways – at the well-head, carbon emission permit auctions, etc.) a monthly $100 deposit can be made automatically in everyone's bank account.
>
> Although energy prices will rise, you can bet your bottom dollar that lower and middle income people will figure out how to reduce energy use enough that, overall, they come out ahead. And in doing so, moving to more energy-efficient products, they will spur economic activity and create jobs. The tax-and-dividend approach not only minimizes public backlash against climate and energy policies, it also has the characteristics needed to make those policies work. (Hansen 2008a)

This excerpt is from a May 29, 2008, message to Hansen's email list. From that point onward, "carbon tax and 100% dividend"—later "fee and dividend"—was a staple of Hansen's writings and public talks.

Hansen credited Barnes with introducing him to the dividend idea. ("The proposed 'tax and 100% dividend' is based largely on the cap-and-dividend approach described by Peter Barnes in *Who Owns the Sky*," he explained in a June 23, 2008, speech [Hansen 2008b]. He also credited "Peter Barnes and others" in a June 4, 2008, email bulletin [Hansen 2008c].) Hansen recalls that he might have first heard Barnes talk about climate dividends somewhat earlier than May 2008. "Peter Barnes probably suggested the dividend earlier. I remember talking with him about how to implement a dividend and he emphasized the low cost of doing it electronically—give a debit card to those people who do not have a bank account" (personal communication).

One important distinction between Hansen's vision of carbon dividends and Barnes's is that Hansen proposed to raise the price of carbon with a tax or fee, rather than by capping emissions and selling permits. In 2008, climate change was on the U.S. political agenda. Presidential candidates Barack Obama and John McCain were both campaigning on promises to take action on climate change, and it was almost foreordained that that action would take the form of "cap-and-trade" rather than a carbon tax, since conventional wisdom held that Americans were allergic to discussions about taxes. The *New York Times* compared the positions of the two candidates on the topic not under the heading "Climate Change Mitigation Policy" or "Carbon Pricing," but rather "Details on a Cap-and-Trade Program" (Revkin et al. 2008). Hansen, experienced in the ways of Washington, considered "cap-and-trade" ripe for abuse. And the cap-and-trade legislation that eventually was put up for consideration in 2009 (passing the House, but not the Senate) was indeed a boondoggle, as Hansen predicted it would be, full of giveaways to the regulated community.

Hansen has held firmly to his commitment to a fee-based approach, while Barnes continues to advocate for a carbon cap. As we will see below, Hansen's main criticisms of the cap-based approach are easily remedied when the once-customary but entirely unnecessary "and-trade" is pried away from it. The fee-based (price-based) approach and the cap-based (supply-based) approach are both workable. In practice, each has its own distinct advantages.

Carbon Dividends Advocacy in the U.S.

Today, more than a decade after the U.S. failed to adopt cap-and-trade, fee-and-dividend is the most popular carbon pricing option on the table in policy circles. Much of the credit goes to Citizens Climate Lobby (CCL), a grassroots lobbying organization founded in 2007 that now has around 600 chapters in the U.S. and around the world. According to Marshall Saunders, CCL's founder, it was a presentation by Hansen in December 2009 that convinced him that fee-and-dividend was the right policy for the organization to be advocating. ("Before that," he wrote later in an email to Hansen, "we were lobbying for cap and trade and offsets even though we didn't understand it and couldn't explain it" [as quoted in Hansen's forthcoming *Sophie's Planet*, per personal communication].) Fee-and-dividend is in fact very straightforward and easy to explain, and in that respect it is a good fit for citizen lobbying. The CCL website summarizes it in four bullet points. In promotional materials, CCL highlights the fact that in addition to being an effective climate change mitigation policy, fee-and-dividend will financially help low- and middle-income citizens, will be revenue neutral, and enjoys bipartisan support.

Carbon dividend legislation was introduced as early as 2007, and various such bills competed (ineffectually) with the Democratic leadership's preferred cap-and-trade scheme in the critical legislative session of 2009. Legislation sponsored by Representative John Larson (D-Conn.) in 2007, 2009, and subsequent sessions would have allocated carbon tax revenue for infrastructure investment, research and development, low-income assistance, and individual tax rebates. A bipartisan 2009 bill introduced by Representative Bob Inglis (R-S.C.) would have used carbon tax revenue to fund Social Security, and would have reduced payroll taxes proportionately. The 2009 "Carbon Limits and Energy for America's Renewal (CLEAR) Act" of Senators Maria Cantwell (D-Wash.) and Susan Collins (R-Maine) would have established a cap, auctioned 100% of permits rather than giving them away for free, and issued 75% of the proceeds as dividends. Another cap-and-dividend bill, an even purer incarnation of Barnes's "Sky Trust" (calling for auctioning of permits and rebating 100% of proceeds as dividends), was introduced by Representative (now Senator) Chris Van Hollen (D-Md.) in 2009 and in subsequent sessions. The most recent incarnation of this bill, at the time of writing, is the 2019 Healthy Climate and Family Security Act co-sponsored by Van Hollen and Representative Don Beyer (D-Va.).

Since 2018, the CCL's own version of fee-and-dividend has had legislative sponsors. The "Energy Innovation and Carbon Dividend Act," a bipartisan bill introduced by Representative Ted Deutch (D-Fla.), calls for a carbon tax that rises on a fixed schedule and the establishment of a trust that returns the revenue to citizens in equal monthly full shares for adults and half-shares for children.

Legislation introduced in 2019 by Senator Chris Coons (D-Del.), Senator Dianne Feinstein (D-Calif.), and Representative Jimmy Panetta (D-Calif.) (the "Climate Action Rebate Act of 2019") would allocate 70% of carbon fee revenues to monthly dividends sent to households with incomes below 150,000 USD, with adults getting full shares and children getting half-shares, similar to the CCL bill. The remainder of the revenue would go to infrastructure investments, research and development, and transition assistance for workers and communities.

In 2017, a major new carbon dividend proposal entered the stage, co-authored by veteran Republican administrators James A. Baker, III and George P. Shultz. A project of the Climate Leadership Council (CLC), the Baker–Shultz Carbon Dividends plan has garnered endorsements from thousands of professional economists, including 27 Nobel laureates and four former chairs of the Federal Reserve. Organizational sponsors and endorsers include environmental groups like the World Resources Institute and the World Wildlife Federation, corporations like IBM, Microsoft, Ford, GM, Santander, Goldman Sachs, and—most impressively—energy companies like ExxonMobil, Shell, and ConocoPhillips.

In substance, the Baker–Shultz CLC plan is very similar to the CCL plan. The most significant difference is the numbers: the Baker–Shultz plan starts with an initial surcharge of 40 USD per ton of CO_2-equivalent emissions and then increases the fee by 2.40 USD per year, while the CCL plan starts with a low initial surcharge of 15 USD per ton and increases by 10 USD per year (leading to higher prices than the Baker–Shultz plan within five years). Also, the Baker–Shultz plan calls for quarterly distribution of dividends rather than monthly. The Baker–Shultz plan touts a rising carbon price as an alternative to "cumbersome regulations" and calls for the dismantling of most Obama-era climate change regulations, which it claims will no longer be needed (CLC 2020, ii, 2). This angle is played up in the CLC's promotional materials and no doubt plays some part in the plan's appeal to Republicans and the business community. But it does not really set the Baker–Shultz plan apart from the CCL plan, which also provides for suspension of regulations. Lerman (2018) suggests that adapting the Social Security system to distribute dividends, as CCL proposes, would be more felicitous than CLC's idea of distributing dividends via the federal tax system (74–75).

Curiously, despite the backing of what CLC (2020, vi) describes as "the broadest climate coalition in U.S. history," the Baker–Shultz plan has not (as of the time of writing, in 2020) been introduced in Congress. This surely reflects not a lack of interest on the part of prospective Republican (and Democratic) sponsors, but rather deference to a Republican Congressional leadership whose legislative agenda, coordinated with the Trump White House, does not have room for climate initiatives.

We can expect that when Congress next turns to climate change mitigation policy, two of the main options on the table will be the CCL and CLC carbon dividend programs. Alternatives like the Van Hollen and Beyer bill will also be in the mix. James Boyce, whose 2019 *The Case for Carbon Dividends* is perhaps the best book-length treatment of the topic of carbon dividends, offered this take in a July 1, 2020, interview: "One at this point should be fairly open-minded about the specifics of what [an eventual carbon pricing] bill will and will not include. I think what will end up happening in Washington when momentum builds for such a policy will be a process of give and take amongst the proponents of different alternatives, and what emerges will be some sort of compromise that is capable of winning broad-based support" (This is Democracy 2020).

Carbon Dividends in Action

While Washington, D.C. has been indecisive, other nations, regions, and subnational units have been proceeding apace to meet commitments made under the Kyoto Protocol and the Paris Climate Agreement. As of 2020, there are 61 carbon pricing initiatives around the world that are in operation or scheduled to launch, together covering about 22% of global greenhouse gas emissions. These are almost evenly split between 31 cap-and-permit systems and 30 carbon tax systems. Altogether, carbon pricing programs raised more than 45 billion USD in 2019. According to a World Bank report, "almost half of the revenues were dedicated to environmental or broader development projects, and more than 40 percent went to the general budget [of the implementing governments]. The remaining share was dedicated to tax cuts and direct transfers" (World Bank 2020a, 7).

So roughly ten percent of carbon pricing revenues are being refunded by governments to individuals and other parties (e.g., corporations) as direct transfers and tax cuts. What is the nature of these programs, and where are they located? The following table provides an overview (Table 4.1).

"Revenue recycling" (as tax cuts and rebates are called) is relatively rare among cap-and-permit systems. There are two examples, and both happen to be in the United States. RGGI returns a small percentage of permit auction revenues to low-income households as electricity rate relief. California, as one element of its carbon pricing program, grants permits to electric and natural gas utilities (i.e., energy distributors, not generators) at no cost. The permits are then sold at auction, to be redeemed by the utilities' suppliers (electricity generators and natural gas suppliers). The money raised at auction is not retained by the utilities but refunded in full to their customers. Approximately 85% goes to residential customers, in the form of a combination of rate reductions and equal per-household statement credits (CPUC 2012). The amount of the annual California Climate Credit, delivered in twice-yearly installments or on some other schedule, varies from utility to utility. In 2019 it ranged from 28 USD for PG&E's electric customers to 160 USD for Pacific Power's electric customers.

Among carbon tax systems, revenue recycling is quite common. The Scandinavian countries led the way early on, using the new revenue stream to lighten the burden of corporate taxes (in a bid to improve economic

Table 4.1 Carbon pricing programs that recycle revenue

Jurisdiction	*Carbon pricing mechanism*	*Effective date*	*Total annual revenue (2019)*	*Percent of revenue "recycled" to citizens and other parties*	*Form of revenue recycling*
Finland	Carbon tax (select sectors, covering 36% of emissions)	1990	1,420M USD	~50%	Individual and corporate tax rebates
Sweden	Carbon tax (heating and transport sectors, covering 40% of emissions)	1991	2,314M USD	50%	Reductions in income taxes and corporate taxes
Norway	Carbon tax (by sector and fuel, covering 62% of emissions)	1991	1,374M USD	~30%	Reductions in corporate taxes
Denmark	Carbon tax (primarily building and transport sectors, covering 40% of emissions)	1992	520M USD	~45%	Reductions in income taxes and corporate taxes
Estonia	Carbon tax (industry and power sectors, covering 3% of emissions)	2000	3M USD	Information not available	Reductions in income taxes and corporate taxes
British Columbia	Carbon tax (upstream, covering 70% of emissions)	2008	1,145M USD	100%	Individual and corporate tax rebates and direct payments
Regional Greenhouse Gas Initiative (RGGI), a coalition of eastern U.S. states	Cap-and-permit (electric power generation, covering 18% of emissions)	2008	284M USD	~12%	Electric utility rate relief, targeted in some states and universal in others
Switzerland	Carbon tax (select sectors, covering 33% of emissions)	2008	1,235M USD	~67%	Flat universal rebates to households; employer payroll tax rebates

(continued)

Table 4.1 (continued)

Jurisdiction	*Carbon pricing mechanism*	*Effective date*	*Total annual revenue (2019)*	*Percent of revenue "recycled" to citizens and other parties*	*Form of revenue recycling*
California	Cap-and-permit (multiple sectors, covering 85% of emissions)	2012	3,065M USD	35–40%	Flat rebates to households from electric and natural gas utilities, plus rate reductions
Australia	Carbon tax (select sectors, covering 60% of emissions)	2012; cancelled 2014	not applicable	53%	Increases in pensions, allowances, and family payments; income-tax cuts targeted at lower income households
France	Carbon tax (multiple sectors, covering 35% of emissions)	2014	8,968M USD	Information not available	Reduction of income taxes and corporate taxes; energy assistance to low-income households
Portugal	Carbon tax (multiple sectors, covering 29% of emissions)	2015	281M USD	Information not available	Reduction of income taxes
Alberta	Carbon tax on fuel (information not available on coverage)	2017; cancelled 2019 (province now covered by Canadian federal program)	not applicable	Information not available	Rebates for low- and middle-income families; cuts in small business tax rate

(continued)

Table 4.1 (continued)

Jurisdiction	*Carbon pricing mechanism*	*Effective date*	*Total annual revenue (2019)*	*Percent of revenue "recycled" to citizens and other parties*	*Form of revenue recycling*
Canada (federal backstop, covering about 50% of provinces)	Fuel tax (covering 19% of emissions)	2019	1,371M USD	100%	Individual tax rebates

Sources Carl and Fedor (2016), Navigant and The Generation Foundation (2018), and World Bank (2020b)

efficiency) and personal taxes (making them more progressive). Over time, many other jurisdictions have devoted at least some of their carbon tax revenues to tax-shifting. The British Columbian system stands out for recycling fully 100% of carbon tax revenue. A portion of the funding goes to tax credits for low- and middle-income families. As of 2019, the maximum value of the annual Climate Action Tax Credit stood at 154.50 CAD per adult and 45.50 CAD per child (about 115 USD and 35 USD) (British Columbia 2019). The success of the British Columbian tax-and-dividend experiment, in terms of both emissions reduction and economic performance (see, e.g., Elgie and McClay 2013), appears to have played a role in the decision to replicate it at the federal level with a fuel tax. (The Canadian federal government has a separate system of pricing industrial carbon emissions; that revenue goes to other purposes.)

The Swiss individual rebates, which go to all residents in an equal amount, are delivered via health insurers as the middleman, since health insurance in Switzerland is mandatory and health insurers have the most up-to-date records of residents' addresses. The rebate amounts are effectively deducted from health insurance premiums (Swiss Federal Office for the Environment 2020). In 2018, the yearly lump-sum rebate received by each Swiss resident was equivalent to 89 USD (World Bank 2019, 44).

The Australian experiment is a sad tale. The carbon tax-and-dividend policy was implemented by the Labor party in 2012 as a concession to the Greens, a junior coalition partner, and then shut down by the Liberal (i.e., conservative) party on taking power in 2014. During the two years that the carbon tax-and-dividend policy was in effect, it was striking effective in reducing emissions. According to one post-mortem, the policy was a victim not only of right-wing climate-contrarian propaganda, but also malign neglect from the Labor party, which failed to promote it in the public sphere and explain its benefits, and sought instead to claim independent credit for the nation's solid economic performance and lower tax rates and higher pension payments during the period (Komanoff 2020). The annual 3.5 billion USD that Australia was rebating to households during the program's short existence made it one of the highest-volume revenue recycling programs in carbon pricing history.

Policy Design for Carbon Pricing and Dividends

The debate between carbon taxes and cap-and-permit schemes can be confusing. What makes a good carbon pricing policy? For that matter, why put a price on carbon at all, why not just invest in clean energy technologies? And if we do price carbon, what considerations should go into the decision to issue dividends? Here we will seek to shed some light on climate change mitigation policy design and the place of dividends in that policy.

In evaluating policy options, we are mindful of two imperatives: one is to determine what will be most effective in mitigating climate change. The other is to determine what will conform best to the principle of fair sharing of wealth from common resources articulated by Paine and Hammond and Barnes. These two imperatives largely coincide, but they are not identical.

Why Price Carbon at All?

Successful climate change mitigation will require changes in behavior and infrastructure: individuals deciding not to travel by plane, households deciding to purchase energy-efficient appliances, utilities deciding to build a solar farm rather than a coal-fired power plant. Billions of decisions like these will be necessary. But without a rising price on carbon, they will be ineffective. This can easily be seen from a thought experiment. Suppose I decide to cut petroleum out of my life. I turn in my gas-guzzling sedan and invest in a bicycle. Will this help reduce climate change? On the contrary, my action will produce a very slight reduction in demand for petroleum, which will produce a very slight decrease in the price of petroleum, which will make it a little more attractive to other users of petroleum.

Suppose that an entire nation or region—let us say the European Union—decides to entirely abandon fossil fuels. With discipline and vision and a robust program of research and development, European administrators and business leaders successfully put in place a new infrastructure that meets the region's energy needs entirely with renewables and next-generation nuclear plants. Will this make a dent in climate change? Again, the answer is no: when Europe stops purchasing coal and oil and natural gas in the global marketplace, the prices of those commodities will fall, and that will stimulate more consumption in nations that lack the Europeans' foresight and conscientiousness.

This phenomenon is called "rebound."[4] There are three possible antidotes to rebound, in theory. The first two—entirely unrealistic—are to make everyone equally foresighted and conscientious (i.e., to change human nature), or to use command-and-control regulation to *enforce* virtuous behavior in every corner of the economy. The third is to provide clear incentives that do not depend on either goodwill or coercion. That is what putting a price on carbon does. This is the solution of Adam Smith, who understood that the economy delivers the meat, beer, and bread we need and want not because the butcher, brewer, and baker understand and endorse society's grand goals, but because they understand and respond to price signals ([1776] 1986, 119).

Sending a price signal to those who use fossil fuels is a *necessary* policy intervention if we are to meet our climate change mitigation targets. However, most would agree that it is not sufficient. If we want consumers to trade in their internal combustion engines for bicycles and electric cars, the public sector needs to make investments in infrastructure for those alternatives, and there is a lot of scope for other government action to smooth the way for a quick transition, including funding R&D, creating financial incentives (and eliminating counterproductive fossil fuel subsidies), and promoting public education. We need both a rising price on carbon (via a rising fee or a descending cap) *and* action to generate viable low-carbon alternatives—the stick and the carrot.

[4]The rare outright critique of cap-and-dividend usually fails to grasp the issue of rebound. See, for example, Food & Water Watch's issue brief, "Dividend and Conquer: Cap-and-Dividend and Environmental Betrayal" (Food and Water Watch 2013).

How to Price Carbon (Carbon Tax Versus Cap-and-Permit)

When we talk about putting a price on carbon, what we mean is using the dynamic relationship between supply, demand, and price to limit the *supply* of fossil fuels delivered by the economy. We can manipulate either of the other two variables, and this means there are two basic approaches to carbon pricing. A carbon tax artificially raises the *price*, depressing both the effective demand and the amount supplied. A cap-and-permit system artificially limits the *demand*, which raises the price and depresses the supply. In the abstract, either should be equally effective.

In the real world, experience in over sixty jurisdictions shows that either *can* be effective. But each has its own unique concerns and pitfalls.

- *Political acceptability.* Though both policies will hit consumers in the pocketbook, the carbon tax might have a harder time being adopted simply because it takes the form of a tax. A taboo against taxes made cap-and-trade the default option in the 2008–2009 debates in the U.S., and evidently prompted Hansen and the Citizen's Climate Lobby to advocate for "fee-and-dividend" rather than "tax-and-dividend." Knee-jerk dislike of taxation evidently played a role in the death of the Australian carbon pricing program, as it had earlier done for Hammond's initial vision of Bristol Bay, Inc. (see Chapter 3), despite considerations of both sound management and financial self-interest in both cases.
- *Ease of implementation.* Here, the carbon tax shines. Taxation is a core function of government; it is easy for a government to marshal the expertise necessary to administer a carbon tax fairly and effectively. Cap-and-permit systems are more complex and difficult and expensive to administer and there are many things that can go wrong (to be discussed below). A tax is also more convenient than a cap for the regulated community, since a reliable price for carbon takes much of the guesswork out of their planning and budgeting.
- *Assurance of effectiveness in hitting environmental targets.* In a cap-and-permit approach, the declining cap can be set at levels that will precisely meet science-based emissions targets. With a tax, on the other hand, we can only make educated guesses about what the effective demand will be at a given price. To put it another way, there is a necessary trade-off: a reliable carbon price comes at the expense of uncertainty about environmental outcomes, while reliable

environmental outcomes come at the expense of uncertainty about price. There are workarounds: For example, a cap-and-permit system can have a floor price (to be discussed below). And a carbon tax can be designed with a built-in mechanism for periodic adjustment to improve alignment with emissions targets. The Swiss carbon tax includes such a mechanism (Hafstead et al. 2016). But such a mechanism includes a lag, and it might not perform equally well in all regulatory contexts, and it would eliminate one of the carbon tax's main selling points, the predictability of prices.

The final consideration alone—assurance that the program will be environmental effective—could be enough to make cap-and-permit the preferred alternative. The consequences of getting the quantities wrong when calibrating prices are both graver and more difficult to mitigate than the consequences of volatile prices.[5]

Designing a Carbon Tax

In designing a carbon tax, one of the main questions is where the tax will be imposed: upstream, where fossil fuels enter the economy? Midstream, where businesses use and process them? Or downstream, at final consumer use?

As a general rule, the further upstream the tax is imposed, the easier it will be to administer, since it will be imposed on fewer entities. A Treasury Department report on the subject (Horowitz et al. 2017) declares that either an upstream or midstream approach to taxing carbon, or even a hybrid, would be perfectly workable. There are some technical consideration that would need to be addressed in each case.[6] But the smaller

[5] Compare the argument for commodity-based rather than price-based controls in Martin L. Weitzman's classic paper "Prices vs. Quantities" (1974).

[6] Some fossil fuel products are used in ways that might not lead to carbon emissions (e.g., petroleum use as feedstock in the manufacture of plastics—but note that even plastics can be a source of greenhouse gas emissions when they degrade (Royer et al. 2018) or are incinerated). Excluding fossil fuels destined for these uses from taxation, via a system of exemptions or credits, will add more complication to an upstream tax than a midstream tax. Conversely, some quantity of fossil fuels may be consumed (or, in the case of natural gas, simply leak into the atmosphere) before the point of taxation, a circumstance that will also require special provisions. This will complicate midstream taxation more than upstream taxation. Whether a midstream or upstream approach is taken, technical considerations like these will be manageable (Horowitz et al. 2017, 6).

number of tax filers and their greater sophistication make the upstream approach clearly preferable. An upstream approach in the U.S. might involve as few as around 2,000 entities (Hargrave 1998, 6–7). Imposing the tax would require only modest modifications to an existing tax form, according to the Treasury Department (Horowitz et al. 2017, 6).

A carbon tax typically includes a "border adjustment" component. Imports will be subject to a fee at the border that is equivalent to the tax paid by domestic producers. Exports will be subsidized to mark down their price so they can compete on a level playing field abroad. In the case of a trade partner that has a carbon pricing program of its own, the import fees and export subsidies could be reduced or eliminated. The border adjustment would presumably apply not only to fossil fuels but also to energy-intensive products such as iron and steel, paper, aluminum, cement, and bulk glass (Horowitz et al. 2017, 15).[7]

Designing a Carbon Cap-And-Permit System

The design of a cap-and-permit system involves a number of technical considerations.

- **Will permits be auctioned, or given away for free (e.g., allocated based on historical emissions)?** For many reasons, auctioning is preferable. Only via auctioning will the system produce revenue that can be issued as dividends or used for other public priorities. Auctioning can provide some assurance that the permits will be distributed efficiently (i.e., that they will go to the companies that will need and use them); giving them away for free does not, and *requires* that some other mechanism like trading be added to the program so the permits can be reallocated to produce an efficient distribution. Auctioning provides a way of establishing a market price for the permits; giving them away for free does not. Giving permits away for free also raises intractable questions of fairness. Why should this company be given X dollars' worth of permits, while that company is given Y dollars' worth of permits? Basing the distribution on historical emissions only rewards past pollution. Although it is quite common in practice for permits to be given away for free, there is in fact no principled justification for it that stands up to any

[7] For more detail on carbon tax design, see Partnership for Market Readiness (2017).

sort of scrutiny—one suspects that all too frequently it comes down to political patronage. (Sometimes permits are granted for free to protect companies in trade-sensitive sectors from being at a disadvantage in international competition. While the motivation here is legitimate, the practice is flawed for the reasons stated above. Allocation of permits and border adjustments should really be treated as two separate issues.)

- **How will auctions be handled?** An auction is a game, and it carries risks: Participants might find ways to cheat (e.g., by colluding to rig the price). If the game is complex it might favor larger participants with more resources to spend on research and consultants' fees, unfairly punishing smaller participants. And depending on how the rules are written, participants might face perverse incentives that lead them to pursue strategies that inadvertently make the auction price misrepresent the market price. But if it is designed well, an auction can be a very effective way to allocate permits. To illustrate how an auction can work, one decent and relatively simple approach is the so-called "ascending clock." The auction takes place over multiple rounds. In each round, the auctioneer states a price (starting with a low price), and participants privately tell the auctioneer the number of permits they would be willing to buy at this price. (This bidding process is simple enough that it could be conducted over the Internet.) If the sum of permits requested (the total demand) at this price exceeds the number of permits available (the cap), the price is rejected and the auction continues with another round and a slightly higher price. From round to round, as the price rises, participants can bid for the same number of permits as before or a smaller number, but not a larger number. (This is to prevent gaming.) When a price is reached where the demand for permits no longer exceeds the cap, the price is settled and everyone pays their final bid at that price. (If some permits are left over, they could be allocated based on the bids that were received in the second-to-last round.) Auctions can also be designed such that participants bid prices rather than quantities of permits, or submit entire schedules of how many permits they will want to buy at a range of prices, but these introduce complications of various kinds.[8]

[8] For a good introduction to carbon permit auction design, see Cramton and Kerr (1998). Lopomo et al. (2011) provides a useful synthesis of subsequent research.

- **Will trading be permitted?** In the eyes of many, trading is the essence of a cap-and-permit system. For years, the alternative to a carbon tax was conventionally called "cap-and-trade," and even today international institutions are more likely to use the expression "emissions trading scheme" (ETS) than "cap-and-permit." Of the 31 carbon cap-and-permit systems operating in 2020, every single one allows some kind of trading. But trading is ***not essential*** to a cap-and-permit system, and it introduces new complexities and new opportunities for market failure and gaming. The layer of middlemen involved in secondary market transactions (brokers, consultants, etc.) will have their fees, and those costs will be built into the prices that permit holders charge consumers. Some permit trading schemes, bizarrely, allow even non-regulated entities (investment banks, private traders, etc.) to participate in auctions and to buy and sell permits. Whatever profit these players derive from temporarily holding permits will also come at the expense of the regulated entities that need to redeem the permits, and will also be passed on to consumers.

  The theoretical justification for trading, with its associated costs, is that it provides economic efficiency by helping permits flow into the hands of the parties who will make the most efficient use of them. But there are simpler ways to ensure efficient allocation. The first condition of a well-designed cap-and-permit system is a well-designed auction, as described above. Auctions (and permit holding) will be limited to regulated entities. As with a well-designed carbon tax, the regulated entities will be ***upstream*** entities—the relatively small number of companies whose main business is carbon and who will be well-equipped to forecast demand and bid intelligently. Auctions will take place fairly regularly (say, monthly or quarterly rather than annually), so participants can easily modify their permit holdings in response to changing market conditions. Participants will be allowed (within limits, to prevent gaming) to "***bank***" permits, i.e., to save them for use them in a later period than the one for which they were nominally purchased, so they need not fear buying too many at auction.
- **How will border adjustments be handled?** There are several options, including requiring importers to purchase permits at auction, granting free permits to companies in trade-sensitive industries (not ideal, as discussed above), or using a system of fees and

subsidies to adjust prices at the border just as under a carbon tax system.

The design of a carbon tax or cap-and-permit system can be much more complex than indicated here. For example, there might be provisions for *offsets*: alternative actions that are meant to provide equivalent environmental benefits, like planting trees. Experience has shown that offsets are often of dubious value (e.g., there is no guarantee that planted trees will grow to maturity, and regardless of how many trees we plant we should also necessarily be reducing emissions), and offset provisions often end up becoming loopholes. A well-designed carbon policy will not include offsets. There will certainly need to be provisions for monitoring, reporting, and verification (MRV). In general, the simpler the program design (e.g., the further "upstream" in the economy the carbon is taxed or capped), the easier and more straightforward will be the MRV requirements.[9]

Benchmarking

Designers of a carbon tax will need to decide what the initial price will be and how quickly it will rise. Similarly, designers of a cap-and-permit system will need to decide where the cap will initially be set and how quickly it will fall. These benchmarks could be established by law, or left to the discretion of regulators, or pegged to projections produced by scientists (e.g., in regular IPCC reports) of the reductions in emissions that will be required to meet defined climate change mitigation goals.

Target prices (or per capita caps) might not be the same from country to country. The well-regarded "contraction and convergence" model (Meyer 2000) would have a declining overall global emissions target, allocated among nations in such a way that per capita carbon usage rises (temporarily) in less-developed nations and falls among more-developed nations until they converge, and then they fall together. Until convergence is reached, those nations using more than their per capita share may compensate those using less than their per capita share.

[9] For more detail on cap-and-permit program design, PMR and ICAP (2016) is a good resource, with the caveat that this report, like most others, assumes that permits will necessarily be tradable. Boyce (2019) is a useful corrective in this regard.

It is not uncommon for carbon pricing programs to incorporate "floors" and "ceilings" to keep prices within an expected range. In cap-and-permit systems, this can be accomplished by releasing additional permits if the price gets too high or repurchasing permits if the price gets too low. One problem with carbon taxes, and with cap-and-permit programs with ceilings, is that we really have very little idea of how high prices will need to rise in order to be environmentally effective. Economic demand for fossil fuel energy is fairly *inelastic* (see discussion in Boyce and Riddle 2007, 9; Boyce 2018, 56; Boyce 2019, 45–49). That means even large changes in price produce relatively small changes in demand. This makes sense if we think about how a good deal of our energy is consumed. When the price of gasoline rises, the commuter who does not have a convenient public transportation option will continue to drive to work. When the cost of fuel oil rises, the homeowner will continue to heat their home. This points to the importance of complementary policies like investing in infrastructure (public transportation, bicycle lanes, renewable energy sources, etc.) while also putting a price on carbon. It also points to the importance of not being squeamish in letting carbon prices rise. If we are serious about reducing carbon emissions, we will need to let prices rise far more dramatically than they have done to date.

How to Use the Revenue

A carbon pricing program—as long as it is not a cap-and-permit program that gives away the valuable permits for free—will generate revenue. We have already seen that governments today put this revenue to a variety of uses, including spending it on climate change mitigation priorities, spending it as part of their general budget, reducing personal and corporate taxes, and issuing dividends.

Why issue dividends? There are three main justifications.

First, there is the argument from justice that was articulated by Peter Barnes, echoing Thomas Paine, as described at the beginning of this chapter. The atmosphere is part of our common heritage. If its capacity as a carbon sink is to monetized, every person deserves a share in the wealth that is generated.

Second, there is an argument from realpolitik. The prospect of receiving dividends ought to make the policy attractive to voters. And when voters start receiving the dividends, they should become a powerful constituency for preservation of the program, as Alaskan voters are a powerful constituency for the Alaska Permanent Fund. There is undoubtedly some truth to this, even if it is not a hard and fast rule. The rejection by Australian voters of their quite generous carbon tax revenue recycling system can be cited as a counterexample, but arguably the cards were stacked against it. Barnes makes the quite plausible case that the Australian carbon pricing program would have fared better with the public if the dividend component had been more prominent and better publicized (Carbon Tax Center 2020).

Finally, there is an argument from sound policy design. This often gets lost in the discussion of carbon pricing, but in fact dividends are *not an optional add-on* to an effective carbon pricing policy. Universal dividends (or something very much like them) will be *essential*.

This follows from the discussion of price inelasticity above. In order to generate the market pressure to develop and adopt alternatives to fossil fuels, carbon prices will need to rise much higher than they have to date. We will also need to do away with the subsidies that have kept fossil fuel prices artificially low. Boyce (2018, 54) reports that with all the subsidies heaped on fossil fuels, the average net carbon price in the world today is *minus 8 USD*. All of this means that during the transition, ordinary households will face significantly higher prices than they have in the past for transportation, heating, and electricity (to the extent they are not yet weaned off of fossil fuels), plus all goods and services that contain significant embodied fossil fuel energy (including food items produced via industrial agriculture) or are transported over long distances. It is likely that low- and even middle-income households will not be able to simply swallow these higher costs, but will *require* financial assistance to handle them. Universal uniform dividends will be an obvious way to provide that necessary relief.

Since the dividends are universal and uniform while the higher carbon costs are dependent on purchasing decisions and lifestyles, the dividends, though they provide financial relief, provide no disincentive to making the changes to purchasing decisions and lifestyles that will decarbonize our economy. Those who use less fossil fuel energy will come out ahead.[10]

[10] By contrast, consider a peculiar alternate scenario offered by Marron and Maag (2018), in which every household receives a tax rebate *in the amount of the higher carbon costs it has paid*. That would muddy the incentive to decarbonize, and for some consumers possibly even counteract it.

What will be the distributional effects of carbon pricing and of universal dividends? As a rule, the poor use less energy than the wealthy, but their energy budget consumes a larger proportion of their income. This means a carbon pricing program on its own will be regressive, while a carbon pricing program with 100% recycling of revenue as universal uniform dividends will be a progressive financial arrangement that is protective of the most vulnerable households. Numerous quantitative studies have demonstrated this, focusing on the U.S. context (CBO 2000; Dinan and Rogers 2002; Boyce and Riddle 2007; Fremstad and Paul 2018). The U.S. Treasury Department's Office of Tax Analysis finds that a tax-and-dividend policy would increase net income for 70% of households (with the poorest decile seeing a 9% increase) and lower net income for 30% of households (with the highest-income decile seeing a 1% decrease) (Horowitz et al. 2017, 25). Using the revenue to reduce the deficit or reduce the corporate income tax, on the other hand, would have regressive effects (Rosenberg et al. 2018, 6).

"Horizontal" disparities (variations in the economic effects of price-and-dividend policies within each income decile) get less attention in the literature, but research by Cronin et al. (2017, 1) indicates that they could be significant. "Because of heterogeneity of income sources and expenditures, any package of reforms is likely to create winners and losers within each income group.... Even if retirees could be compensated by expansion of social security benefits, poor families in harsh climates still bear a higher carbon tax burden than families of similar means residing in temperate areas." Even dividends, then, will not necessarily fully protect all of the most vulnerable households from the financial effects of a robust climate pricing program.

REMI and Synapse (2014) produced a rare study that not only calculates the cost of carbon pricing to households and the size of the dividend, but also attempts to capture secondary costs and benefits as the economy is reshaped by the policy. The study concludes that although costs and benefits are not evenly distributed across regions and industries, over the course of ten years a program that delivers a 33% reduction in carbon dioxide emissions would add 2.1 million jobs over the baseline (business-as-usual) scenario and increase GDP by a margin of 80 million USD or more, as well as preventing 13,000 premature deaths as an ancillary benefit of improving air quality. Balanced against that, the cost of living after ten years of fee-and-dividend would be around 3% higher than under the baseline scenario.

How close could we get to 100% revenue recycling? Boyce (2019, 83–84) cites precedents indicating that administrative costs should be fairly small. Overseeing a cap-and-permit system with auctions, naturally, would be more expensive than administering a tax. Of carbon pricing programs in existence at the time of writing, only those in Canada and Switzerland recycle more than 50% of funds to households. There are plenty of other good uses to which carbon pricing revenue could be put, but statements like this one from the World Bank (2019, 44)—that "just a fraction of the revenues raised" is sufficient to ameliorate the regressive effects of carbon pricing—must be taken with a grain of salt. Such a statement might be true of today's "pilot" carbon pricing programs, but it is unlikely to remain true when carbon costs rise to levels that will be environmentally effective.

Boyce and Riddle (2008) point out that about 28% of fossil fuels consumed in the U.S. are consumed by local, state, and federal government. Policy-makers might be tempted (and legislators might be pressured by administrators) to reserve a portion of carbon pricing revenue to make up carbon-price-related shortfalls in government budgets, to (in Boyce and Riddle's words) "make government whole." As a rule, this would be shortsighted. First, government too needs incentives to make the shift from fossil fuels, and with its large purchasing power and ability to make investments in infrastructure, government is well-positioned to lead the way and should do so. Second, if dividends to households are taxed as income (and there is no reason they should not be), government will already recoup most of the shortfall. Boyce and Riddle (2008, 4) estimate that about 24% of the dividend wealth will return to government in taxes, leaving a shortfall of only about 4%—though there will be a net transfer from local governments, which spend a lot on fuel, to higher levels of government that collect income tax. If government does need more funding, then the logic of the Sky Trust and the logic of the resource curse (discussed the previous chapter) would both argue for increasing taxes rather than raiding a revenue stream to which households have a claim. Boyce and Riddle (2008) point out that issuing 100% dividends and then taxing back 24% results in a more progressive income distribution outcome than government retaining 24% off the top and issuing the rest as dividends.

How should children be treated? Most plans assign half-shares to children. Hansen proposed limiting children's dividends to a maximum of two per household, but most plans set no limit. Slowing population growth can help reduce carbon emissions, but it seems unlikely that limiting the availability of dividends for children will affect family planning decisions. From a Sky Trust perspective, it is important that dividends be truly universal. My right to a share of the sky is not dependent on how many siblings I have. Some plans would place children's shares in accounts on their behalf, to which they will be entitled on reaching adulthood.

The Future of Carbon Dividends

We have seen that many carbon tax programs and some cap-and-permit programs currently include revenue recycling. None of them have all the features of a "Sky-Trust"-type dividend (universal payments in uniform amounts, distributed conspicuously by check or direct deposit), but some come close—notably the universal payments made in California as utility bill rebates and in Switzerland as health insurance premium rebates, and the bold, well-publicized British Columbian experiment with recycling 100% of carbon tax revenues, now being replicated nation-wide with Canadian fuel tax revenues.

We have seen reason to believe that as carbon pricing programs ramp up further to brake emissions, and consumer prices for fossil fuels rise much higher than they are today, policy-makers will come to recognize that direct revenue recycling to households will be an essential element of successful carbon pricing programs.

Even today, there is a growing public appetite for carbon dividends. In the U.S., this has been seen recently not only in the growth of CCL's grassroots advocacy and the emergence of CLC as a voice for dividends in the business community and among Republicans, but also in the endorsement of carbon dividends by a number of Presidential candidates in the 2019 Democratic presidential primaries, including Andrew Yang, whose campaign helped to widen the national conversation about basic income more generally.

In Europe, local chapters of CCL and other climate change mitigation advocates launched a petition in 2019 for a Europe-wide fee-and-dividend program. It did not receive the required one million signatures, but it raised the profile of fee-and-dividend as a policy option.

Some have envisioned a global carbon dividend system. Given the logic of the "Sky Trust" model, according to which the atmosphere is a global commons of which all of humanity are the trustees and should be the beneficiaries, what better way could there be to implement it than globally?

As early as 1992—a decade before Barnes's opening salvo—British economist and sustainability advocate Richard Douthwaite proposed in his book *The Growth Illusion* that every person on the planet should be granted a coupon or ration card representing their equal share of the worlds' (capped) annual fossil fuel budget, which they could redeem when purchasing fuel, or sell on the open market, or even destroy (Douthwaite 1992, 211ff). Around 2004, possibly prompted by the growing interest around Barnes's work, Douthwaite and colleagues at the Ireland-based think tank Feasta began actively developing and promoting the idea. It was the subject of a 2008 Feasta report, *Cap & Share: A Fair Way to Cut Greenhouse Emissions* (Feasta 2008).

The proposal continued to evolve over time, and in 2014–2015 (in time for COP21[11] in Paris) it was rebranded as CapGlobalCarbon (https://www.capglobalcarbon.org/). The vision is a global trust that would distribute universal dividends out of carbon pricing revenue entrusted to it by ratifying nations. In 2017, Feasta submitted to the Irish Citizen's Assembly a proposal to kick-start CapGlobalCarbon by setting up a bilateral Cap and Share partnership between Ireland and a nation from the Global South that has lower emissions but a similar population size, such as Liberia or Eritrea. A single trust would collect revenue from permit auctions in the two countries and distribute the revenue in equal amounts to residents of both countries (CapGlobalCarbon 2017, 3ff). "Were this to happen, Ireland would effectively be subsidizing the other country's transition to a zero-carbon economy. This would show significant support for climate justice and could potentially help to address the refugee crisis, providing badly needed stability and security. It would also ensure that Ireland itself became zero-carbon" (Feasta 2017, 12).

A couple of observations are worth making about CapGlobalCarbon. First, the coupon idea was dropped in favor a trust model *a la* Barnes. The idea of coupons was inspired by the rationing systems that Britain and other nations employed during times of shared sacrifice in the past, like World War II, according to Douthwaite (1992, 211). It may have been suggested as well by the privatization reforms being implemented at the time of writing in the early 1990s in the former Soviet Union and other

[11] This is the conventional shorthand for the meeting that was the twenty-first annual session of the Conference of the Parties to the UNFCCC.

Eastern bloc countries. It was not uncommon for a former Communist nation to privatize state-owned businesses by issuing shares to all citizens, which they could hold or sell. In theory, this was an equitable and democratically empowering way to introduce market reforms. In practice, the reform was subject to the sorts of failures that attend unequal access to information and markets. Most citizens got only a pittance for their shares, selling them to bundlers who then turned around and made a killing by reselling them to oligarchs, foreign investors, and corporations. As admirable as Douthwaite's original vision was, the redemption of carbon coupons distributed to every corner of the world would likely be subject to a similar dynamic. An advantage of the trust model that Feasta ended up adopting is the *inalienability* of shares—the shares are a birthright that cannot be bargained away or sold.[12]

Second, is it realistic to think that civil society could put together an institution like a global climate trust? It does strain the imagination, but Feasta argues that there are precedents. "The idea that an international institution could arise from a citizen's initiative is not new. There is the inspiring example of Henri Dunant whose actions, after he had seen 40,000 soldiers left dead or dying on the battlefield at Solferino in 1859, led to the formation of the International Committee of the Red Cross. A parallel initiative today is the current project to create an International Court for the Environment. Other examples of environmental governance beyond the state include the Forest Stewardship Council" (CapGlobalCarbon, n.d.).

Barnes, in company with a number of distinguished sustainability thought leaders, mostly U.S.-based (including Robert Costanza, Paul Hawken, David Orr, and Elinor Ostrom), made a separate case for a global trust, the "Earth Atmospheric Trust," in *Science* magazine in 2008, during the critical run-up period to the latest concerted attempt at climate change mitigation legislation in the U.S. Congress (Barnes et al. 2008). The pitch is brief and focuses more on the advantages

[12]The idea of rationing remains attractive to those who are concerned about ensuring equitable access when fossil fuels become truly scarce (e.g., Fleming and Chamberlin 2011). It is possible to imagine a situation, for example, when the phase-out of fossil fuels is far along, where a small, wealthy group of consumers (or, say, the military) would be willing to purchase the entire stock of fuel, regardless of cost. Despite dividends (which may involve a time lag, and which don't guarantee access to suppliers), the average consumer might be unable to acquire fossil fuels without a policy of rationing. For some historical perspective on challenges associated with rationing, see Cohen (2011).

of the scheme (efficient, manifestly fair, relatively immune to political manipulation, and offering solutions to problems of both climate change mitigation and global poverty) than the details of implementation.

While Barnes has focused more on national implementation (e.g., McKibben and Barnes 2010), his collaborator Costanza continues to advocate for a global program. In the wake of COP21 in Paris in 2015, Costanza and colleagues launched "Claim the Sky" (https://claimthesky.org/), a campaign that aims to generate citizen and civil society pressure for climate change mitigation action through the courts under the *public trust doctrine*, a concept that will be discussed in more detail in the next chapter. In brief, the public trust doctrine is a legal principle that holds that government has a fiduciary responsibility to hold natural assets in trust for the public good. "The public trust doctrine has been used in many countries in the past to protect water bodies, shorelines, fresh water, wildlife, and other resources," Costanza writes (2015, 21). Climate is more complicated since the atmosphere is a global asset, but "the fact that nations are *co-trustees* makes them no less responsible for protecting the asset than individual sovereigns are for protecting assets like shorelines or open water bodies that occur exclusively within their borders" (Costanza 2015, 21).

Costanza envisions legal action being taken against polluters by governments, spurred on by citizen pressure (Costanza 2015, 21–22). This could result in fines or in the establishment of carbon taxes or cap-and-permit systems as punitive measures. A natural first step (though, curiously, Costanza's call to action does not emphasize it) would be to take legal action against governments themselves for derogation of public trust responsibilities. This would be consistent with precedents cited on the "Claim the Sky" website: courts in Washington State and the Netherlands have ruled in favor of citizen and civil society plaintiffs, requiring government defendants to take action on climate change mitigation. The establishment of a global "Atmospheric Trust" or "Earth Atmospheric Trust" in the spirit of the public trust doctrine would make it possible to deliver global citizen dividends. The website does not discuss dividends, but a 2020 paper (Costanza et al. 2021) lays out a vision of paying "a fraction of the revenues to all people on Earth in the form of an annual per capita payment," in an amount that may be insignificant to those in developed nations but will alleviate global poverty, and using the remainder "to enhance and restore the asset, to encourage both social and technological innovations, and to run the Trust."

Another proposal for global carbon dividends was launched in 2020 by World Basic Income (WBI), a U.K.-based advocacy group. Under this plan, the revenue from a global cap-and-permit system would go into a global sovereign wealth fund. The fund would invest in development of renewable energy infrastructure and related research. As with the Alaska Permanent Fund, the principal would be husbanded while the *investment income* would be distributed as cash payments to every individual worldwide. The payments would be made on a monthly basis.

WBI cites several advantages of a global approach, in addition to the arguments from justice (fair sharing of compensation from those who pollute a common resource), equity (avoiding a situation where "the highest polluting countries... end up with most of the dividends"), and humanity (the transfers "would contribute significantly to an ending of extreme poverty, as well as a boost to local economies and employment in low-income areas") (WBI 2020, 14). As a practical matter, an international approach would in some ways be easier to administer than a patchwork of national programs. A national program generally requires calculating embodied fossil fuel energy in a range of trade products, while a global program could take a 100% upstream approach and a focus exclusively on the relatively small number of fossil fuel providers (14–15). Furthermore, WBI argues, when fossil fuel production ramps down, the accumulated capital will still be in place and can serve as the basis for an ongoing worldwide basic income. (One possible concern, however, is whether fund earnings and dividends in the early years will be high enough to enable households to weather higher energy prices.)

The problem of how the global cap-and-permit system is to be established is touched on only lightly by WBI. (WBI simply states that the plan could be adopted by the United Nations or set up independently.) But WBI devotes some attention to the question of *distribution* and makes a compelling case that this problem is tractable.

> A few years ago this might have been close to impossible, but a mixture of bank transfers and mobile money transfers could now get money to most people worldwide at the click of a button.
>
> Mobile money transfers use innovative banking services initially developed in Kenya in 2007. Using a text message-style service, people can receive and spend money using an old-style mobile phone. Nearly two thirds of people worldwide now have a mobile phone, and many of the

> remaining third are children who will receive their dividend via their parents.
>
> This leaves a small group of adults who will need extra help to access their dividend. These individuals could be given a cheap mobile phone (potentially supplied by mobile network companies, as it is in their long-term interests to create more phone users) or paid their dividend via a charge card, similar to how cash payments are distributed to some refugees. (WBI 2020, 20)

Registering recipients and validating their identities to prevent fraud will be a challenge in nations without effective national ID programs, but WBI believes these challenges can be overcome, citing as an example the progress made by Mannabase, an emerging blockchain-based universal basic income platform (WBI 2020, 20–21). The World Bank, it is worth noting, is equally sanguine on the question of distribution: "Increasing use of electronic cash transfers in developing countries and widespread uptake of mobile money accounts suggest that technology could make... transfer programs simpler and more efficient in future" (World Bank 2019, 44). Feasta's CapGlobalCarbon initiative has also studied the question of global distribution and found reason to be optimistic (Whyte 2016).

In sum, we are well on our way to establishing carbon pricing systems in nations around the world, using well-validated carbon tax and carbon cap-and-permit models. As carbon prices ramp up, we can expect that dividends will become an essential component of these programs due to simple economics (the need to relieve households that are burdened with higher energy costs). We are far from establishing a worldwide cap-and-dividend program, but a worldwide program would have some distinct advantages, and many of the technical problems associated with it are tractable.

References

Barnes, Peter. 1971. "Reconsidering Henry George." *The New Republic* (December 11).

Barnes, Peter. 2001. *Who Owns the Sky?* Washington, DC: Island Press.

Barnes, Peter. 2006. *Capitalism 3.0*. San Francisco: Berrett-Koehler.

Barnes, Peter, Robert Costanza, Paul Hawken, David Orr, Elinor Ostrom, Alvaro Umaña, and Oran Young. 2008. *Science* 309 (February 8): 724–726.

Block, Ben. 2008. A Look Back at James Hansen's Seminal Testimony on Climate, Part Two. *Grist* (June 18). https://grist.org/article/a-climate-hero-the-testimony/.

Blunden, J., and D. S. Arndt, eds. 2020. *State of the Climate in 2019*. Special Supplement to the *Bulletin of the American Meteorological Society* 101 (8, August).

Boyce, James K. 2018. Carbon Pricing: Effectiveness and Equity. *Ecological Economics* 150: 52–61.

Boyce, James K. 2019. *The Case for Carbon Dividends*. Medford, MA: Polity.

Boyce, James K., and Matthew Riddle. 2007. *Cap and Dividend: How to Curb Global Warming While Protecting the Incomes of American Families*. Political Economy Research Institute. Working Paper No. 150. November.

Boyce, J.K., and M.E. Riddle. 2008. *Keeping the Government Whole: The Impact of a Cap and-Dividend Policy for Curbing Global Warming on Government Revenue and Expenditure*. Political Economy Research Institute. Working Paper No. 188. November.

British Columbia. 2019. Climate Action Tax Credit Boost Helps B.C. Families. Ministry of Finance Information Bulletin (July 2). https://archive.news.gov.bc.ca/releases/news_releases_2017-2021/2019FIN0065-001371.htm.

Brulle, Robert. 2018. 30 Years Ago Global Warming Became Front-Page News—And Both Republicans and Democrats took it seriously. *The Conversation* (June 19). https://theconversation.com/30-years-ago-global-warming-became-front-page-news-and-both-republicans-and-democrats-took-it-seriously-97658.

Burtraw, Dallas, and Samantha Sekar. 2014. Two World Views on Carbon Revenues. *Journal of Environmental Studies and Sciences* 4: 110–120.

CapGlobalCarbon. 2017. Submission to the Irish Citizens' Assembly. August 11. https://www.capglobalcarbon.org/wp-content/uploads/2017/08/cgc-citizens-assembly.pdf.

CapGlobalCarbon. n.d. The Thinking Behind CapGlobalCarbon. https://www.capglobalcarbon.org/the-thinking-behind-capglobalcarbon/.

Carbon Tax Center. 2020. Where Carbon Is Taxed. Online Resource: https://www.carbontax.org/where-carbon-is-taxed. Accessed August 30, 2020.

Carl, Jeremy, and David Fedor. 2016. Tracking Global Carbon Revenues: A Survey of Carbon Taxes Versus Cap-and-Trade in the Real World. *Energy Policy* 96: 50–77.

Congressional Budget Office (CBO). 2000. *Who Gains and Who Pays Under Carbon-Allowance Trading?* June 1. https://www.cbo.gov/publication/12342.

Ciais, P., C. Sabine, G. Bala, L. Bopp, V. Brovkin, J. Canadell, A. Chhabra, R. DeFries, J. Galloway, M. Heimann, C. Jones, C. Le Quéré, R.B. Myneni, S. Piao, and P. Thornton. 2013. Carbon and Other Biogeochemical Cycles. In

Climate Change 2013: The Physical Science Basis. Contribution of Working Group I to the Fifth Assessment Report of the Intergovernmental Panel on Climate Change, ed. T.F. Stocker, D. Qin, G.-K. Plattner, M. Tignor, S.K. Allen, J. Boschung, A. Nauels, Y. Xia, V. Bex, and P.M. Midgley. Cambridge, UK: Cambridge University Press. https://www.ipcc.ch/site/assets/uploads/2018/02/WG1AR5_Chapter06_FINAL.pdf.

Climate Leadership Council (CLC). 2020. *The Baker Shultz Carbon Dividends Plan: Bipartisan Climate Roadmap, Issued by the Broadest Coalition in U.S. History*. https://clcouncil.org/Bipartisan-Climate-Roadmap.pdf.

Cohen, Maurie J. 2011. Is the UK Preparing for 'War'? Military Metaphors, Personal Carbon Allowances, and Consumption Rationing in Historical Perspective. *Climatic Change* 104 (2): 199–222.

Costanza, Robert. 2015. Claim the Sky! *Solutions* 6 (1, January–February).

Costanza, Robert, Paul W.B. Atkins, Marcello Hernandez-Blanco, and Ida Kubiszewski. 2021. Common Asset Trusts to Effectively Steward Natural Capital and Ecosystem Services at Multiple Scales. *Journal of Environmental Management* 280 (15 February): 111801. https://doi.org/10.1016/j.jenvman.2020.111801.

California Public Utilities Commission (CPUC). 2012. CPUC Issues Proposal on Use of Revenue from Sale of Greenhouse Gas Allowances by Utilities. Press Release. November 16. https://docs.cpuc.ca.gov/PublishedDocs/Published/G000/M034/K966/34966395.PDF.

Cramton, Peter, and Suzi Kerr. 1998. *Tradable Carbon Allowance Auctions: How and Why to Auction*. Center for Clean Air Policy.

Cronin, Julie-Anne, Don Fullerton, and Steven Sexton. 2017. *Vertical and Horizontal Redistributions from a Carbon Tax and Rebate*. Center for Economic Studies and if Institute (CESifo). Working Paper No. 6373.

Daily, Gretchen C., Susan Alexander, Paul R. Ehrlich, Larry Goulder, Jane Lubchenco, Pamela A. Matson, Harold A. Mooney, Sandra Postel, Stephen H. Schneider, David Tilman, and George M. Woodwell. 1997. *Ecosystem Services: Benefits Supplied to Human Societies by Natural Ecosystems*. Published as *Issues in Ecology* 2 (Spring).

Dinan, Terry, and Diane Lim Rogers. 2002. Distributional Effects of Carbon Allowance Trading: How Government Decisions Determine Winners and Losers. *National Tax Journal* 55 (2, June): 199–221.

Douthwaite, Richard. 1992. *The Growth Illusion: How Economic Growth Has Enriched the Few, Impoverished the Many, and Endangered the Planet*. Bideford, Devon: Green Books.

Elgie, Stewart, and Jessica McClay. 2013. *BC's Carbon Tax Shift After Five Years: Results. An Environmental (and Economic) Success Story*. Sustainable Prosperity. July.

Feasta. 2008. *Cap & Share: A Fair Way to Cut Greenhouse Emissions*. May. https://feasta.org/documents/energy/Cap-and-Share-May08.pdf.

Feasta. 2017. *Submission to the Citizens' Assembly*. August. https://www.feasta.org/wp-content/uploads/2017/08/Feasta-Citizens-Assembly.pdf.

Fleming, David, and Shaun Chamberlin. 2011. *TEQs (Tradable Energy Quotas): A Policy Framework for Peak Oil and Climate Change*. House of Commons All-Party Parliamentary Group on Peak Oil, and The Lean Economy Connection.

Food & Water Watch. 2013. *Dividend and Conquer: Cap-and-Dividend and Environmental Betrayal*. Issue Brief. January 11. https://www.foodandwaterwatch.org/sites/default/files/dividend_and_conquer_ib_jan_2013.pdf.

Fox, Justin. 2020. A 1988 Climate Warning Was Mostly Right: NASA Scientist James Hansen's Famous Global Warming Forecast Ran Through 2019. It Wasn't All That Far Off the Mark. *Bloomberg Opinion* (January 30). https://www.bloomberg.com/opinion/articles/2020-01-30/1988-global-warming-forecast-by-james-hansen-proved-mostly-true.

Fremstad, Anders and Mark Paul. 2018. *Disrupting the Dirty Economy: A Progressive Case for a Carbon Dividend*. People's Policy Project. September. https://www.peoplespolicyproject.org/wp-content/uploads/2018/09/CarbonTax.pdf.

Hafstead, Marc, Gilbert E. Metcalf, and Roberton C. Williams III. 2016. *Adding Quantity Certainty to a Carbon Tax: The Role of a Tax Adjustment Mechanism for Policy Pre-Commitment*. Resources for the Future. Discussion Paper. October. RFF DP 16–43. https://media.rff.org/documents/RFF-DP-16-43.pdf.

Hansen, James. 1988. Statement of Dr. James Hansen, Director, NASA Goddard Institute for Space Studies. In *Greenhouse Effect and Global Climate Change: Hearings Before the Committee on Energy and Natural Resources, United States Senate, One Hundredth Congress, First Session ... November 9 and 10, 1987*, 39–41. Washington, DC: U.S. Government Printing Office.

Hansen, James. 2007. Testimony Before the Iowa Utilities Board on November 5, 2007, in re: Interstate Power and Light Company. http://www.columbia.edu/~jeh1/mailings/2007/IowaCoal_20071105.pdf.

Hansen, James. 2008a. Dear Governor Greenwash. Mailing to Email List on May 29, 2008. http://www.columbia.edu/~jeh1/mailings/2008/20080529_DearGovernorGreenwash.pdf.

Hansen, James. 2008b. Global Warming Twenty Years Later: Tipping Points Near. Talk delivered June 23, 2008, at the National Press Club and at a Briefing to the House Select Committee on Energy Independence & Global Warming. http://www.columbia.edu/~jeh1/2008/TwentyYearsLater_20080623.pdf.

Hansen, James. 2008c. Carbon Tax and 100% Dividend—No Alligator Shoes!. Mailing to Email List on June 4, 2008. http://www.columbia.edu/~jeh1/mailings/2008/20080604_TaxAndDividend.pdf.

Hansen, James. 2009. *Storms of My Grandchildren: The Truth About the Coming Catastrophe and Our Last Chance to Save Humanity*. New York: Bloomsbury.

Hargrave, Tim. 1998. *U.S. Carbon Emissions Trading: Description of an Upstream Approach*. Center for Clean Air Policy. March.

Heron, Scott F., Ruben van Hooidonk, Jeffrey Maynard, Kristen Anderson, Jon C. Day, Erick Geiger, Ove Hoegh-Guldberg, Terry Hughes, Paul Marshall, David Obura, and C. Mark Eakin. 2018. *Impacts of Climate Change on World Heritage Coral Reefs: Update to the First Global Scientific Assessment*. Paris: UNESCO World Heritage Centre.

Horowitz, John, Julie-Anne Cronin, Hannah Hawkins, Laura Konda, and Alex Yuskavage. 2017. *Methodology for Analyzing a Carbon Tax*. U.S. Treasury Department, Office of Tax Analysis. Working Paper 115. January.

Hughes, J. Donald. 1994. *Pan's Travails: Environmental Problems of the Ancient Greeks and Romans*. Baltimore: Johns Hopkins University Press.

Intergovernmental Panel on Climate Change (IPCC). 2014. *Climate Change 2014: Synthesis Report. Contribution of Working Groups I, II and III to the Fifth Assessment Report of the Intergovernmental Panel on Climate Change*. https://ar5-syr.ipcc.ch/index.php.

IPCC. 2018. Summary for Policymakers. In *Global Warming of 1.5°C. An IPCC Special Report on the Impacts of Global Warming of 1.5°C Above Pre-Industrial Levels and Related Global Greenhouse Gas Emission Pathways, in the Context of Strengthening the Global Response to the Threat of Climate Change, Sustainable Development, and Efforts to Eradicate Poverty*. https://www.ipcc.ch/sr15/chapter/spm/.

Kalmus, Peter. 2017. *Being the Change: Live Well and Spark a Climate Revolution*. Gabriola, BC: New Society Publishers.

Komanoff, Charles. 2020. Australia's Brief, Shining Carbon Tax. Carbon Tax Center. January 7. https://www.carbontax.org/blog/2020/01/07/australias-brief-shining-carbon-tax/.

Lerman, Allen H. 2018. Paying Dividends to American Residents from Carbon Fee Revenue. Prepared for Citizens' Climate Education—Coronado, CA. May.

Lopomo, Giuseppe, Leslie M. Marx, David McAdams, and Brian Murray. 2011. Carbon Allowance Auction Design: An Assessment of Options for the U.S. *Review of Environmental Economics and Policy* 5 (1, Winter): 25–43.

Marron, Donald, and Elaine Maag. 2018. *How to Design Carbon Dividends*. Urban-Brookings Tax Policy Center.

McKibben, Bill, and Peter Barnes. 2010. A Simple Market Mechanism to Clean Up Our Economy. *Solutions* 1 (1, January): 30–38.

McSweeney, Robert. 2020. Tipping Points: Explainer: Nine 'Tipping Points' That Could Be Triggered by Climate Change. *Carbon Brief* (October 2). https://www.carbonbrief.org/explainer-nine-tipping-points-that-could-be-triggered-by-climate-change.

Meyer, Aubrey. 2000. *Contraction & Convergence: The Global Solution to Climate Change*. Cambridge, UK: Green Books.

Myhre, G., D. Shindell, F.-M. Bréon, W. Collins, J. Fuglestvedt, J. Huang, D. Koch, J.-F. Lamarque, D. Lee, B. Mendoza, T. Nakajima, A. Robock, G. Stephens, T. Takemura, and H. Zhang. 2013. Anthropogenic and Natural Radiative Forcing. In *Climate Change 2013: The Physical Science Basis. Contribution of Working Group I to the Fifth Assessment Report of the Intergovernmental Panel on Climate Change*. Cambridge, UK: Cambridge University Press. https://www.ipcc.ch/site/assets/uploads/2018/02/WG1AR5_Chapter08_FINAL.pdf.

Navigant and The Generation Foundation. 2018. *Raising the Acceptability and Effectiveness of Carbon Pricing: The Crucial Role of Carbon Revenue Recycling*. https://www.genfound.org/media/1657/carbon-revenue-recycling-final-paper-december-2018.pdf.

Partnership for Market Readiness (PMR) and International Carbon Action Partnership (ICAP). 2016. *Emissions Trading in Practice: A Handbook on Design and Implementation*. World Bank. https://icapcarbonaction.com/en/?option=com_attach&task=download&id=364.

Partnership for Market Readiness (PMR). 2017. *Carbon Tax Guide: A Handbook for Policy Makers*. World Bank. https://www.connect4climate.org/publication/carbon-tax-guide-handbook-policy-makers.

Ranalli, Brent. 2012. Can International Regimes Be Effective Means to Restrain Carbon Emissions? In *Controversies in Globalization*, 2nd ed., ed. Peter M. Haas and John A. Hird, 283–304. Thousand Oaks, CA: CQ Press.

Regional Economic Models, Inc. (REMI) and Synapse Energy Economics, Inc. (Synapse). 2014. *The Economic, Climate, Fiscal, Power, and Demographic Impact of a National Fee-and-Dividend Carbon Tax*. June 9. https://citizensclimatelobby.org/wp-content/uploads/2014/06/REMI-carbon-tax-report-62141.pdf.

Revkin, Andrew C., Shan Carter, Jonathan Ellis, Farhana Hossain, and Alan Mclean. 2008. On the Issues: Climate Change. *New York Times*. https://www.nytimes.com/elections/2008/president/issues/climate.html.

Rosenberg, Joseph, Eric Toder, and Chenxi Lu. 2018. *Distributional Implications of a Carbon Tax*. Urban-Brookings Tax Policy Center. July. https://www.taxpolicycenter.org/publications/distributional-implications-carbon-tax.

Royer, Sarah-Jeanne., Sara Ferrón, Samuel T. Wilson, and David M. Karl. 2018. Production of Methane and Ethylene from Plastic in the Environment. *PLoS ONE* 13 (8): e0200574.

Schröter, Matthias, Emma H. Van der Zanden, Alexander PE. van Oudenhoven, Roy P. Remme, Hector M. Serna-Chavez, Rudolf S. De Groot, and Paul Opdam. 2014. Ecosystem Services as a Contested Concept: A Synthesis of Critique and Counter-Arguments. *Conservation Letters* 7 (6): 514–523.

Schwartz, John. 2020. Overlooked No More: Eunice Foote, Climate Scientist Lost to History. *New York Times* (April 21). https://www.nytimes.com/2020/04/21/obituaries/eunice-foote-overlooked.html.

Shabecoff, Philip. 1988. Global Warming Has Begun, Expert Tells Senate. *New York Times* (June 24). https://www.nytimes.com/1988/06/24/us/global-warming-has-begun-expert-tells-senate.html.

Smith, Adam. [1776] 1986. *The Wealth of Nations Books I–III*. London: Penguin Classics.

Swiss Federal Office for the Environment. 2020. Redistribution of the CO_2 Levy. Webpage Last Updated 8 November 2020. https://www.bafu.admin.ch/bafu/en/home/topics/climate/info-specialists/reduction-measures/co2-levy/redistribution.html.

This is Democracy. 2020. Podcast Episode 103: "Carbon Dividends: Solving our Climate Crisis" (July 1).

United Nations Framework Convention on Climate Change (UNFCC). n.d. The Paris Agreement. https://unfccc.int/process-and-meetings/the-paris-agreement/the-paris-agreement.

Walsh, J., D. Wuebbles, K. Hayhoe, J. Kossin, K. Kunkel, G. Stephens, P. Thorne, R. Vose, M. Wehner, J. Willis, D. Anderson, S. Doney, R. Feely, P. Hennon, V. Kharin, T. Knutson, F. Landerer, T. Lenton, J. Kennedy, and R. Somerville. 2014. Ch. 2: Our Changing Climate. Climate Change Impacts in the United States. In *The Third National Climate Assessment*, ed. J.M. Melillo, Terese (T.C.) Richmond, and G.W. Yohe, 19–67. U.S. Global Change Research Program. https://doi.org/10.7930/J0KW5CXT.

Weart, Spencer. 2003. *The Discovery of Global Warming*. Cambridge, MA: Harvard University Press.

Weitzman, Martin L. 1974. Prices vs. Quantities. *The Review of Economic Studies* 41 (4): 477–491.

World Bank. 2019. *Using Carbon Revenues*. August. Partnership for Market Readiness Technical Note 16. https://openknowledge.worldbank.org/handle/10986/32247.

World Bank. 2020a. *State and Trends of Carbon Pricing 2020*. Washington, DC. https://openknowledge.worldbank.org/handle/10986/33809.

World Bank. 2020b. Carbon Pricing Dashboard. Data last updated April, 01 2020. https://carbonpricingdashboard.worldbank.org/map_data. Consulted August 2020.

World Basic Income (WBI). 2020. *International Carbon Charge and Dividend: A Practical Mechanism for Climate Justice*. July. http://www.worldbasicin

come.org.uk/uploads/7/8/9/3/78930716/international_carbon_charge_and_dividend_-_final.pdf.

Whyte, Caroline. 2016. Tackling Climate, Poverty and Inequality Together: Managing the Share in CapGlobalCarbon on a Global Level. June 5. https://capglobalcarbon.org/2016/06/05/tackling-climate-poverty-and-inequality-together-managing-the-share-in-capglobalcarbon-on-a-global-level/.

CHAPTER 5

Common Wealth Dividends, Generalized

In the preceding three chapters, we examined three classes of common wealth that can be tapped to generate broad-based financial dividends: land, natural resources, and ecosystem services. The task of this chapter is to see how far the idea can reasonably be generalized beyond these three domains. Does it extend, for example, to man-made commons, as many authors assert (e.g., Andersen 1996, 227ff; Barnes 2014, 139ff; Flomenhoft 2012; Farley et al. 2015; even Paine [1797] 1945)?

We attack this problem from two directions. We explore ***theories and principles*** that may be able to tie together what we have observed so far and extend it to man-made commons, and we examine candidate *examples* of potential sources of dividends in the human economy. Some of the examples and some of the theories may be more compelling than others. Readers may decide for themselves which approaches they find most convincing and how broad a circle they would draw when identifying sources of common wealth suitable for funding broad-based dividends.

This chapter is bookended by two other topics. We start with a discussion of ecological sustainability. The imperative of sustainability places some constraints on how and when Nature should be treated as a source of universal dividends, so we clarify this before moving on to discuss man-made sources of dividends. We close the chapter by touching on some of the practical questions of how a program (or, more likely, a collection of

B. Ranalli, *Common Wealth Dividends*,
Exploring the Basic Income Guarantee,
https://doi.org/10.1007/978-3-030-72416-0_5

programs of various sizes and scales) to gather and distribute common wealth dividends would operate.

Natural Wealth and the Demands of Sustainability

Nature is more than a source of financial dividends; it literally sustains and permeates us. Our relationship with Nature is shot through with ethical implications, and if we want to develop a general theory of common wealth dividends we need to situate it within that larger ethical domain.

In the first place, there is *Nature as gift*. Theists like Grotius and Locke viewed Nature as a gift from the God of the Old Testament, with particular conditions and strings attached. Most cultures have adhered to some variation on this theme, whether the giver is a sky god or a mother goddess or a pantheon or a world of spirits, or even if the rivers and forests and beasts give themselves as gifts. As Lewis Hyde explains in *The Gift* ([1983] 2007), a classic study of art and anthropology, the recipient of a gift incurs ethical obligations. The obligation may be to reciprocate or, if the gift is of such magnitude as to make reciprocation impossible, to live in a state of gratitude and grace and to pay the gift forward. Practices like offering "first fruits" to protecting spirits are examples of reciprocation; Robin Wall Kimmerer explains in *Braiding Sweetgrass* (2013) how such rituals foster an ethic of conservation and can also serve to enhance and protect the landscape. A monotheistic religion like Christianity may seek to cultivate a generalized stewardship ethic (e.g., Pope Francis 2015). The "gift" frame is not scientific, but it is nearly universal in human history because it is functional—it helps cultures maintain the resources they need to sustain themselves.

The insights of modern science allow for an even more firmly grounded environmental ethic. Earth is the only spot in the entire universe, as far as we know, where life has developed, and every single species alive today is the product of millions upon millions of years of evolution, and the life cycles of visible and microscopic organisms are bound together in ways that we have only begun to comprehend. An understanding of how unlikely and precarious life on Earth is leads to an appreciation of how precious it is. Aldo Leopold articulated well the corollary ethical principle: "A thing is right when it tends to preserve the integrity, stability, and beauty of the biotic community. It is wrong when it tends otherwise" ([1949] 1989, 224–225). The fossil record shows that Earth has experienced five mass extinctions in its deep history. It is currently undergoing a sixth, for which we (humans, and especially moderns) are directly responsible. We are erasing the product of millions of years of evolution, a loss that is incalculable, not only on a planetary but also very likely on a galactic or possibly even universal scale. It is certainly possible that when the extinction episode draws to an end the planet will bounce back and flourish even more than before, but here and now the single greatest and most absolute positive good we can do is to conserve and preserve and shepherd as many species and functioning ecosystems as we can through this bottleneck.

Seen in this light: if we face a choice between disrupting ecosystems to generate financial dividends—even dividends shared equitably—or allowing ecosystems to flourish, we should let ecosystems flourish.

Nevertheless, living in a bubble apart from Nature is not an option. We necessarily interact with Nature. In addition to ethical imperatives that value Nature for its own sake, there are ethical imperatives that value Nature as resources for human use and sustenance. In a nutshell, these concern *sustainability*. As a matter of prudence and courtesy, we have an obligation to refrain from fouling our nest, an obligation to leave future generations with sufficient "natural capital" (resources, ecosystem services, etc.) to live good lives—ideally, to enlarge the natural capital account of future generations rather than allowing it to diminish.

What does sustainability require? Environmental economists generally distinguish between renewable and non-renewable resources when discussing sustainability. A renewable resource is like an asset that earns interest. In fairness to future generations, we should consume only (at most) the interest; we should leave the capital intact. That is: we should limit our harvest of fish to an amount that will allow the fishery to continue to thrive at the same level from year to year. We should limit our emissions of carbon to a rate that earth systems can safely absorb. We should replenish the nutrients in soils as we deplete them.

The case of a non-renewable resource is harder. When a resource like a fossil fuel deposit or an ancient groundwater reserve is gone, it is gone. A reasonable approach is to use the depletion to capitalize some other kind of asset that will continue to provide benefits to future generations when the original asset is gone—as the State of Alaska uses oil revenue to capitalize a Permanent Fund, and as many nations around the world, from Norway to Nigeria, have in recent decades started capitalizing (typically non-dividend-issuing) sovereign wealth funds from oil and other mineral revenue (Cummine 2016). Prudence also requires budgeting the non-renewable resource carefully: to ensure that it is drawn down cautiously and made to last as long as possible, and that it is put to the highest possible uses.

That simple description is certainly not the last word in sustainability. On long timescales, like those at which fossil fuels form and deep aquifers are replenished, the distinction between renewable and non-renewable resources becomes blurred. On even longer timescales, like that of the solar system, nothing is sustainable. Even on human timescales, changes in technology can change what kinds of resources are valuable to people and worth preserving. Norwegian economist Rögnvaldur Hannesson (2001, 1–2) tells the cautionary tale of a sustainability-minded Irishman who carefully stewarded the peat on his property to provide income for his children and grandchildren—and then was overtaken by the Industrial Revolution, which rendered the peat obsolete and valueless as fuel. Petroleum was once a resource with no commercial value, as was uranium. Medical researchers regularly discover that some rare plant or animal species holds the key to a breakthrough; the loss of species is not only an objective impoverishment of the universe, it also impoverishes our human pharmacopeia. We should also expect that our understanding of what constitutes a "sustainable yield" from a fishery or other renewable resource will necessarily be imperfect. If we are not cautious, we risk inadvertently drawing down the capital. So a precautionary approach is called for.

Although there are some bright spots in our record, on the whole we are failing to live up to the obligations of sustainability. Researchers have determined that our global "ecological footprint" began to exceed the capacity of the Earth around the year 1970, and by 2016 our annual consumption would have required over 1.5 Earths to be genuinely sustainable (Wackernagel and Beyers 2019, 59). Put another way, we tend to consume a year's worth of resources by sometime in August each year: in 2020, "Earth Overshoot Day" fell on August 22, according to https://www.footprintnetwork.org/our-work/earth-overshoot-day/. By living far beyond our means, running at over 150% of our budget, we are depleting the capital (water, soil, and forest resources, etc.) that we and future generations will depend on.

We can and must do better at living up to the requirements of sustainability. On the assumption that we will aspire to sustainability, thinking like an environmental economist can help us see what financial flows are generated from sustainable use of resources, and how those flows could and should be treated as sources of common wealth dividends.

In the case of non-renewable resources, we want to ensure that those resources are exploited in a way that is measured rather than hasty, and that they go to their highest use. We also want, if possible, to capitalize some other asset that will continue to generate benefits for future generations, providing some compensation for the loss of the resource itself. These requirements imply the following: Stewardship of the resource and the revenue generated by it should be in the hands of a dedicated government organization or some other body with a mission of public responsibility. This steward will be responsible for gradually selling the resource (or selling a concession to exploit the resource). The pace of sale/drawdown will be determined by prudence. The price will be determined by the market. The steward of the resource should drive the hardest possible bargain: to maximize value for future generations (or to put it another way, to ensure that none of the value of the capital stock is lost when it is monetized),[1] to slow the pace of exploitation and reduce waste, and to put the resource to (arguably, according to the market) its highest use. The steward's judgment may need to be brought to bear when evaluating highest use. The steward of an aquifer might determine, for example, that irreplaceable groundwater should not be used to irrigate thirsty crops like alfalfa and rice, even if growers of those crops are willing to pay top dollar.

Ideally, 100% of the receipts should be used to capitalize other resources that will benefit future generations.[2] (Compare the stingy-seeming 11–14% that goes to the APF [Erickson and Groh 2012, 42].) It could be used to provide some sort of equivalent service, like using fossil fuel revenue to build nuclear or renewable energy infrastructure, or using

[1] Basu and Pegg (2020, 1374) point out that framing matters. "Maximize revenue" and "tolerate zero loss" may be mathematically equivalent when it comes to exploitation of non-renewable resources, but "maximize" is a fuzzy directive—one that a person can fall short of and still feel satisfied—while "zero loss" is a strict directive, and it is galvanizing. Humans tend to be loss-averse. (Cf. the researches of Kahneman and Tversky [1979] on prospect theory: "Losses loom larger than gains" [79].)

[2] This is in accordance with what is known in environmental economics as "weak sustainability," which posits a degree of substitutability between natural capital and other types of capital. Foundational writings include Solow (1974) and Hartwick (1977). The idea that society should invest all rents from exhaustible resources in reproducible capital goods is known as "Hartwick's Rule."

groundwater revenue to (perhaps) develop surface water resources or diversify a predominantly agricultural economy. Some or all, alternatively, could go into an investment fund like the APF. Basu and Pegg (2020) argue for investing the preserved liquid capital in a global portfolio of low-cost mutual funds.

For the steward to distribute dividends directly out of the resource or concession revenue would be highly irresponsible. But to distribute dividends out of the profits of a revenue-funded investment portfolio would be acceptable, prudent (to build a political constituency to preserve the fund), and arguably even imperative, as the investment portfolio itself would effectively be a sort of renewable resource. Dividends from earnings would allow citizens to benefit in a concrete and equitable way from the funds invested in their name. In her book about the future of sovereign wealth funds, *Citizens' Wealth*, Angela Cummine argues that other sovereign wealth funds should follow Alaska's example in this regard (2016, 135ff).

For renewable resources, sustainability requires preserving the natural capital and harvesting only a sustainable yield. Accomplishing these goals means, again, that authority to make and enforce rules should be invested in some government body or other institution with a public mission. Rules must be designed to ensure that the resource does not become degraded, including ensuring that harvests do not exceed a sustainable yield. For example: The manager of a fishery may establish rules about acceptable technologies and practices to limit by-catch, and may establish a permit system. The managers of a park may establish rules about waste management and use of fire, and may limit the number of simultaneous visitors or the number of visitors per year.

If demand exceeds supply, the limited fishing permits and park passes will have some market value. The manager of a renewable resource is not under a ***moral obligation*** to maximize receipts from permits and passes (as the steward of a non-renewable resource is under an obligation to drive the hardest bargain to preserve capital stock), but selling them at full market price is one option for distributing them. Considerations of fairness might point in other directions: for example, instituting a lottery system, or reserving some free or subsidized permits or passes for those with limited income, or giving preference to groups with a vested interest (as parks sometimes give discounts to local residents, and some fisheries might give precedence to long-established fishing families). To the extent that charging for permits and passes is consistent with the demands of fairness, it has the advantage of providing revenue that can be put to good use—and charging full market value for permits and passes maximizes that revenue. The revenue must be used first and foremost to ensure sustainable management of the resource. If net revenue remains beyond that, that money—raised in the name of the public—should be put to some use of public benefit. Issuing it as dividends is one option. Other options would include investing it in something of public benefit or adding it to the general revenue of the state.

We have already discussed in Chapter 3 the drawbacks of using resource revenue to fund the state. I would like to focus here on the question of when it is particularly appropriate to issue dividends from renewable resource revenue, as this will help tie together the topics of Chapters 2 and 4. First of all, it must be recognized that both land (Chapter 2) and ecosystem services (Chapter 4) come under the heading of renewable resources. What makes the case for issuing dividends in the case of land use so strong, and for charging full market value so as to maximize dividends, is that land is an asset that can generate income. It can serve as a factor in production (e.g., for farming, or as a site for other commercial activity), it has rental value, and it is an investment whose value may appreciate over time. Those who do not have a permit or pass (i.e., a deed) for exclusive use of a plot of land are missing out on economic opportunities. The same is true of those who do not receive a permit or pass to harvest fish from a fishery, and true in spades of those who do not receive a permit or pass to emit carbon. It is *not* true of those who are deprived of a permit or pass to camp in Yellowstone National Park or scuba dive around the Great Barrier Reef. We can broadly distinguish between permitting systems that create economic winners and losers and permitting systems that do not. For the former type, a strong case can be made for charging full market value for permits and returning the revenue to the public as compensation. For the latter type, charging full market value and redistributing is an option, but (as discussed above) other considerations could also come into play, like ensuring equality of opportunity to take advantage of a recreational resource.

It is worth revisiting the question of what is to be done with carbon pricing revenue. The Earth systems that regulate climate are a renewable resource, and the requirements of sustainability would seem to demand that any revenue raised by stewards of the resource should be spent first and foremost on protecting the resource. Yet in Chapter 4, we argued forcefully that dividends should be central to any plan for spending carbon pricing revenue. How can this be reconciled? The answer, in a nutshell, is the exceptional scope and scale of the climate crisis. Solving it will require mobilizing society-wide resources and making investments on a scale that will dwarf the revenue of the carbon pricing system itself. In terms of facilitating climate change mitigation, the great value that the climate pricing system provides is not the revenue it generates but the price signal it sends throughout the economy. To preserve the price signal, we need to ensure that the carbon pricing system itself remains viable. And that means keeping the public on side. Issuing dividends can awaken and reinforce the public's sense of ownership over the shared resource, as Barnes proposed. And making the dividends robust enough to ensure that households can keep their head above water during the decarbonization transition is not only good policy, it is also—similar to the PFD in Alaska—good politics. It can help forestall public opposition to climate action (like the "yellow vest" movement in France) and can even recruit the public as a constituency for carbon pricing (Boyce 2021). Is it necessary for 100% of the revenue to be issued as dividends? Costanza and Farley (2010) argue that some of the revenue—perhaps a variable proportion, to be monitored and adjusted as needed—should be reserved for investments. They worry that "private" investments, spurred by the carbon price signal, may be inadequate, and in particular that "if research and development is left up to the private sector, new technologies will be patented," and this will retard their dissemination (33). The response to this argument is that public investment will certainly be necessary as well. Public–private partnerships can be designed to ensure that new technologies are quickly disseminated and that innovators are fairly compensated. The resources available for public investment are bottomless—we regularly see that in any emergency (war abroad, disaster relief, financial meltdowns, pandemic), governments with sovereign control over their currency instantly call up resources in the needed amount. (See the section on money creation, below, for an explanation.) In consequence, it is not *necessary* to tap into carbon pricing system revenue to fund investments in decarbonization. It is certainly *possible*. Investment in decarbonization would not be an objectively bad use of the funds (as long as enough remain to ensure households can weather the transition). But I would argue that the cleanest way to ensure that dividends are adequately funded is to insist that 100% of carbon pricing system revenue go to dividends as a core element of program design. Allowing some percentage to go to other purposes would be to invite continual political wrangling over allocation.

Some readers might be surprised to have read so far into a book about our common interest in natural resources and encountered no discussion of the so-called "tragedy of the commons." This is a good time to address the topic. Garret Hardin's classic essay by that title describes the overuse and degradation that can be expected to occur when a limited resource is not subject to any kind of collective management. The conclusion Hardin reaches is precisely that some kind of collective management is necessary: "mutual coercion, mutually agreed upon" (Hardin 1968, 1247). (Years later, Hardin (1991, 178) acknowledged that the famous paper should really have been titled "The Tragedy of the *Unmanaged* Commons.") Subsequent scholars, picking up the thread of Hardin's work, have shown that the ease or difficulty of setting up a management regime, and the most optimal type of regime (e.g., centralized management or distributed property rights), will depend in large part on a resource's characteristics—most importantly, how difficult it is to divide it up, and how difficult it is to exclude parties from using it. They have also shown that even in the most challenging cases—so-called "common pool" resources, like pastures and fisheries—it is quite possible to devise regimes to manage such resources sustainably, and that societies around the world have often done so, in creative and diverse ways.[3] So when in the discussion above I state simply that some governmental or other body should be empowered to steward non-renewable resources and manage renewable resources, it can be taken as understood that it might be easier in one case and more difficult in another, but that it in all cases it is possible in principle.

The following table sums up the conclusions reached so far about the applicability of the concept of common wealth dividends to renewable and non-renewable resources in a management regime focused on sustainability (Table 5.1).

Other questions arise when we envision sustainable management of natural resources. For example, *who* should manage the resources? In *Nature's Trust: Environmental Law for a New Ecological Age*, Mary Christina Wood (2013) makes a compelling case that stewardship of natural resources for the benefit of the public and future generations is

[3]A good entry point into the vast literature on common pool resources is the short 1999 article "Revisiting the Commons: Local Lessons, Global Challenges" by Elinor Ostrom and colleagues (Ostrum et al. 1999).

Table 5.1 Applicability of common wealth dividend concept to renewable and non-renewable resources

Type of natural resource	*Non-renewable*	*Renewable*	
		Managed for use on market terms	*Managed for public preservation*
Management goals	Maximize long-term value: • Monetize sparingly • Charge the highest rates the market will bear ("zero loss") • Invest as much as possible in financial or other assets that will produce ongoing wealth	1. Long-term stewardship of resource and the ecological systems in which it is embedded 2. Financial security for the trust 3. Equitable distribution of rental income	1. Long-term stewardship of resource and the ecological systems in which it is embedded 2. Financial security for the trust 3. Socially optimal allocation of use in accordance with public mission (e.g., education, recreation)
Mandate to issue dividends?	• From original non-renewable resource: No (in fact, it is imperative to *not* issue dividends) • From new perpetual asset: Yes, weak (mandate to provide tangible benefits, possibly in the form of dividends)	Yes, a strong mandate	No mandate
Examples	Minerals; fossil fuels; fossil groundwater	Fisheries; most land, rivers, lakes, and oceans; the atmosphere	Unique or sensitive parts of the landscape

an essential function of government, and in fact an inalienable element of sovereignty. The "public trust doctrine" appears in law codes as far back as ancient Rome, and it is perennially, if sporadically, invoked as a common law principle by courts in settings as diverse as the United States, the Philippines, and India.

Wood quotes a standard explanation of the responsibilities of a trustee: "The trustee... is obligated to the beneficiary to do all acts necessary for the preservation of the trust *res* which would be performed by a reasonably prudent man employing his own like property for purposes similar to those of the trust" (2013, 167). The *res* (Latin for "things" or "objects") is the thing which is to be managed, and the beneficiary is the party on whose behalf and for whose benefit the trust operates. When the *res* is a natural resource, and the beneficiary is the public at large, including future generations, the responsibility of the trustee amounts to protecting the resource, preventing its diminishment, maximizing the societal value it provides, restoring it when damaged, and obtaining recompense from those that injure it (Wood 2013, 167). Not surprisingly, this maps fairly neatly onto our working understanding of the demands of sustainability, described above. With this ideal of trust management clearly in view, the actual record of natural resource management by governments frequently stands in stark and appalling contrast. (Think, for example, of the record of the U.S. Forest Service, which has been so eager to service the logging industry that in some years it has actually *lost* money for the public when conducting timber sales, or the U.S. mineral rights regime, which since 1872 has allowed any private party to claim and exploit non-renewable resources on federal land for paltry up-front fees and no payment of royalties.) Wood explains why this should be so: legislators take no fiduciary oath; natural resources are only one of many issues that command their attention; their job is structured to make them responsive to the demands of constituents and patrons on a timescale of months and years rather than responsive to the requirements of long-term stewardship (Wood 2013, 191–192). The executive agencies that are responsible for managing resources on a day-to-day basis, in their turn, are accountable to the legislature and its whims, and to political leadership with a similarly narrow time horizon.

Wood offers suggestions for making legislatures and executive agencies into better trustees (e.g., lengthening the amount of time agency officials have to wait before becoming lobbyists, strengthening reporting and disclosure requirements for agency employees, and reforming the legislative process to place some limits on the use of "riders" that favor special interests [2013, 193–200]), but these frankly do not inspire much hope of real change. In his forthcoming *Ours: A Case for Universal Property*,

Barnes (2021 [in press]) proposes that rather than waiting for governments to behave more like trusts, we should literally employ trusts to manage our natural resources. A variety of trusts could be commissioned to manage forests, lakes, mines, etc. Their authority would be granted by the government that establishes them, but their primary mode of accountability would be not *democratic* accountability (i.e., accountability to constituents or their political representatives) but *fiduciary* accountability to the terms of their charter, enforceable by the courts.

There are examples that one can point to as models of such trusts. In Britain, the National Trust for Places of Historic Interest or Natural Beauty (commonly known as the "National Trust") is an independent charity whose mission has been defined and refined by successive Acts of Parliament. The National Trust owns, operates, and manages historical houses, castles, gardens and parks, and over 960 square miles of land in England, Wales, and Northern Ireland, making it one of the largest landowners in Britain. On a smaller scale, in Massachusetts, the Trustees of Reservations is a non-profit organization that was founded by the state legislature in 1891 (but is not funded by the state, except via competitive grants). The Trustees manage and preserve "places of ecological, scenic, and historic importance" throughout the Commonwealth. These organizations, and others like them, may offer free public admission to some sites and charge admission at others, depending on circumstances (e.g., level of demand, cost structures, imperatives to serve the public and to protect against overuse). They generally also require outside sources of income, including endowments and donations, to fulfill their mission. The nature of their niche (specializing in properties of primarily public recreational or conservation value rather than commercial value) dictates that these trusts do not have a strong mandate to issue dividends. If we commission trusts to manage other types of land and other natural resources and ecosystem services, some of these other trusts would (and should) have strong mandates to issue dividends.

What else would be different in a world where land and natural resources and ecosystem services are governed by trusts?

There would naturally be questions of jurisdictional boundaries to be resolved—but that is true even today of the many local, regional, and national government bodies that oversee natural resources. That is not an obstacle, just a set of technical issues to be worked out.

It is easy enough to imagine a trust established to sustainably manage a fishery or a lake or a bay or a nation's mines or public forests. It is a little harder to envision a trust established to manage ***land*** per se (by which I mean land that is treated as a commodity for private or commercial or governmental use, as opposed to land that has distinctive features and would belong under the authority of a boutique trust like the National Trust or the Trustees for Reservations, described above), for the simple reason that much land is privately owned and transferring ownership to a trust would be quite disruptive (not to mention unpopular). This is an instance where working through existing government channels might be better than establishing a new institution. Private landowners are already subject to a range of public-interest restrictions on how they may use their property (like zoning laws, rules about applying pesticides, rules about disposal of waste, etc.) and incentives; these restrictions and incentives can be optimized for ecological sustainability. And private landowners already pay something like a Georgist tax on land values—except that in most cases (a) the tax is not set precisely at the full rental value of the land, and (b) the value of the land is not separated out from the value of buildings and other improvements. That would be easy enough to optimize as well. In the United States at least, real estate taxes are collected at the local level and used to fund local schools and services. Fairer would be to pool the revenue more widely across jurisdictions, and (according to the principles we have set out) to distribute this kind of revenue equitably as dividends, and to use other means (e.g., income tax, sales tax, allotments from central government) to fund schools and local services. Changes like these would be somewhat disruptive, but certainly more feasible than transferring title of all commercial and residential real estate to a trust.

Just how broad should the jurisdictions of natural resource trusts be? That is: should they be local, and issue dividends to local residents only? Or should they be wide in scope, or even global? In principle, the question comes down to: who has a claim on the resource? For a global ecosystem service like the atmosphere as a carbon sink, the principled answer would be "every person in the world." Some might want to think globally in the case of a mine or a fishery as well, but a compelling argument could also be made in those cases to favor locals instead—though just how wide or narrow to draw the circle will be a question of judgment. For land, a principled answer might be "anyone who lives within the relevant jurisdiction," which might be a nation-state. In practice, the nation-state—or in federated systems, possibly the state or province or canton, etc.—is the scale on which trusts are most likely to form, simply because that is where it is easiest to find and exercise the authority necessary to establish them.

So the oil revenue from Alaska's North Slope did not flow only to local Inuit villages, it flowed to the whole state via Anchorage. And carbon dividend systems are likely to be mostly national programs (though there is always the possibility that the will could be found, over time, to federate them at a trans-national level).

General Theories and Principles

As already discussed, in most cultures throughout history it has been customary to treat Nature as a gift, and that perception of Nature as Gift has implied ethical obligations. Depending on how the Gift myth is framed, those ethical obligations could include not only conservation (as discussed in the previous section on sustainability) but also equitable sharing. "The Yakut refuse to believe," according to anthropologist Claude Lévi-Strauss, "that somewhere in the world people could die of hunger, when it was easy to go and share a neighbor's meal" (Hyde [1983] 2007, 86). The Christian tradition had its own versions of this sharing imperative as well. The doctrines of Aquinas and the natural law arguments of thinkers like Grotius that we surveyed in Chapter 2, arguing for equity (in one degree or another) in the distribution of land and natural resources, were grounded in a Gift myth, the story of a bequest made by the God of the Old Testament to Adam as humanity's common ancestor.

Gift-myth arguments are made, or at least implied, even today in our modern, secular culture. Barnes and other contemporary writers refer, for example, to "gifts of Nature." I have used the phrase myself. The phrase is rhetorically useful, implying an imperative to share equitably. But it does not stand up well to analytical scrutiny. (Is Nature a conscious agent? Are these gifts necessarily granted to humanity as a whole, or can they not just as well be seen as granted to the individuals who take them?) And traditional formulations are equally flimsy. The same Adam-and-Yahweh story that Grotius used to argue for equal rights to the fruits of nature, Filmer used to justify inequality.

To clarify and give more weight to the moral intuition we have been exploring in this book, it seems that we would need to set it on some firmer foundation. In this section we explore three principles, from three different domains (political theory, property theory, and microeconomics), that could potentially provide that firmer foundation. They are largely compatible, but they are not identical. Each has its merits; the reader may decide how compelling they are as explanations/justifications for common wealth dividends.

Political Theory: Public Trust Doctrine

The public trust doctrine was already introduced above. "The doctrine," writes Wood (2013, 125), "holds government, as trustee of ecological assets, to a quintessential duty of protection.... The citizens stand as beneficiaries holding a clear public property interest in these natural resources." The government has a right and responsibility to ensure that natural resources, the necessities of life and prosperity, are managed sustainably for the benefit of current and future citizens.

Wood explains that public trust doctrine is, like police power, "a fundamental attribute of sovereignty." In the words of one federal district court, "The trust is of such a nature that it can be held only by the sovereign, and can only be destroyed by the destruction of the sovereign" (Wood 2013, 129). For this reason it is found in positive law codes, in one form or another, from ancient Rome to the present day. (The Alaska Constitution's declaration that natural resources are to be managed by the state "for the maximum benefit of its people," cited in Chapter 3, is just one example.) The doctrine is also a well-established common-law principle, and it is not uncommon for judges to enforce it when lawmakers fail to heed it.

The focus of the public trust doctrine is on sustainably managing common resources, not on monetizing them or issuing dividends. But the doctrine does serve as a foundation of sorts for the idea of common wealth dividends. It clearly identifies citizens as the beneficiaries of natural resource management. And in a democratic polity, with equal rights before the law, that beneficiary status cannot be anything other than equitable. So it follows from the doctrine that *if* natural resources are monetized (which should only be done in a manner consistent with sustainable management), that money should be used to benefit all equally—whether in services or otherwise (e.g., in cash).

Property Theory: The Labor Theory of Property

As noted above, early natural law theorists working in the Christian tradition, like Grotius, had a ready-made justification for common ownership of Nature in the Genesis story. They believed that the God of the Old

Testament had granted title to the natural world to Adam, and they reasoned that as Adam's heirs every person inherits a share in that original title. A leading interpreter of Paine, Gregory Claeys, assuming that this same logic—an "original community of property established on earth by God"—must undergird Paine's own natural law argument for equal right to the land in *Agrarian Justice*, chastises the professed Deist for a presumed lapse into theism (Claeys 1987, 21; cf. Claeys 1989, 2016). But Paine does not actually make the theistic argument (Ranalli 2020). Nor does he need to. Another justification is available that is entirely secular, and the essence of it is found in Paine's insistence that "Man did not make the earth" (1797, 13).

The principle that Paine is appealing to is known variously as the "responsibility principle," the "natural rights theory of property," or the "labor theory of property" or LTP. This principle assigns property rights based on effort: one has a right to that which one has produced oneself. (More precisely: *initial property rights* are assigned to the agent who created the property. They can of course then be exchanged or gifted. In principle, any legitimately held claim to property ought to be traceable back through free exchanges (or gifts, or court settlements, etc.) to the individual(s) who created the property.) Though the principle is "essentially primordial" (to quote a leading contemporary LTP theorist, the economist and political scientist David Ellerman [2016, 330]), it is most often associated with the thought of John Locke. Locke ([1690] 2017, 287–288) wrote that "every Man has a *Property* in his own *Person*. This no Body has any Right to but himself. The *Labour* of his Body, and the *Work* of his Hands, we may say, are properly his." However, Locke might not actually be the best authority to cite for this principle, since (as we already saw in Chapter 2) he also claims to have the right to the products of his *servant's* hands as well as his own, which implicitly negates the principle (Locke [1690] 2017, 289). John Stuart Mill (1875, 133) did better at stating the principle concisely and consistently when he wrote that "the institution of property, when limited to its essential elements, consists in the recognition, in each person, of a right to the exclusive disposal of what he or she have produced by their own exertions."[4]

[4] Ellerman takes pains to distinguish the labor theory of property from the so-called labor theory of value (LTV), which states that a product's value can or should be measured by the amount of human labor embodied in it. The labor theory of value (which is problematic—it falls apart completely when we consider that natural resources have value)

In Ellerman's hands, the responsibility principle provides the basis for a radical critique of the modern corporation, specifically of the employment contract, which he argues constitutes "human rental." The responsibility principle would assign the risks and rewards of a collective enterprise to all and only those individuals who directly participate in the enterprise (rather than, say, to those who supply capital to the enterprise, or even to the founders and managers of the enterprise exclusively). The principle is violated when participating persons—i.e., workers—are treated merely as "factors of production" (employees) rather than partners. "When private property is refounded on the responsibility principle (or the labor theory of property), then a very different system emerges, in which firms are worker co-operatives (or similar workplace democracies)" (Ellerman 2016, 320).

But as Ellerman (2016, 320) goes on to note, the responsibility principle "provides no basis to treat the products of nature as if they were ordinary private property." As these resources were created by no person, the principle assigns them to no person. Ellerman refers to this insight as the "negative" application of the labor theory of property (2016, 321). Again, John Stuart Mill (1875, 140, 142) expresses it elegantly: "The essential principle of property being to assure to all persons what they have produced by their labor and accumulated by their abstinence, this principle cannot apply to what is not the produce of labor, the raw material of the earth.... No man made the land. It is the original inheritance of the whole species."

Furthermore, if a person uses or consumes something, the labor theory of property assigns them the liability for (i.e., cost of) that consumption. For your use of a house that I constructed, you owe compensation to me. But for your use of the land underneath, a piece of "the original inheritance of the whole species," to whom should you pay your compensation?

In Ellerman's words, "some common ownership arrangement is required" (2016, 321). Some formal structure is needed, such as atrust, to receive payments made by those who use and consume that which "no man made," and then to use or redistribute the funds in a way that makes

goes back at least to Adam Smith, but is associated particularly with Marxist economics. Some early economists had a tendency to muddle the LTP and LTV together, or to justify one on the basis of the other, but they are analytically distinct.

beneficiaries of "the whole species." Ellerman emphasizes that beneficiaries are not limited to the current generation; future generations should also receive consideration (Ellerman 2016, 341). Thus, the labor theory of property, applied negatively to the natural world, leads Ellerman to reconstruct practically the whole logic of Paine and Barnes, including the sustainability requirement discussed earlier in this chapter.

The negative application of the LTP is a good fit for Nature. It would almost seem paradoxical to try to apply it to that which is "man-made." But in our discussion below of examples of man-made commons (where Nature and human effort are intermingled), we will have occasion to refer to this principle.

Microeconomics: Economic Rent

Several authors (e.g., Barnes 2014, 45; Flomenhoft 2012, 88–89; Fitzgerald 2013; cf. Gaffney 2009) identity *economic rent* as a general principle that can extend to manmade commons the principle of collectivizing and equitably distributing common wealth.

In everyday use, *rent* is a payment made to a property owner for use of the property, and especially to a landlord for use of land and/or a dwelling. The technical sense in which economists use the term "economic rent" (sometimes just "rent") is different from the everyday usage, but derives from it. Adam Smith ([1776] 1986, 247ff) wrote about rent in the eighteenth century in the context of landholding. Smith considered there to be three basic categories of income: wages to labor, profits to entrepreneurial risk-taking, and rent to landlords. Rent accrues to landlords "independent of any plan or project of their own." That is, it is not earned. Smith considered rentiers as a social class, in their passive accumulation of wealth generated by others, to be characterized by indolence and ignorance (356–357).

Smith recognized that it is not only landlords who reap where they never sowed. Monopolists too, by suppressing competition, "rais[e] their profits above what they naturally would be, [and] levy, for their own benefit, an absurd tax upon the rest of their fellow-citizens" ([1776] 1986, 358). Since Smith's time, economists have generalized the concept of rent beyond landholding to include all sorts of "excess earnings," including monopoly profits, profits attributable to "positional advantages," and more (Khan 2000, 1; Bebchuk and Fried 2004, 62). The portion of an individual's or firm's income that is attributed to rent is typically quantified by subtracting what they could have earned if they had instead pursued their next-most-lucrative option. So we encounter in the literature normative definitions of rent, like "an amount of money earned that exceeds that which is economically or socially necessary" (Hayes 2020) and "unearned income" in excess of "real costs" (Hudson 2016), alongside technical/operational definitions like "a return in excess of a resource owner's opportunity costs" (Tollison 1982, 575) and "the excess earnings over the amount necessary to keep [a productive] factor in its current occupation" (Shepherd 1970, 209).[5]

Social costs associated with rent include not only unfairness (parties capturing income beyond their merits) and economic inefficiency, but also the waste of resources and political and economic distortions associated with *rent-seeking*—activities conducted simply to capture and maintain rents. Such activities include lobbying for subsidies, tax preferences, etc. Watchdog organizations have calculated that during fiscal years 2014 through 2017, Fortune 100 companies spent two billion USD in lobbying in Washington, D.C. and secured 399 billion USD in federal funding (mostly contracts, plus 3.2 billion USD in grants) (Andrzejewski and Smith 2019). Lobbying being now a standard part of the "corporate business model" of the modern American corporation (Andrezejewski 2019), those figures indicate a return on investment (ROI) of somewhere between around 150% (based on grants alone—already an astonishing rate of profit) and 20,000%. Given such returns, it is no wonder businesses of all sizes and types find lobbying an irresistible temptation.[6]

Government favors (and gaming of tax and regulatory systems, etc.) and monopolistic practices (and oligopoly and monopsony and other anti-competitive practices) may cause rent to accrue to particular businesses. In addition, rent can accrue to entire industries. Today, industries in the so-called FIRE sector (finance, insurance, and real estate) and, in the U.S. at least, the healthcare industry, are often held up as examples of industries whose rates of profit are egregiously inflated by rent (Bezemer and Hudson 2016; Stiglitz 2018; *The Economist* 2018).

[5] The analysis of economic rent presented here largely follows the classifications used in Khan's (2000) chapter-length study of the topic. An alternative framework is Boyce's four-part classification (2019, 13ff), which offers a distinction between *extractive* rent (rent that accrues to those who exploit natural resources) and *protective* rent (rent paid by those who make use of ecosystem services), one rewarding exploitation and the other encouraging conservation.

[6] Corporate lobbying was not always so intense; it emerged as a core element of American business operations in the 1970s. For an explanation of how that transition occurred and a review of relevant literature, see Ranalli et al. (2018).

Compensation of individuals can also be egregiously inflated by rent. Commonly cited examples include corporate executives, professionals working in the finance industry, and professional athletes and others in the entertainment industry (Stiglitz 2016; Morrison 1996).

On its face, the idea that people should retain only so much of their income as they have earned or merited sounds very similar to the negative application of the labor theory of property. The (perfectly valid and orthodox) definition of rent given Flomenhoft (2012, 88–89) reinforces this resemblance: "all unearned income from ownership of a resource, from a monopoly, from scarcity, or any other reason resulting in *unearned excess profits not due to work, risk, or enterprise*" (emphasis added). It might be tempting to view the rent critique as a simple translation of the negative application of LTP from the domain of property theory to the domain of microeconomics. But it is not quite that neat and tidy. The labor theory of property can be taken as a foundational principle in property theory that admits of no exceptions, while rent is a multifaceted and even contested concept in economics. As we will see, it would be neither feasible nor just to extract and share every kind of rent as common wealth dividends, and it would also be difficult, perhaps impossible, to frame a simple rule about when rent could justifiably be extracted for public benefit.

To see why it is neither feasible nor just to extract every kind of rent from its possessor, we need look no further than the ordinary supply-and-demand graph from introductory microeconomics (Fig. 5.1).

The graph shows that supply and demand are in equilibrium at quantity Q_1. The "last" unit produced during the period, bringing the total quantity to Q_1, brings in exactly enough revenue (OP_1) to cover the cost of producing that unit. (Producing and selling even one more unit—pushing to the right of the equilibrium point—would require the producer to take a loss on that unit, and would also push the price of *all* units downward, below the equilibrium price P_1.)[7] The "first" unit produced, on the other hand, all the way on the left, cost its producer much less. Sold at the market price P_1, it covers production costs (that is, OA) and brings

[7] In this simple and stylized example, it is necessary to assume that there are multiple producers and consumers in competition, that all products are of identical quality, that every unit produced during the period is sold during the period, and that all sales take place simultaneously at the end of the period (or at least in full knowledge of what the total production during the period will be).

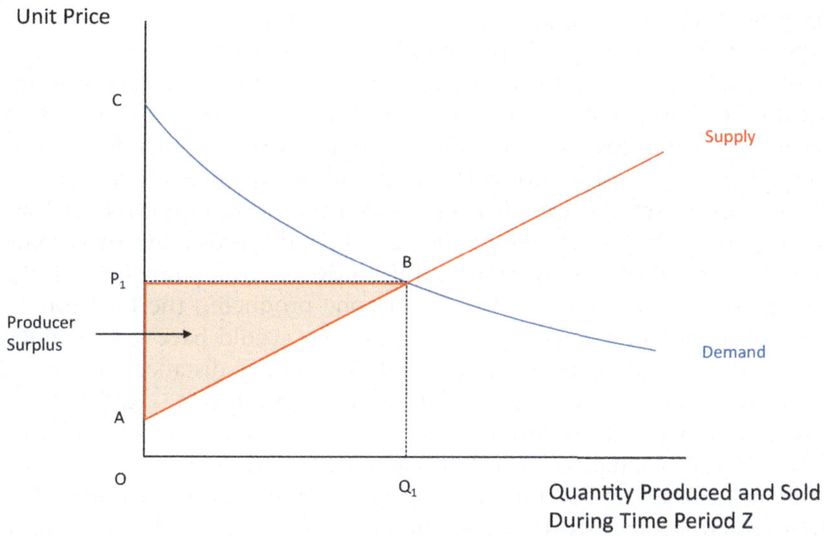

Fig. 5.1 Producer surplus

in additional income AP_1. That additional income AP_1 is rent—revenue beyond the minimum the producer would have been willing to accept. In this example, every unit produced and sold during the period, right up until the last one, brings in some amount of rent. The triangle ABP_1 illustrates the total amount of rent taken in by producers in this example of a simple market equilibrium. It is conventionally called the ***producer surplus***.

The producer surplus is an example of what could be considered "good" rent. Economists count it as one component of the social welfare produced by a market in static equilibrium. (The other component is the ***consumer surplus*** represented by the shape BCP_1. That is the extra value that consumers receive from the transaction beyond the minimum they would have been willing to accept.) A producer surplus will emerge whenever the supply line has a positive slope, and this will happen when there are differences among firms that cause production costs to differ. For example, imagine that on market day, different families with eggs to sell have different distances to travel to reach town. Since the eggs are identical, buyers will pay the same price for all of them. Those who live closest to the market and have the lowest travel costs will pocket the most revenue per egg. Those who live furthest away and have the highest travel costs might barely break even. The extra revenue taken in by those who live closest is economic rent. It is "unearned excess profits not due to work, risk, or enterprise." But it is not the sort of rent that would justify extraction and sharing as common wealth dividends. For one thing, this excess profit is not being taken out of anyone else's pocket; it is generated precisely by a market mechanism that makes everyone at least as well off as they were before. For another, the possibility of earning some amount of rent is an important incentive to even *participate* in the market. If every producer—not just the one producing the final unit at Q_1—was only barely covering costs, producers would have just as much reason to sit on their hands as to produce. Besides distance to market, other factors that could explain differences in producers' costs and the existence of a producer surplus could include: different costs for other factors (labor, capital, etc.), economies of scale, different technologies, different management techniques, and more. Within certain bounds (like labor laws to protect workers), we should be perfectly willing to let those who have achieved economies in any of these areas keep whatever excess profits they receive by producing at lower cost than their competitors.

This brings us to a second example of "good" rents, *Schumpeterian rents*, which come into play in a dynamic rather than static economic analysis. Schumpeterian rents are the extra earnings that a firm temporarily receives when it *innovates* (e.g., via technology or management) to produce goods (of equal or better quality) more cheaply than rivals. Sooner or later the rivals will catch up, and the industry's whole supply curve will shift down and to the right, increasing overall social welfare. But temporarily, the innovative firm will be earning extra revenue that will look something like a monopoly rent (Khan 2000, 16). If Schumpeterian rents are taxed away by an overzealous state, or if they are negated by rivals catching up too quickly, the incentive to innovate will be dampened, and the economy as a whole will suffer in the long term. This is a reason not to treat Schumpeterian rents as a source of common wealth dividends, and also a reason to ensure that genuine innovations are given temporary protection as intellectual property. On the other hand, if Schumpeterian rents continue too long, they may ossify as monopoly rents—"bad" rents—and it may be a sign that the intellectual property regime is broken and needs reform.

Natural resource rents (think fisheries and mines) are "good" rents—"good" in the sense that they will accrue if property rights are assigned to one or more parties who will manage the resource so as to maximize its economic value, and they will fail to accrue if property rights are left unassigned and the resource is squandered as a costless input (as an unmanaged open-access resource, per the tragedy of the commons). In this case, the "good" rent, minus the cost of administration and sound management, is ripe for extraction and sharing—not because it is rent, but because it represents the value of a natural resource, which does not *belong* to the party managing it but has been *assigned* to them to manage.

Khan (2000) provides additional examples of rents that can be considered "good." Usually, as with Schumpeterian rents, their status as "good" is conditional. Depending on how firms behave and whether the state provides adequate oversight, potentially "good" rents can turn out "bad," harmful to social welfare. And usually, as with Schumpeterian rents, as long as they are "good" rents they are serving a purpose and are not suitable for extraction and sharing.

Prime examples of "bad" rents are those associated with monopoly (and other anti-competitive practices) and those associated with positional advantage (favors obtained from buyer or seller or state, or information asymmetry vis-à-vis buyer or seller or state). These can generally be corrected in one of three ways. First, the source of the rent can sometimes be eliminated: for example, by breaking up monopolies or by eliminating subsidies. Second, in the case of a *natural monopoly*, where barriers to entry for competition are prohibitive, the state can intervene to ensure that the firm receives only a fair profit and not exorbitant rents. This is the normal procedure with utilities like electric companies and providers of drinking water and wastewater services. (It would make little sense, clearly, for one neighborhood to be serviced by two competing water companies, laying down duplicate pipes under every street, each of which might operate at only half capacity.) Prices charged by utilities are not determined by market forces, but rather they are set with the review and approval of a governing authority. Third, if the rents cannot be prevented, they can be extracted—e.g., by taxes and fees. In this last case, the revenue could conceivably be eligible for distribution as common wealth dividends.

In general, the first two solutions, if feasible, are preferable, because they *prevent* harm to social welfare. Breaking up a monopoly and eliminating unnecessary subsidies and regulating the rates charged by an electric company help to ensure that firms do not unfairly take advantage of customers and taxpayers. The third solution holds the potential to *remediate* harm that has already occurred. If extraction and sharing of rent does occur, ideally redistribution will be directed to the harmed group (e.g., customers, taxpayers).

Capital gains from *speculation*, or purchasing an existing asset and then selling it later at a higher price,[8] can also be considered a type of economic rent (Shepherd 1989). It satisfies the conventional criteria: revenue from speculation bears no relationship to effort expended, and when it is positive it exceeds that which is economically or socially necessary. Speculation can exist in pure form or it can be mixed with genuine productive activity in the form of investment. Shepherd (1989) effectively refutes arguments that capital gains from speculation are necessary for economic efficiency, and enumerates the costs. Capital gains can therefore be considered a "bad" form of rent, taxation of which at high rates would introduce no economic inefficiency and might provide societal benefits in terms of reducing unnecessary risk-taking, improving social morale, and freeing up productive assets (including high-value human capital) for productive activities. Speculation is an example of a bad rent where taxation, rather than prevention, might be the most efficient corrective.

Having already mentioned that some kinds of "good" rents (e.g., those associated with innovation) can turn bad (monopolistic), it is also necessary to point out that even rents associated with positional advantage—typically "bad"—might sometimes not be bad at all, or it might be hard to judge. Take government subsidies, recalling again the report about Fortune 100 companies receiving billions of dollars in grants and contracts. The truth is that subsidies (and protective tariffs, tax privileges, etc.) might be granted for any number of reasons. They might be venal political backscratching, or they might be economically valuable or vital to national security, or they might be all at once. Depending on who you ask, government subsidies for high-tech and renewable energy will either be essential to keep a nation at the forefront in emerging economic sectors or examples of regulators inappropriately "picking winners"; agricultural price supports will either be vital to long-term food security or gross pork-barrel politics. And to take an example of positional rent that does not even involve government: a successful union campaign to raise workers' wages could be viewed as a victory for economic justice or a blow to economic efficiency and economic competitiveness. In the words of E.C.

[8] Or even "shorting" the asset—signing a contract to sell it before one has purchased it.

Paseur, Jr. (1987, 132), "there is no objective procedure" to distinguish virtuous from wasteful interventions (positional rents) or virtuous from socially detrimental lobbying (rent-seeking). It is irreducibly a question of values and politics. While this insight in no way diminishes the fact that rent-seeking in general is an important social and economic problem (135), it should make us cautious when attempting to frame solutions.

With these caveats and complications in mind, we can ask: how well does a "rents" critique do at unifying the imperatives for common wealth dividends presented in the previous chapters on land, natural resources, and ecosystem services, and linking them up with potential man-made sources of dividends?

A Georgeist tax on land, to go right back to the base example—the one that occupied Adam Smith and inspired the whole concept of "economic rent"—is a 100% tax on the producer surplus in the market for leasing land, on the notional assumption that every marketable parcel (commercial, residential, and otherwise) is on the market. The value of the lease is indeed "rent" in the technical economic sense since the next-best alternative to leasing it at market price is understood to be *not* leasing it and earning no income from it. (In the case of manufactured products, or anything involving labor, there is usually some next-based alternative that involves using people's time and energy to some other remunerative purpose. That is not the case here.[9]) As we have seen, as a general rule, the producer surplus is a "good" rent that does not merit extraction. The justification for making an exception in the case of land is that (a) it disincentivizes speculation and hoarding, and therefore puts into circulation in greater quantities and at lower prices a particular economic input (land) that is necessary for practically all other productive activity, and (b) it puts the value of the land—to which all have a legitimate claim—to work supporting everyone rather than propping up a minority as an elite leisure class. So the justification for extracting and possibly redistributing rents in this case is based not on the nature of the rent, but on the nature of the resource.

[9]As a consequence of there being no labor component to land and hence no "next-best" use other than no use—and as a consequence of its immobility—land has the curious property that taxing it at 100% creates no distortions in supply. I.e., when the alternative is letting the land lie idle, the owner has just as much incentive to rent it out for an after-tax income of \$1 as for an untaxed income of \$1,000. George was aware of this fact and used it as a selling point for his Single Tax.

We have already seen the case of natural resource rents, which covers renewable and non-renewable resources that involve extraction over time at variable rates, like fisheries (and forests, etc.) and mines (and oil fields and most aquifers, etc.). Again, natural resource rents are "good" rents in the sense that collection of rents by a manager or owner(s) promotes economic efficiency, which goes a long way toward sound management and stewardship. Extracting the rents for the benefit of the wider public, perhaps for distribution as dividends—after the costs of administration and sound management/stewardship have been covered—is, in this case too, justified not by the nature of the rents but by the nature of the resource.

When an ecosystem service is managed with a cap, permits to use the service become a factor of production whose scarcity can place limits on production, in much the same manner that the scarcity of land can place limits on production. The same dynamic applies. Taking carbon pricing as an example: Instead of landowners leasing land periodically to residential and commercial customers on the real estate market, we have an agency (or, in the case of California, a set of electricity and natural gas distribution utilities) selling permits periodically to fossil fuel energy suppliers at auction. The income from the auction is rent, a producer surplus. Due to the nature of the resource (not the bald fact that it is rent, or a producer surplus), the income should not be retained by the agency or utility holding it; rather, 100% of it should be used for public purposes. (The situation with a carbon tax is not as easy to visualize as rent as the permit system, but it is mathematically equivalent.)[10]

What about rents that have no essential connection to Nature? As we have already discussed, a producer surplus is an example of a "good" rent that does not harm social welfare. From the examples of land and carbon permits, we might extract a general rule that if, for policy purposes, a factor of production is rationed by a central authority, it should not only be done by charging full market value (for the sake of efficient allocation),

[10]We might even consider the permit auction concept to be even purer and more paradigmatic than the land tax. A Georgeist land tax is functionally equivalent to an auction of permits to use parcels of land, an auction in which the *users* of land participate and the nominal owners have no role. In this visualization, the agency that issues permits (for land use, carbon emissions, etc.) at auction puts the revenue to public use not because it is a producer surplus but because—like the authority overseeing the use of renewable or non-renewable resources in the earlier example—it is merely a *manager* of the resource, not an owner.

but the revenue (the entire producer surplus) should be recycled back to the base of consumers for the reason discussed in Chapter 4: it completes the circulation of revenue back to the firms who pay for the privilege of using the factor of production. If the cycle is incomplete, the pumping of money to government by firms will leave government with an excess of funds and consumers with a deficit. This rule of thumb would seem to be valid for any essential/limiting factor of production rationed by a central authority, even one unconnected to Nature—though no such example readily springs to mind. (It may be that anything at all that legitimately requires rationing can be convincingly tied back to Nature.)

Anti-competitive (e.g., monopoly) rent is, possibly without exception, "bad" rent, rent that diminishes social welfare in aggregate and unfairly burdens some parties with unnecessary costs. As a rule, anti-competitive rents can be eliminated by either introducing/restoring competition (e.g., breaking up monopolies) or, in the case of natural monopolies, regulating the prices charged by utilities. So there would be no particular call for extracting rent that could be distributed as dividends. One possible exception could be monopolies that form as a result of the *network effect*. The network effect is the tendency of larger market players to grow and smaller players to be edged out in domains where interoperability is a factor. The larger the critical mass of people that use (for example) a leading business software platform or social media service, the greater will be the pressure and incentives for others to join. Calls to "break up" Facebook, as one would break up a market-dominating airline or phone company, are therefore misguided. The network effect practically guarantees that one social media platform or another will become dominant in the niche that Facebook previously occupied. In a sense, then, a network-effect monopoly is a kind of natural monopoly. Regulating the prices that a network effect monopoly charges customers or advertisers, as one would regulate a utility, might be an option. But if—as is the case with Facebook and other leading social media platforms—the company's business model is not to charge customers but to gather users' data and then charge advertisers, a case could be made that rather than reducing the rents charged to advertisers, the state should tax the rents and return that revenue to the users whose data is providing so much value to the company. There have been calls for this kind of reform. See, for example, the "Data Dividend Project" (https://www.datadividendproject.com/). DDP seeks to represent U.S. consumers in collective bargaining with big tech companies, taking advantage of laws such as the California Consumer

Privacy Act. In a sense, this kind of reform too would close a revenue loop: money would circulate from consumers to advertisers to the social media platform and back to consumers again.

Rents from positional advantage (government subsidies, tax advantages, etc.) can be eliminated by revoking those advantages. As we have seen, not all positional rents are necessarily bad, and there may be considerable grey area in determining which are actually detrimental. It would probably be rare that *extracting* positional advantage rents by taxes or fees would be preferable to simply nullifying them.[11]

As discussed above, taxation may be the most effective way to neutralize rent associated with speculation.

Let us close by briefly discussing some of the most high-profile examples of putative bad rents in today's economy, as identified earlier: finance sector profits, executive pay, and celebrity pay.

The absurdly high profits that the finance sector has consistently reported in recent decades, despite the 2008 financial crisis and despite technological advances that ought to have reduced barriers to entry and increased competition, puzzle even experts (Crotty 2008; Smith 2016). Some explanations that have been advanced include (a) asymmetry of information between the finance sector and consumers, and between the finance sector and regulators; (b) oligopolistic behavior, where players compete in terms of offerings and convenience, etc., but refrain from competing on price; and (c) since a large portion of the finance sector is not consumer-facing, firms in the sector largely service each other, creating a weightless environment where practically unlimited wealth can be created backed by practically unlimited debt, as long as someone else in the industry is willing to buy that debt (in an escalating game of musical chairs that can destabilize the sector, as happened in the 2008 financial crisis).[12] As this complex mix of apparent anti-competitive and positional rents would be quite difficult to disentangle, it could be argued that a reasonable approach would be to simply cut the Gordian knot

[11] As an example, consider the rents that accrue to holders of taxi licenses when the supply is kept artificially low by regulators. One Australian inquiry determined that over 100 million AUD of public revenue could be raised in Victoria by jacking up the license fee to extract the rent from existing license-holders. But the more practical solution—and the one that better served consumers, the "long-suffering taxi users"—was rather to issue more licenses, leading to lower prices and reduced rents (Fitzgerald 2013, 33).

[12] See Huber (2020) on the effects that the metastasizing "non-GDP" (i.e., nonproductive) finance sector has on the real economy.

with taxes/fees. There is plenty of precedent for levying a windfall tax on firms with egregious profits. A robust capital gains tax, as discussed above, would generate enormous revenue and reduce speculative trading. Further, a Tobin tax—a very small surcharge on the riskiest kinds of trades—could also generate significant revenue while dampening speculation and thus reducing systemic risk. Arguably, broad distribution as dividends would be an appropriate use of any of these revenue streams. (See Barnes (2014, 143) and Flomenhoft (2012, 103) on a financial transaction tax as a potential source of revenue for dividends.)

The absurdly high compensation packages of corporate executives are easier to explain. It is positional advantage: compensation is overseen by boards of directors that for a variety of reasons are deferential to the executives they nominally oversee (Bebchuk and Fried 2004). Legal and institutional reform to resolve the problem of capture would be the best long-term solution. And (absent other context-specific reasons to share them more broadly) excess funds in the compensation pool would presumably be most appropriately shared with workers. There are a variety of mechanisms for that, including, in the U.S., the Employee Stock Ownership Plan or ESOP (Mackin 2011).

Top earners in the entertainment industry unquestionably receive high rents—far more income than they would receive in any next-best occupation. But as Rodney Morrison (1996) points out, fans who decry the "greed" of professional athletes rarely stop to think about the inflated earnings of the franchises that employ them. Franchises tend toward *monopsony*, an anti-competitive situation where a powerful buyer can dictate terms and prices to sellers (the mirror image of monopoly). Historically, before players could negotiate as free agents, financial exploitation by U.S. sports franchises was a significant problem, and even today new players and players without free agent status may be paid notably less than their marginal contribution to the earnings of the franchise (265). Sports franchises frequently receive tax breaks and subsidies from cities and states, and on top of that they enjoy legal exemptions from federal anti-trust laws (263). In a sense, outrageous pay for star players is simply a way of sharing a little more equitably the absurdly large income of the franchises. So any attempt to address the issue of economic rent in sports (and the same is true of other branches of the entertainment business as well) would need to consider the industry as a whole, not just the salaries of highly visible stars.

In summary: Rents do provide a framework in which natural and man-made sources of common wealth dividends can be analyzed together. But it is neither simple nor straightforward. Rents associated with land, natural resources, and ecosystem services are as a rule "good" rents, rents whose accumulation does not reduce social welfare or even enhances it. The justification for extracting those rents and redistributing them as common wealth dividends is not the raw fact that they are rents, but the fact that they are common wealth. There are also "bad" rents (e.g., anti-competitive and speculative and some positional rents) whose accumulation *does* reduce social welfare, and which therefore could, *qua* rents, potentially be sources of broad-based dividends. Only in some cases will the best way of neutralizing "bad" rents involve extracting them in a way that could potentially fund dividends; in other cases, the best way will be to prevent their formation in the first place. The natural scope of distribution for dividends funded by "bad" economic rent would be those populations that are harmed by the accumulation of the rent: often this will be (roughly) all residents or taxpayers of a nation.

The justification for treating "bad" rents as sources of common wealth dividends is, essentially, social utility: not only sharing the wealth, but also extracting it for sharing, will improve economic efficiency or productiveness or resilience, or will correct an unfairness. Unquestionably, raising and sharing such dividends will be socially beneficial. But does the confiscated rent genuinely count as common wealth in the same sense as revenue from land and natural resources? And can receipt of these dividends be viewed as a *right* as convincingly as receipt of dividends raised in accordance with the public trust doctrine and/or the labor theory of property? We leave that for the reader to decide.

Man-Made Sources of Common Wealth

The preceding discussion has already touched on several candidate sources of wealth that are not derived directly from Nature but could plausibly be seen as sources of common wealth dividends. Of these, the financial sector and the ad-driven social media sector are probably the most promising. In both cases, as discussed above, (a) firms take in economic rents that cannot be justified on grounds of social utility, and (b) the economic rent is more easily taxed away than eliminated at the source.

In this section we will examine several additional (or overlapping) sources of wealth that are man-made, or have a distinctly man-made component, and evaluate their suitability as candidate sources of common wealth dividends. They are:

- The contribution of social context to land values
- The common stock of culture and science and technology that we have inherited from previous generations
- Our collective social, political, and economic institutions
- The electromagnetic broadcast spectrum
- Our system for assigning Web domain names
- Our system of money creation

This list is by not meant to be comprehensive; it is merely meant to capture some topics that have been discussed in the literature or raise points of particular interest.

The Contribution of Social Context to Land Values

This first example is not a new source of revenue for us to consider, but a clarification that a source of revenue already discussed—the value of land, presented in Chapter 2—is not based on Nature alone, but owes something to human activity.

The value of a parcel of land lies partly in its own biological and geological characteristics (its unique features and beauty, the productivity of its soil, the plants and animals of commercial value present, its suitability for siting a building or drilling a well, etc.). But the value of the parcel also lies partly in what is available nearby, and that includes human activities and institutions. The vibrancy of the human environment is the reason an acre of weeds and broken concrete in Manhattan will cost many times more than an acre of rich farmland in rural Idaho.

We do not ordinarily distinguish these two components of land value (what Nature contributes and what social context contributes). But we could distinguish them just as carefully as the Georgist distinguishes their sum (the total value of the land) from the value of on-site buildings and other on-site improvements. On one occasion, Ellerman (1988) outlined a proposal to do just that, treating property values as divided into three components: levying local property taxes based on the value contributed by social context (fittingly enough—having members support the community in taxes in proportion to the value the community adds to each member's property), while the value contributed by Nature—the balance of the Georgist tax—goes to support central government, and the portion of the property value contributed by buildings and other improvements goes untaxed.

The social context can be thought of as a diffuse, collective, *indirect* good contributed by many individuals, past and present, beyond whatever direct good each individual may already have been compensated for in accordance with the labor theory of property. We can justify this component of the Georgist tax by saying that those who enjoy the diffuse good should contribute something proportional back to the community at large on the grounds of negative LTP. Or we might even appeal to the positive LTP and say that as the *community* (reified as an actor) generated the good, the *community* merits compensation.

Of course there are bads as well as goods when it comes to social context. Crime can depress property values just as surely as symphony orchestras can raise them.

Cultural Inheritance

Like Nature, *culture*—literature and music and art, our accumulated scientific knowledge and technical know-how—is rightly seen as part of our common heritage (see, e.g., Andersen 1996, 227ff). But it is not a credible potential source of universal dividends. To the extent that innovations are protected for a limited number of years by copyright and patent law, income is assigned by the labor theory of property to their individual creator(s). When those property rights (if any) expire, and the cultural works enter the public domain, they are by their nature infinitely sharable, not at all scarce—so no one need pay for them, and there is therefore no stream of income to be collected and distributed. This is true, for example, of the technologies and protocols that underpin the Internet; these were deliberately placed in the public domain by their creators (Bollier 2003, 101ff; Flomenhoft 2017, 93–94).

Social, Political, and Economic Institutions

Barnes, a former entrepreneur, points out how amazing it is that for a small fee one can incorporate a business and obtain a "license to enter the American marketplace, with its 300 million consumers and all the legal, financial, and physical infrastructure Americans have built over the generations," including "limited liability and perpetual life," and a guarantee of protection of the corporation's physical, intellectual, and financial property by state and federal governments. Further, he observes that if he and his partners had taken their business public, they would have further reaped a "liquidity premium," adding significantly to the value of the company (Barnes 2014, 45ff; cf. Flomenhoft 2017, 87). The lesson he draws is that, as a rule, people who become wealthy do not do it all on their own; they are embedded in social and economic and political systems that facilitate the accumulation of wealth. In a sense, this is very similar to the auxiliary argument made by Paine in *Agrarian Justice*, when he turns from land to other types of wealth and declares that "personal property is the effect of society; and it is as impossible for an individual to acquire personal property without the aid of society, as it is for him to make land originally" ([1797] 1945, 620).

There are several things to parse out here. First, we can consider specific services provided by public and semi-public institutions that secure and amplify flows of wealth. Well-regulated financial markets ensure the reliable and equitable provision of liquidity to businesses. Law enforcement agencies and the courts protect tangible and intellectual property. Those who make the most use of such government services generally get more value out of them than they contribute to them in taxes. Considerations of fairness may suggest ideas like the payment of user fees or transaction fees. User fees or transaction fees could perhaps be paid into a trust fund for distribution to the general public, as Barnes has suggested (2014, 143), but a compelling principled argument could also be made that such fees should be used to support the work of the public agencies providing the services.

Then, there is what Barnes (2014, 61) calls "'wealth of the whole'— the value added by the scale and synergies of our economy itself," citing Adam Smith's insight that we all benefit from specialization and distribution of labor. This is perhaps closest to what Paine meant in his auxiliary argument quoted above. But if we take Smith as our guide here, there is not really any flow of wealth to distribute. Smith's argument is that every participant in the economy automatically benefits from the specialization and distribution of labor ([1776] 1986, 110ff). Consumers have more and a wider variety of goods available at lower cost; entrepreneurs and workers have additional and more varied productive opportunities.[13]

Finally, Barnes suggests that those who amass great fortunes often do so by gaming our collective institutions to capture economic rents (2014 45ff). This is a productive line of inquiry, as we have already seen above in our discussion of economic rents. Examining great fortunes and extraordinary profits—"following the money"—can help us to identify rents whose accumulation is detrimental to social welfare, and among those which are best dealt with by eliminating rent at the source, and which by extraction that could fund broad-based dividends. This will need to be done on a case-by-case basis, by looking at particular firms and industries. Some cursory industry-level analysis was given in the discussion of economic rents above, and more is given in the sections that follow.

Broadcast Spectrum

The broadcast spectrum is a limited resource—there are a range of broadcast frequencies, roughly from 3 kHz to 300 GHz, that are suitable for transmitting radio, television, and cell phone signals, etc. If multiple parties attempt to use the same broadcast frequency at the same time and are in too close geographic proximity to one another, their signals will interfere. So it is generally accepted that some authority is needed to make assignments. At the international level, that authority is the International Telecommunication Union (ITU). Like most United Nations agencies, the ITU's role is primarily one of coordination; its charter "recogniz[es] the sovereign right of each State to regulate its telecommunication" (ITU, n.d.).

Each nation allocates bands of the broadcast spectrum to different users for different purposes. Some frequencies are assigned to television and radio broadcasters, some to cell phone service providers. Some are reserved for military and law enforcement and public safety and

[13] For a critical perspective on this argument of Adam Smith's, see Ranalli (2016a, b). Interestingly, years before Smith made his famous use of the "invisible hand" argument in *Wealth of Nations*, he test-drove it in *The Theory of Moral Sentiments*, writing (somewhat rashly, and prefiguring George H. Evans) that "The rich... are led by an invisible hand to make nearly the same distribution of the necessaries of life, which would have been made, had the earth been divided into equal portions among all its inhabitants" (Smith [1759] 1976, 304).

navigational uses. Some are assigned for radioastronomy and satellite communications. Some are set aside for amateur radio.

It is easy to draw an analogy with land here. The broadcast terrain is limited and therefore valuable.[14] It was created by no one. (In fact it could be considered a natural resource, a most perfectly regenerable sort of renewable natural resource.) By negative-LTP logic, then, government should lease the parcels out to users at market rates and use the proceeds for public benefit (perhaps issuing dividends—so argue Barnes (2014, 145) and Flomenhoft [2012, 99–100]). A regime like this, with government owning the resource and leasing it to private users, would fulfill in the domain of broadcast spectrum what James Bronterre O'Brien once envisioned for land, as discussed in Chapter 2.

In practice, in the earliest days the regulatory authorities in the U.S. (to take this nation as a pioneering example) extended broadcast rights to television and radio companies at no charge.[15] What the government did require was that users of the public airwaves serve the "public interest." Over time this requirement was partly codified in rules about decency (e.g., nudity and profanity) and also what was called the "fairness doctrine," a requirement to present controversial public topics in ways that are equitable and balanced, ensuring that viewers and listeners are exposed to a range of views.

In the 1980s, under the Reagan Administration, the Federal Communications Commission (FCC) repealed the fairness doctrine. The primary justification offered for repealing the fairness doctrine was that it inhibited First Amendment rights to free speech, placing restrictions on radio and television broadcasters that were not shared by print journalists. The rebuttal that the radio and television broadcasters had additional public responsibilities because they were using public airwaves was not sufficient to carry the day. The demise of the fairness doctrine led to the rise of conservative talk radio and "shock jock" programming, and prefigured

[14] How fungible (interchangeable) are frequencies? Lower frequencies can more easily be broadcast over a wider geographic range, and they can also better penetrate obstacles like walls. High frequencies can pack information more densely and generally require less power to transmit. For any particular application, the entire range of the spectrum might not be suitable, but most likely a very wide range of it will be.

[15] For an account of the origins of the wireless property rights regime in the U.S. and parallel developments in Europe, see Kruse (2002). In addition, a classic work on the use and regulation of the radio spectrum in the U.S. is Levin's 1971 *The Invisible Resource*.

the further siloing of media on wired cable television, Internet, social media, etc. (which being nominally independent of the broadcast spectrum are not subject to the FCC's public interest requirements). Siloed media today present a serious problem to democratic governance—as the Trump presidency has recently made clear, with pro- and anti-Trump factions immersed in separate, often diametrically opposed, and sometimes fantastical narratives of U.S. and world events, including the outcome of the 2020 U.S. election itself. But solving that problem will require much more than reinstating the fairness doctrine for the subset of media that use the broadcast spectrum. When it comes to *ensuring that users of the broadcast spectrum serve the public interest*, a more meaningful and appropriate focus will be ensuring that they adequately compensate the public for their use of the airwaves.

A shift in that direction began in the 1980s. Cellular phone service was first commercially licensed in 1984 (Rosston 2014, 222). The emergence of this new market, alongside increasing saturation of the radio and television spectrum bands, created a perceived crisis of spectrum scarcity. In response, in 1983 Congress permitted the FCC to begin awarding licenses by lottery. This was a highly unsatisfactory solution. Many licenses were awarded to parties who were not technically competent to make use of them, and some of them turned out to be speculators who participated in the lottery "solely... in the hopes of extracting rents through the resale of 'won' spectrum to more efficient users" (Connolly et al. 2018, 6). The scandal of speculation, and growing awareness that even legitimate broadcasters had been receiving valuable licenses for free rather than paying for them, led to a demand for change. The FCC moved in the direction of auctioning new spectrum assignments. The first auction, held in 1994, brought in 617 million USD (Christopher 2016). Adopted and adapted by other regulators, the auction model has since been used to raise over 200 billion USD in public funds worldwide from spectrum users (Christopher 2016).

Subsequent decades have seen increased demand for spectrum, further innovation by regulators to accommodate this demand, and further technological advances that allow spectrum users to do more with less. In the second decade of this century, the FCC undertook to "repack" UHF television broadcasters more compactly in a narrower section of the spectrum, so freed-up wavelengths could be auctioned off for new uses (primarily cell phone service). The repacking was made possible by a shift from analog to more efficient digital encoding of television signals. It also relied on the FCC's first ever "reverse auction," in which the government paid television stations for making voluntary bandwidth concessions. More recently, FCC is pioneering a model of licensing that allows multiple tiers of users to share a single segment of bandwidth (the so-called Citizens Broadband Radio Service or CBRS band), with prices based on the right-of-way priority assigned to each tier.

Even more advanced is what is sometimes called *cognitive radio*—the use of transmitting and receiving devices that monitor traffic and automatically migrate their signals to portions of the spectrum where interference will be minimized. The technical requirements of cognitive radio can be achieved via the flexibility of *software-defined radio*, which digitally simulates the circuitry hardware of traditional receivers and transmitters. Cognitive radio makes possible a vision of a future for broadcast spectrum where "smart" devices, programmed to obey rules of the road like driverless cars, could make allocation of broadcast spectrum by regulators unnecessary. Such advances have even led some to question the whole notion of spectrum scarcity. With the right technology, and with the dismantling of regulations that create artificial scarcity (see, for example, Hazlett's (1997) critique of the FCC as from the beginning "captured" by incumbent broadcasters who wished to stifle new competition), we could enter a whole new paradigm of spectrum use characterized by abundance rather than scarcity (Werbach 2002; Ryan 2005). The controlling metaphor for spectrum on this view should perhaps not be *land* at all, with its connotation of scarcity, but rather air (which is "theoretically limitless" [Goodman 2004, 272]) or the sea ("so vast that it doesn't need to be parceled out" [*The Economist* 2003; cf. Werbach 2002, 2]).

Granting that the efficiency of spectrum usage will be drastically improved by technological advance and by moving beyond regulators' traditional approach of allocating spectrum in generously spaced blocks and bands, it still seems unlikely that we will have any need of a new paradigm. However finely we divide the spectrum, and however efficiently we use it, it will remain a finite resource. And as technology advances and the efficiency of spectrum allocation/distribution improves, lower prices will surely drive increases in demand. It is reasonable to assume that spectrum scarcity (both physical scarcity and effective economic scarcity) will always be with us (cf. Gaffney 2009, 359–360).

Even the proposed alternative metaphors fail to offer a genuine alternative paradigm. Air and sea might suggest to us limitless abundance, but so did land once (the seemingly boundless abundance of North America, as discussed in Chapter 2), and we know perfectly well now that the atmosphere and oceans have their limits too (not least as carbon sinks, as discussed in Chapter 4).

Thus we can expect that spectrum will continue to have market value. How will rents, then, be collected for the public?

In the first place, as a practical matter, we can expect that large-scale auctions of spectrum will continue. Despite advances in technology that make possible the sharing of spectrum, it is likely that regulators will continue to allocate at least some spectrum in large exclusive (or nearly exclusive) blocks. Large corporations with large customer bases expecting reliable phone service and high-definition television broadcasts will insist on leasing large blocks of spectrum for exclusive use and will be willing to pay a premium for them. It is also possible that regulators will adapt to fast-changing technology by auctioning or leasing some bands to "band manager" licensees with carte blanche to divide up and sublet that portion of spectrum as they best see fit (Hazlett 2001, 140). (Historically, the FCC has placed strict controls on the uses approved for particular bands. Only recently has it begun giving licensees more discretion.)

Small commercial users of spectrum may purchase rights at auction (possibly shared use at one or another priority tier), or sublet bandwidth from a commercial band manager. In the case of cognitive radio, selling or leasing bandwidth would not be very workable, since cognitive radio involves many independent actors, each operating across a range of bandwidths. To the extentthat cognitive radio develops a commercial niche that is large enough to impinge on other spectrum traffic, the most sensible (if still crude) way to monetize that usage might be to levy a tariff or tax on sale of the associated equipment/software. In theory, the same could be done for "unlicensed" uses of spectrum such as WiFi, Bluetooth, garage door openers, and remote control gadgets. Such uses are permitted (with restrictions) in certain specially reserved bands of spectrum. Since one of the conditions of unlicensed use is that broadcast take place within a very narrow spatial range (most applications are "household" applications), there is little cause for concern about interference. But if the unlicensed bands should become crowded, and monetization is called for, a surcharge on equipment might be the easiest way to implement it.

At present, noncommercial uses of spectrum (for government, research, etc.) generally involve no compensation. Thus, such uses are effectively subsidized. Subsidizing public-sector activities does not violate the spirit of negative-LTP principles. But subsidizing spectrum usage does lead to economic inefficiencies. Military and other government users in the U.S. have been under pressure for some years now to find ways to economize on their spectrum allocations, to free up more bandwidth for commercial use (Serbu 2014). Putting a price tag on government agencies' spectrum use would enable decision-makers, by harnessing market forces, to more easily find the most efficient solutions. It may be more difficult to obtain payment at market rates from noncommercial users outside the federal government, like researchers and local police and emergency responders, but—if that transition can be managed—doing so would also clearly produce efficiencies (Hazlett 2001, 178ff).

In sum, broadcast spectrum can be a significant source of funds for universal dividends. We have been slowly moving in the direction of monetizing spectrum usage rights and collecting the value of those rents from users rather than allowing users to keep them, and as that trend continues, the amount of funds potentially available to the public will increase. Auctions to large corporate users (especially radio, television, and wireless telephony) will continue to be the largest source of funds, but other sources could potentially come on line as well, including fair market compensation from government and other noncommercial users, and equipment fees from small users.

Web Domain Names

Responsibility for maintaining the registries for domain names in the most prominent top-level domains (.com, .org, and .net) belongs to one sole company, which was known as Network Solutions Inc. (NSI) until it was purchased in 2002 by Verisign (CNET 2002). In the manner of a utility, NSI/Verisign serves as registry administrator under the supervision of the U.S. Department of Commerce and the Internet Corporation for Assigned Names and Numbers (ICANN). An agreement between the Department of Commerce and NSI/Verisign sets the price that the company is allowed to charge for annual registration of a domain name. In 1998–1999, the role of *registrar* was split off from NSI's role of registry administrator (ICANN 2012). Today dozens of companies compete with each other as registrars, in a marketplace governed by ICANN, to register domain names for customers (often packaging that service with others).

Over time, as a market has developed for domain names, in which practically every business and organization and government participates, and many private individuals as well, domain names have taken on much of the cachet of real estate. A domain name is not only a business tool, it is also an investment whose value may appreciate. Speculators purchase domain names with the intention of "flipping" them later at a higher price (Flomenhoft 2017, 91).

By creating a competitive marketplace for registrars and by regulating NSI/Verisign like a utility in its irreducibly monopolistic function of registry administrator, the Department of Commerce and ICANN appear to have taken appropriate steps to tamp down economic rent in the administrative system. But the market for domain names is still a site for economic rent, as the presence of speculation shows. The value of a domain name is composed of several factors. The string of letters and numbers itself, like land, is a limited resource with market value that is made by no one and therefore assignable to no one on LTP grounds.[16] The string may have greater or lesser value depending on its length (shorter domain names are generally more valuable) and the extent to which the sequence of letters and numbers form meaningful combinations, as land may be more or less valuable depending on location and natural features. The value of a domain name also depends on how its owner uses it, much as improvements increase the value of a parcel of land. (So, for example, the domain "Amazon.com" has an inherent value greater than "Anzmao.com" because the letters form a recognizable word, but the greater part of the value of the domain name "Amazon.com" is the brand recognition of the business that is built on it.) The analogy with land can only be taken so far. Domain names are much less fungible than parcels of land. That is, a parcel of land might be suited for many different uses by a wide range of possible owners, but a typical domain name will be of use and interest to only a narrow range of possible owners, often only one if any at all. There is very little scope for rental markets in domain names that could establish market

[16] Are domain names really a limited resource? They are limited to 253 characters, and the final characters in the string must place a domain name in a recognized top-level domain, of which there are over a thousand. So the number of legitimate domain names is finite but enormous. And it is also plastic—a change in the rules could expand or diminish it. What gives domain names market value is not their absolute scarcity, but the scarcity of domain names that are *useful* (short and meaningful). A rough analogy would be to say that the amount of "land" in the galaxy (on dry planets, asteroids, etc.) is finite and indefinitely large, but the market value of land is driven by the limited amount whose location and other characteristics make it viable and attractive to potential users.

prices. Markets disappear altogether when arbitrators (with good reason) recognize the rights of parties to domain names that match their names, trademarks, and copyrights.

What, then, would be appropriate measures to tamp down economic rent in the case of the market for domain names? One possibility would be to charge every domain owner a small annual fee on top of the administrative registration fee, for their exclusive use of a limited common resource. But the fact that domain names are less fungible than land—I would probably have very little use for your domain name, whereas in principle I could probably find some use for your land—makes this less compelling. More useful would be to track down and stamp out sources of speculation. Speculation occurs when a new top-level domain opens up (like ".info" or ".biz"), and opportunists scoop up the shortest and most marketable domain names with an intent to resell them (or arrange for "pay-per-click" advertising, hoping to exploit accidental traffic). It also occurs when domain names expire and scavengers scoop them up, again with intent to resell—possibly even to resell for extortionate rates to the original owner—or to set up an advertising trap. ICANN has taken some steps to discourage speculative activity: notably, by changing its "grace period" policy to discourage registrars from allowing users to register large numbers of domains to test their commercial potential and then return them at no cost (ICANN 2009). Other possible steps might include assigning some domain names, the kinds most sought after by speculators (short, meaningful, free of trademark conflicts), by auction rather than on a first-come, first-served basis. That way the market value will be captured for the public and could be directed into common wealth dividends.

Money Creation

The banking system, like the financial sector generally, is rife with economic rent. Profits are often far out of proportion to the actual business risks involved in running a bank (e.g., Lifschutz 2019). (To speak to the situation in the United States: The FDIC, by insuring individual depositors, has practically eliminated the risk of a "run on the bank." And the Federal Reserve system, by requiring all banks to hold reserves in proportion to their outstanding loans, and by providing liquidity to the sector, has greatly reduced the systemic risk that used to cause periodic collapses of sound and unsound banks alike.) But the banking sector—or to speak more precisely, the monetary system—is the site of an additional possible source of universal dividends, one with a very different story than ordinary economic rent.

In a modern economy, deflation and hyperinflation are avoided by ensuring that the money supply is proportional to the size of the economy. (That is, the *price* of the currency is kept stable by regulating the *supply* of money to match the *demand*.) So money must periodically be created and sometimes also destroyed. Money can be created in two ways: it can be *spent* into existence or *lent* into existence. Lending by banks and credit unions—to households, businesses, and governments—is the bread and butter of money creation.[17] Small amounts of money are sometimes spent into circulation by governments proper. (In the United States, the federal Treasury Department has spent limited amounts of paper money—"United States Notes"—into circulation since the 1860s; since 1971 it has spent only coins into circulation.) Central banks like the Federal Reserve, which have a mission to regulate the money supply, do both: They lend money to other financial institutions and to the government. (Consistent with its public mission, the Fed refunds to the U.S. government the interest it earns from lending at the end of each year.) They also spend money into existence by using new money to purchase financial assets on the open market (typically government debt instruments like Treasury bonds). When they need to destroy money, central banks may siphon it out of the economy by reselling such assets. They can also spend money into existence (or, rather, facilitate its spending) by simply crediting a government checking account with new money.

Allowing private bank lending to play such a large role in shaping the money supply carries some risks. For example, it contributes volatility. As an IMF report puts it: "Sudden changes in the willingness of banks to extend credit must therefore not only lead to credit booms or busts, but also to an instant excess or shortage of money" (Benes and Kumhof 2012, 6). This puts central banks too often in the position of crisis management. There have been proposals—notably the so-called Chicago Plan, worked

[17] To make this point perfectly clear: When modern banks issue a loan, they are not, as laypersons often assume, shifting money from one place to another. They are crediting a deposit account with money that did not previously exist. Since the newly created money is backed by the full faith and credit of the currency-issuing government, banks are performing an inherently public function.

out in the 1930s and extensively studied but nowhere yet implemented—to introduce 100% reserve requirements and rescind the power of money creation from private banks, allowing them to make loans only from liquid assets they hold in their own name—the way private citizens make loans, and closer to the way many laypersons assume banks already do (Benes and Kumhof 2012). Private banks would still do what they do best, like manage deposits, screen loan applicants, provide payment services, etc. They would be free to expand their lending activities by taking (money-creating) loans of their own from a central bank.

Of course, central banks often inspire public distrust, given their great and unique powers, their perceived technocratic elitism, and their seeming lack of accountability. And the main alternative—putting money creation in the hands of elected government officials—seems like an invitation to reckless spending and hyperinflation.[18] In fact, there is a rich and encouraging history of "positive money"—governments directly spending money into existence—that includes the highly successful scrip currencies issued by the British American colonies before the War of Independence, and the "greenbacks" that financed the Union war effort in the 1860s (Brown 2008, 81ff). And as Robert Hockett and Aaron James argue in their 2020 book *Money from Nothing*, subtitled "Why We Should Stop Worrying about Debt and Learn to Love the Federal Reserve," central banks deserve credit as smart and public-spirited institutions that serve us well on the whole—and that could do even more for us if we expand their mission. Ultimately, there are lots of valid ways to manage a money supply, but what is critical is that it be *managed*. The historical record shows that societies whose money supplies have been actively managed—whether by governments issuing scrip, or central banks with a public mission, or some other arrangement—have tended to enjoy stable currencies, and societies that have let private lenders run riot have not (Benes and Kumhof 2012, 12–17).[19]

[18] There are, of course, plenty of other alternatives in the form of different types of local currencies (see, for example, Hallsmith and Leitaer 2011). But as valuable as these alternatives can be in filling niches, they are known as "complementary currencies" for the very good reason that there is no foreseeable lack of demand for widely circulating government-backed currencies.

[19] Benes and Kumhof (2012, 16): "To be fair, there have of course been historical episodes where government-issued currencies collapsed amid high inflation. But the lessons from these episodes are so obvious, and so unrelated to the fact that monetary control was exercised by the government, that they need not concern us here. These lessons are:

Moving beyond the question of private lending versus public management of the money supply, to the more general question of lending versus spending, we can appreciate that our current heavy reliance on ever-expanding lending is not healthy. Lending loads the economy with debt, which reduces its resilience (in the sense that economic shocks are likely to produce more bankruptcies). And ever-expanding lending also effectively locks us into ever-expanding economic activity that is often unnecessary, environmentally deleterious, and detrimental to human health and well-being (Positive Money 2018).

An understanding that money is sometimes *spent* into existence, and that we should perhaps be relying even less on lending and more on spending than we do today, prompts the question: can and should some of that spending be done by households? Economists such as John Maynard Keynes and Milton Friedman have long recognized broad-based distribution as a valid way of introducing new money into the economy, at least in theory (Jackson 2013, 45ff). Recent events have broadened that discussion and brought it into the mainstream.

In the first place, there was the response to the financial crisis of 2008. When the financial sector was on the brink of collapse (i.e., with financial institutions saddled with uncollectable subprime mortgage loans and other debt and therefore unable to make good on their own payments to other parties), central banks bought up billions of dollars of "troubled assets" and other debt instruments held by these institutions using newly created money, in a process known as "quantitative easing" or QE. And in subsequent years they continued to buy more debt instruments from the banks, with the idea of reinvigorating the economy by making it easier for the banks to take on new loans. This well-publicized exercise in new-money creation prompted some criticism about how authorities chose to use the money. Advocates of so-called "QE for the people" ask: why was the newly created money used to bail out and stabilize the banks, when it could have been used to bail out the struggling homeowners instead? (e.g., Blyth et al. 2015) Rescuing the banks does nothing directly to help the homeowners who are "underwater" on their

First, do not put a convicted murderer and gambler, or similar characters, in charge of your monetary system (the 1717–1720 John Law episode in France). Second, do not start a war, and if you do, do not lose it (wars, especially lost ones, can destroy any currency, irrespective of whether monetary control is exercised by the government or by private parties)."

mortgages, but helping the struggling homeowners with their mortgages would simultaneously stabilize the banks. In addition, giving the newly created money to ordinary people to spend—what some call "helicopter money," after Milton Friedman's famous thought experiment (1969), evoking an image of central bankers dropping wads of cash out of helicopters—would be a much better way to reinvigorate a debt-strapped economy than encouraging more lending and borrowing (Jackson 2013).

In the second place, recent years have seen a long spell of unusually low inflation (inflation being the rate at which prices rise over time). Central banks usually aim to maintain low, stable rates of inflation—the Federal Reserve currently touts 2% annual inflation as its goal. When inflation falls below target levels, there is a risk the economy will fall into deflationary territory (where prices tend to collapse—a problem arguably even worse than high inflation). One of the main tools that central banks use to guide inflation is manipulating short-term interest rates: lowering interest rates stimulates lending, which increases the money supply, which should nudge inflation upward (as raising interest rates, conversely, should nudge inflation downward). But if central banks lower the prime interest rate all the way to zero, and low inflation persists, they must look to other, "unconventional" methods of fighting disinflation. Some of these involve increasing the money supply through spending. Ben Bernanke, chairman of the Federal Reserve from 2006 to 2014, has earned the nickname "Helicopter Ben" for his high-profile speeches and writings exploring the topic. In these speeches and writings, he details several ways in which new money can be spent into the economy to fight disinflation:

1. Echoing Friedman, Bernanke argues that the option of turning to the "printing presses"—having the government simply create and spend (or distribute) money, what we identified above as "positive money"—always provides a viable (if in his opinion crude) backstop against deflation (Bernanke 2002).
2. Alternatively, the central bank could create the money and distribute it to people directly. Bernanke (2016) states that this would be technically as effective as other ways to expand the money supply, but in the case of the U.S. he believes that it goes beyond the Fed's mandate—it should be for Congress to decide how money is spent and distributed. This seems like a strange peccadillo in light of the fact that when the Federal Reserve engaged in QE under Bernanke's watch, it already intervened extensively in the private

sector, choosing what kinds of assets to purchase and what kinds of institutions would receive direct aid. Hockett and James (2020), for their part, see a role for an active Fed in this regard. Every U.S. citizen or resident could have a checking account at the Federal Reserve, which the Fed could credit with new money whenever it determines that the money supply needs to be expanded.

3. Bernanke favors solutions that involve collaboration between the central bank and the government. The prototype of this is the "money-financed tax cut" (Bernanke 2002, 2003, 2016). Government injects money into the economy with a tax cut (or, he acknowledges, it could be by some other means—e.g., by making transfer payment to households, or by spending the money directly). The central bank, in turn, "finances" the transfers (or spending) by buying up an equivalent amount of government debt with new money. This option does increase the government's indebtedness, but Bernanke appears to be assuming that by a kind of gentleman's agreement the debt to the central bank will never be called in, it will simply be rolled over into new bonds whenever it comes due. He writes: "the Treasury could issue $100 billion in debt, which the Fed agrees to purchase and hold indefinitely, rebating any interest received to the Treasury" (Bernanke 2016). Bernanke recommended this type of operation in particular for Japan, a country that has struggled with deflation for decades (Bernanke 2003, 18).
4. An even more elegant variant does not involve any debt at all. "The Fed credits the Treasury with $100 billion in the Treasury's 'checking account' at the central bank, and those funds are used to pay for the new spending [or] tax rebate" (Bernanke 2016). This is similar to option #2, but it addresses Bernanke's concern re: option #2 by keeping the central bank itself at arms' length from decisions about how to distribute or spend the new money. In Bernanke's mind, an ideal setup, in terms of separation of powers, would be for Congress to authorize the Fed to specially create a checking account for the Treasury Department for the purpose of "helicopter" operations. The checking account would normally be empty, but using its discretion as monetary authority, the Fed could create money in the account when it believes that money should be spent into the economy. Then, Congress and the Treasury Department can make an independent decision about whether to draw down the

account, and by how much, and how to use or distribute the money (Bernanke 2016).

Finally, the recent COVID-19 pandemic has prompted governments to take extraordinary measures to avoid an economic downturn. These measures have included transfer payments to households, intended to help people meet basic needs and to boost consumer spending. In the U.S., these transfer payments appear to have been financed not using any of the money creation strategies outlined above, but simply by government borrowing. Nevertheless, they set a precedent for transfer payments to households, they demonstrate the feasibility of distribution mechanisms, and they will allow social scientists to study the macroeconomic and other effects of broad-based transfer payments.

So we are led to consider an entirely *sui generis* possible additional source of universal dividends: monetary policy. Either in a crisis or as a routine matter, if policy-makers determine that the money supply should be expanded, universal dividends are one way to accomplish that goal. The dividends could be distributed by check or electronic transfer, or they could even be made as credits to individual checking accounts at a central bank. As an alternative to lowering interest rates to stimulate lending (the conventional method of increasing the money supply), and as an alternative to governments or central banks simply *spending* the newly created money, and as an alternative even to a tax cut, distributing universal dividends offers some distinct advantages. First, in a crisis it provides immediate relief to households. Second, it increases the money supply without simultaneously increasing the debt load. Third, it is manifestly fairer than a government agency or central bank picking and choosing which businesses or individuals to aid. Finally, it can help invigorate the economy by putting the money in the hands of low- and middle-income people who will spend it (whereas a tax cut would disproportionately favor wealthier strata, who may be likelier to save—and simply bid up the price of stocks and other assets—than spend.)

It should be noted that as mainstream economists have been slowly warming up to the idea of making universal dividends a part of the regular monetary policy toolkit, other groups have advocated it for a long time. The populist Social Credit movement, founded by Major C.H. Douglas in the early twentieth century, in many ways took a strikingly modern view of money, including the idea that the money supply should be flexible and independent of the supply of gold or any other metal. Social Credit, which has advocates even today, prescribes the issuance of universal dividends in amounts dictated by overall economic productivity, and also incorporates a unique mechanism to keep inflation in check (Heydorn 2014; Ranalli 2015).

As observed above, sometimes maintenance of a stable currency requires destroying rather than creating money. So the issuance of dividends based on money creation might not be regular as clockwork. It could be cyclical or sporadic, depending on economic conditions, and the seriousness with which we pursue "degrowth" strategies for environmental reasons, and the rate at which money is siphoned out of the economy by taxation, central banks' open market transactions, and other means.

Practicalities

Here we discuss and review some practical issues that arise in the design of a common wealth dividend program.

The Innocent Buyer Problem

Requiring those who operate a mining concession to part with the value of the raw minerals seems straightforward enough. The requirement can be built into the terms of the contract as a severance tax, or it could be imposed afterward as a windfall profits tax. But let us imagine that Company A is operating the mine and pocketing the value of the minerals, and before the windfall profits tax is imposed, Company A sells the concession to Company B. Company B offered a purchase price that reflected the historical profitability of the concession, windfall profits and all. Now, if the state imposes a windfall profits tax, Company B is going to take an unexpected financial hit. If it borrowed money to pay for the purchase, the loss of the windfall profits might make it unable to repay the loan.

This is an example of the "innocent buyer" problem that can affect any change in a tax regime, including the imposition of taxes and fees on common wealth. When parties buy and sell land, mining and forestry concessions, fishing boats, etc., etc., in no expectation that a tax or fee will be imposed, and then the tax or fee is introduced, the current owner is penalized. How can the problem be addressed?

One could simply let the chips fall as they may. This would be analogous to the approach taken to trading in stolen goods. (The analogy is not such a stretch in the case of land, title to which almost invariably traces back to conquest.) If my car is stolen and then sold and resold, a judge would return the car to me, and the current owner will simply be out of luck. The buyer of a forestry or fishing concession who is required to pay a new tax or fee designed to ensure sustainability of the resource arguably has even less to complain of than the individual who must give up the stolen car. The tax or fee is part of a regime intended to ensure the long-term viability of the resource, so it is in the concessionaire's long-term interest. And a prudent buyer of a forestry or fishing concession, knowing the nature of the resource, ought reasonably to *expect* that such measures will be taken when demand begins to overtake supply.

On the other hand, one could take measures to mitigate the hardship on current owners. For example, one could impose the taxes or fees gradually, with plenty of advance warning. This was the approach favored by Henry George for land (e.g., George [1885] 1901). To help protect (many) landowners, one could also reduce taxes on improvements at the same time as raising taxes on land itself. Arguably, mitigating the innocent buyer problem is particularly important in the case of land, since landowners include not only businesses but also households.

Sometimes the innocent buyer problem does not arise. Fossil fuel companies suffer no financial hardship from paying carbon taxes or purchasing carbon permits; they can pass those costs directly on to their customers. The application of carbon pricing to all firms in the sector, plus border adjustments, ensures a level playing field. (Of course, from another perspective, fossil fuel companies *are* subject to the innocent buyer problem. The whole point of carbon pricing is to make fossil fuels less competitive than other energy sources and reduce their market share. But again: anyone purchasing stock in a fossil fuel energy company in the twenty-first century should reasonably expect this.)

To Issue Dividends or not?

How is common-resource revenue to be spent or disposed of? Throughout this chapter, and the book as a whole, there has been a tension between what might be called "Paineite" and "Georgist" answers to this question. George assumed that the revenue would become general income for the state. Paine argued for 100% distribution to individuals.

The theoretical approaches we have examined above (public trust doctrine, LTP, confiscation of socially detrimental economic rent) generally do not dictate an answer to this question. For the most part, they are agnostic: as long as the money is spent or disposed of in a way that benefits all concerned parties equitably, the demands of these theoretical approaches are satisfied.

In the case of natural resources, as we have seen, the demands of sustainability add some parameters. Activities to ensure that a renewable resource will continue to flourish will have first claim on resource revenue; the question of issuing dividends applies to the balance only. Responsible management of a non-renewable resource will involve using resource revenue to capitalize some other quasi-renewable resource (like infrastructure or an investment fund) that could in turn, in principle, be a source of dividends.

Consideration of the resource curse, discussed in Chapter 3, favors issuing dividends to individuals. A government that subsists by taxing its constituents will tend to be accountable to its constituents; a government that has independent sources of income will tend not to be. This argues for keeping common resource funding *out* of the government's general income, i.e., distributing them as dividends. (Of course, the government may recover some of them by taxation—that would allow a society to side-step the resource curse while still using the revenue to fund government activities.) Note that if the revenue is collected by a trust rather than by a government authority, the question of the resource curse does not arise. The resource curse affects the *democratic accountability* of government. As discussed above, a trust's mode of accountability is not democratic but fiduciary. If a trust were ever to misuse common wealth funds, the remedy would be found in the court system. Note also that the issuance of positive money has the potential to create the same kind of moral hazard as the resource curse. That is, if the money a government spends is created ex nihilo rather than derived from taxes (or borrowed—in effect borrowed from future taxes), accountability will be diminished. This provides another strong argument, in addition to those listed above (providing direct relief to households in a crisis, producing a direct "trickle-up" boost to the economy, etc.), for positive money to be issued as dividends and spent by households rather than spent directly by government.

Still other considerations favor the idea of issuing dividends. One is the imperative that funds be used in a way that benefits all beneficiaries *equitably*. As discussed in Chapter 3: since any given government program or service is likely to benefit some individuals more directly than others, government spending is unlikely to be a perfectly equitable use of common wealth revenue. The strictest way to ensure equitability is to write a check to each individual in equal amounts.

Another consideration is the imperative to put money in the hands of consumers when costs are imposed on them by common wealth management policies. This is seen most clearly in the case of carbon permits. Distributing dividends to individuals completes a loop, allowing revenue to cycle among carbon emitters, government, and consumers. We have seen an argument that the same logic applies in the case of land, which is similarly a near-universal factor of production whose costs are built into nearly everything consumers buy. Imposing a Georgeist tax on landowners and then distributing the revenue as dividends ensures that land rent revenue cycles among land users, land owners, government, and consumers. We have also seen an argument that the same logic should apply in the case of data dividends as well (with revenue cycled among advertisers, network-effect-monopoly platforms, governing authorities, and consumers).

On the whole, then, there are several good arguments for issuing as dividends any common wealth funds that are not otherwise spoken for (i.e., not required to cover administrative costs or to address sustainability considerations). A society that issues robust common wealth dividends can be expected to reap many of the benefits that are commonly touted for basic income. Individuals will enjoy more economic freedom (power, autonomy)—freedom to spend more on a higher standard of living, to invest more in their education and skills, or to save more and have more economic security. Some standard concerns about basic income will also apply: for example, the concern that employers will attempt to capture the value of their employees' dividends by reducing wages, or that landlords will attempt to capture it by raising rents. There is also the political concern that a government that provides universal cash payments might attempt to wash its hands of also providing important universal social services for which individual payments are no adequate substitute (Brown 2020). Delving into these questions would take us beyond the scope of this book, but I will repeat what I said in Chapter 1 about the "laziness" argument: such concerns may deserve attention as potential complications of dividend issuance, but they do not constitute a valid reason *not* to issue dividends.

Nevertheless, there could be instances where a community might decide that it will be expeditious to pool common wealth income rather than have it issued directly to individuals. This is especially true when we consider the prospect of exporting the idea of common wealth dividends beyond cultures that are effectively "modern." In the context of climate dividends, Feasta writes: "Distributing [dividends] to individual adults is very much a Western approach[20] and some non-Western societies operate on a more collective or communal basis... However, it should also be said that the nation state is also a Western concept and, just because the distribution to individuals might be inappropriate in some places, that does not mean that the [revenue] should [necessarily] go to a national government instead." Cultural sensitivity would require, rather, that where societies have alternative (e.g., tribal) governance structures in place, some thought should be given to whether pooling dividends at the community level rather than issuing them directly to individuals might be in the best interest of (or at least desired by and not detrimental to) community members (Feasta 2008 Cap-and-Share, 16). An appropriate analogy here would be to the subdivision of tribal land into household plots, an innovation imposed on many North American Native nations in the nineteenth century by neo-European governments that had the effect of undermining tribal governance. An arrangement to pool common-wealth dividends at the community level would be equivalent to tribal members agreeing to put their newly imposed individual plots in a trust to be governed by traditional tribal structures.[21] The imperative of

[20] In this context, I believe "modern" (as opposed to pre-modern or indigenous) would be the correct distinction; plenty of "non-Western" societies share the individualism and nation-state governance that is characteristic of modernity and would be able to incorporate an innovation like common wealth dividends with no significant cultural disruption. For more on this distinction, see Ranalli (2016c).

[21] Observing that opinion polls in Mongolia showed a strong preference for mining revenue to be invested by the state and/or spent on long-term social development (i.e., health and education) rather than distributed as dividends, Cummine (2016, 147) remarks that "in some communities, in-kind benefits may better satisfy the preferences of a recipient population" than cash dividends. It is possible that cultural factors may play a role in explaining the polling results (bearing in mind that Mongolia has been a nation-state for a century and is no longer predominantly pastoral—60% of the population now lives in the capital city (Yeung and Howes 2015, 5)—so it is as "modern" as most nations). But another entirely plausible explanation, as presented in Chapter 3, is that the Mongolian

cultural sensitivity naturally needs to be balanced against an imperative to ensure that individuals are not being exploited or oppressed by alternative governance structures—potentially a tricky ethical problem.

Who Will Issue Dividends?

We have seen that for many types of natural resources, it may be expedient to establish trusts to collect resource rents, conduct resource management activities, and (if applicable) distribute dividends. In the case of land itself (land as commodity), however, the least disruptive option would be to leave tax collection in the hands of local (or other) government where it currently resides, convert real estate taxation to proper Georgeist land taxation, and possibly re-arrange budgeting procedures to free up the land tax revenue for distribution as dividends. Other types of economic rents (i.e., those not involving natural resources) may be recovered by governments or other authorized bodies via taxes, fees, and auctions.

When it comes to distribution of dividends, each trust or government agency could separately write checks (or initiate electronic transfers, etc.). Or efficiency could be improved by centralizing distribution. In the United States, for example, the existing Social Security infrastructure could be adapted as a distribution channel for dividends issued from the whole range of governmental and non-governmental sources (Barnes 2014, 87; Lerman 2018, 74–75).

Who Will Receive Dividends?

As discussed above, the geographic scope of dividend issuance will depend mostly on two factors: the nature of the resource or source of rent, and the geographic scope of the authority that establishes and governs the program. Many would probably agree that dividends from a global resource like the atmosphere as a carbon sink ought to have global distribution, while dividends from a local resource like a fishery ought to be distributed locally. In practice, most dividend programs are likely

people understood that the mining revenue would not last indefinitely, and they preferred that it be directed toward long-term investments, consistent with the sound principles for managing non-renewable resources discussed above.

to conform in their scope to the boundaries of nation-states or subnational units like states and provinces—wherever the authority is found and exercised to establish the programs. For dividend programs operated by independent trusts, the boundaries might be a little more idiosyncratic (e.g., encompassing all cities and townships around a particular lake or bay). In rare instances, it is conceivable that "bad" rent extracted from a particular business or industry would be distributed among affected employees or customers rather than citizens at large.

The public trust doctrine reinforces the idea of redistributing within political boundaries. A strict reading of the labor theory of property, however, would suggest that *all* applicable common wealth dividend programs ought to be universal (global) in scope. Political boundaries, after all, are arbitrary. At present, there is no immediate prospect of a genuinely global common wealth dividend program, but it is certainly something worth contemplating and perhaps aspiring towards. As noted in Chapter 4, there are already voices calling for global carbon cap-and-dividend programs, and even, as a stepping stone toward that goal, proposals for federating national dividend programs on a bilateral basis. Europe, already largely federated, could provide another model if it wished to take a leadership role in this arena. If a global carbon dividend program is established, that will make it a lot easier to think about federating other types of dividend programs and/or globalizing the distribution of other types of dividends.

One of the arguments for keeping dividends local is that in some cases local residents make sacrifices to preserve and sustain resources. Think of the long-time fishing families that (in accordance with management plans) exercise restraint in order to prevent overfishing, and the residents of Maine who (following the law) install septic tanks to avoid fouling the state's aquifers. Naturally these groups deserve more compensation than strangers thousands of miles away. One way to make that happen would be to limit the scope of dividends to local communities. Another would be to compensate locals for their financial sacrifices and losses *directly out of gross revenue (e.g., the budgets for renewable resource stewardship)*, before the balance of the fund is allocated for distribution as universal dividends. Hickel (2012, 133) suggests that this is one way the Alaska model could be improved upon. (Compare also the idea of a transition fund, paid out of gross carbon pricing revenues, to help those displaced by the shift away from fossil fuels, as discussed in Chapter 4.)

Various authors have made other suggestions about scale and scope. Alfred Andersen (1985, 149–156) describes a nested hierarchy of trusts, with revenue shared up and down the hierarchy to moderate local differences. Another option would be to conventionally assign certain types of rents (e.g., from water resources and land values) to local trusts and others (e.g., from oil resources and carbon permits) to national or global trusts (Hartzok 2012, 61; Barnes 2006, 136ff).

By default, we can assume that dividends will be directed to individuals (with the caveat aboutnon-Western cultures above in mind), though there are examples (e.g., in Iran, as discussed in Chapter 3, and California, as discussed in Chapter 4) where households rather than individuals have been the recipient unit. Policy-makers will need to decide whether dividends go to citizens or to residents, and how to handle myriad exceptional cases. Alaska's eligibility rules for residents allow those who leave the state to study or serve in the military, for example, to register for the dividend, as long as they are present in the state for at least 72 consecutive hours during the year and meet other requirements. When it comes to issuing dividends to children, there are several schools of thought, as discussed briefly in Chapter 4. Children could be eligible for less than full dividends (e.g., half-dividends), and/or the dividends might be placed in trust for them until they reach a certain age, which would be similar to Paine's idea of giving each young adult a nest egg when they start out in life.

Conclusion

This chapter does not tie up the idea of common wealth dividends neatly with a bow. We have at least three theoretical frameworks that could be invoked to explain and justify them, and a variety of ways the concept could be extended from the domain of Nature to man-made sources of wealth.

One of the things we can say about the moral intuition we have been examining, then, is that it is generative. As one particular expression of a universal concern for fairness, it shows up in many domains and is adaptable to a variety of circumstances; a variety of disciplines shed light on it and those discussed here perhaps still do not exhaust it.

The case for fair sharing of common wealth has been independently reinvented or rediscovered several times over the last few centuries, in theory and in practice. In some cases, like Alaska's Permanent Fund, it has been put into effect with full knowledge and intention. At other times—like Iran's fuel subsidy phaseout and the many garden-variety carbon pricing programs that return a portion of revenue to taxpayers—policy-makers have implemented it from simple expediency. But even when those who develop and implement programs of sharing common wealth are not aware of the theory or the history recounted in this book, not aware of the work of Paine and George and Hammond and Wilfong and Barnes and Hansen, but are simply putting one foot in front of the other and doing what is necessary and what seems fair, they are still part of that tradition. Those most practical of motives—directing resource revenues to households because it is simply necessary to keep those households financially afloat, and because it is evidently fair, fairer than alternatives on the table—are themselves the essence of Paine's original proposal.

Most flows of wealth in the economy are invisible. With mines, forests, fisheries, aquifers, and carbon sinks not directly before our eyes (even as we stare straight through the blue atmosphere), we do not easily develop the habit of recognizing them as sources of common wealth and ourselves as their natural beneficiaries. The value of the effort made by Paine and Hammond and the other theorists and advocates, and what I hope this book will provide as well, is to encourage us to develop those habits of imagination: to connect those dots and see ourselves and each other as having the added dignity of being natural beneficiaries of the common wealth of our planet and civilization, and to be ready to demand that policy conform better to that reality.

References

Andersen, Alfred F. 1985. *Liberating the Early American Dream*. New Brunswick, N.J.: Transaction Books.

Andersen, Alfred F. 1996. *Challenging Newt Gingerich, Chapter by Chapter*. Eugene, OR: Tom Paine Institute.

Andrzejewski, Adam. 2019. How the Fortune 100 Turned $2 Billion in Lobbying Spend Into $400 Billion of Taxpayer Cash. *Forbes* (May 14).

Andrzejewski, Adam, and Thomas W. Smith. 2019. *Federal Funding of Fortune 100 Companies: Open the Books Oversight Report*. https://www.openthebooks.com/federal-funding-of-fortune-100-companies--open-the-books-oversight-report/.

Barnes, Peter. 2006. *Capitalism 3.0*. San Francisco: Berrett-Koehler.

Barnes, Peter. 2014. *With Liberty and Dividends for All*. San Francisco: Berrett-Koehler.

Barnes, Peter. 2021 [in press]. *Ours: The Case for Universal Property*. Cambridge, UK: Polity Press.

Basu, Rahul, and Scott Pegg. 2020. Minerals are a Shared Inheritance: Accounting for the Resource Curse. *The Extractive Industries and Society* 7 (4): 1369–1376.

Bebchuk, Lucian, and Jesse Fried. 2004. The Managerial Power Perspective. In *Pay Without Performance: The Unfulfilled Promise of Executive Compensation*, ed. Lucian Bebchuk and Jesse Fried. Cambridge, MA: Harvard University Press.

Benes, Jaromir, and Michael Kumhof. 2012. *The Chicago Plan Revisited.* IMF Working Paper WP/12/202. August.

Bernanke, Ben S. 2002. Deflation: Making Sure 'It' Doesn't Happen Here. Remarks Before the National Economists Club, Washington, DC. November 21. https://www.federalreserve.gov/boarddocs/speeches/2002/20021121/default.htm.

Bernanke, Ben S. 2003. *Some Thoughts on Monetary Policy in Japan: Remarks before the Japan Society of Monetary Economics, Tokyo, Japan.* May 31. https://fraser.stlouisfed.org/title/statements-speeches-ben-s-bernanke-453/thoughts-monetary-policy-japan-8879.

Bernanke, Ben S. 2016. What Tools Does the Fed Have Left? Part 3: Helicopter money. Brookings Institution. April 11. https://www.brookings.edu/blog/ben-bernanke/2016/04/11/what-tools-does-the-fed-have-left-part-3-helicopter-money/.

Bezemer, Dirk, and Michael Hudson. 2016. Finance Is Not the Economy: Reviving the Conceptual Distinction. *Journal of Economic Issues* 50 (3, August 11): 745–768.

Blyth, Mark, Eric Lonergan, and Simon Wren-Lewis. 2015. Now the Bank of England Needs to Deliver QE for the People. *The Guardian* (May 21). https://www.theguardian.com/business/economics-blog/2015/may/21/now-the-bank-of-england-needs-to-deliver-qe-for-the-people.

Bollier, David. 2003. *Silent Theft: The Private Plunder of Our Common Wealth.* New York: Routledge.

Boyce, James K. 2019. *Economics for People and the Planet: Inequality in the Era of Climate Change.* London: Anthem Press.

Boyce, James K. 2021. A Litmus Test for the Climate. *Bangor Daily News* (January 26). https://bangordailynews.com/2021/01/26/opinion/contributors/a-litmus-test-for-the-climate/.

Brown, Ellen Hodgson. 2008. *Web of Debt: The Shocking Truth About Our Money System--the Sleight of Hand That Has Trapped Us in Debt and How We Can Break Free*, 2nd ed., Expanded and Updated. Baton Rouge, LA: Third Millenium Press.

Brown, Halina. 2020. The Perils of Privatization. Contribution to GTI Forum, "Universal Basic Income: Has the Time Come?" November. https://greattransition.org/gti-forum/basic-income-brown.

Christopher, Ben. 2016. The Spectrum Auction: How Economists Saved the Day. *Priceonomics*. August 19. https://priceonomics.com/the-spectrum-auction-how-economists-saved-the-day/.
Claeys, Gregory. 1987. Paine's Agrarian Justice and the Secularisation of Natural Jurisprudence. *Bulletin of the Society for the Study of Labour History* 52 (3): 25.
Claeys, Gregory. 1989. *Thomas Paine: Social and Political Thought*. London: Unwin Hyman.
Claeys, Gregory. 2016. Paine's Rights Reconsidered. In *New Directions in Thomas Paine Studies*, ed. Scott Cleary, Ivy Linton Stabell, and Quinlan Short. New York: Springer.
CNET. 2002. VeriSign Buys Network Solutions in $21 Billion Deal. January 2. https://www.cnet.com/news/verisign-buys-network-solutions-in-21-billion-deal/.
Connolly, Michelle, Nelson Sá, Azeem Zaman, Chris Roark, and Akshaya Trivedi. 2018. *The Evolution of U.S. Spectrum Values Over Time*. Brandeis Working Paper 2018/121.
Costanza, Robert, and Joshua Farley. 2010. What Should Be Done with the Revenues from a Carbon Cap and Auction System? *Solutions* 1 (1, January–February): 33.
Crotty, James. 2008. If Financial Market Competition Is Intense, Why Are Financial Firm Profits so High? Reflections on the Current 'Golden Age' of Finance. *Competition & Change* 12 (2): 167–183.
Cummine, Angela. 2016. *Citizens' Wealth: Why (and How) Sovereign Funds Should be Managed by the People and for the People*. New Haven: Yale University Press.
The Economist. 2003. Freeing the Airwaves: Should Radio Spectrum be Treated as Property, or as a Common Resource?" (May 29). https://www.economist.com/finance-and-economics/2003/05/29/freeing-the-airwaves.
The Economist. 2018. Which Firms Profit Most from America's Health-Care System? (March 15). https://www.economist.com/business/2018/03/15/which-firms-profit-most-from-americas-health-care-system.
Ellerman, David. 1988. *Cooperative Farming Communities: A Model Based on Mondragon and Moshav Principles*. Prepared for the Research Center for Rural Development of the State Council of the People's Republic of China. Industrial Cooperative Association. July.
Ellerman, David. 2016. Rethinking Common Versus Private Property. *American Journal of Economics and Sociology* 75 (2): 319–345.
Erickson, Gregg, and Cliff Groh. 2012. How the AP and the PFD Operate: The Peculiar Mechanics of Alaska's State Finances. In *Alaska's Permanent Fund Dividend: Examining Its Suitability as a Model*, ed. Karl Widerquist and Michael W. Howard, Chapter 3. New York: Palgrave Macmillan.

Farley, Joshua, Robert Costanza, Gary Flomenhoft, and Daniel Kirk. 2015. The Vermont Common Assets Trust: An Institution for Sustainable, Just and Efficient Resource Allocation. *Ecological Economics* 109 (January): 71–79.

Fitzgerald, Karl. 2013. *Total Resource Rents of Australia: Harnessing the Power of Monopoly*. Prosper Australia. https://www.prosper.org.au/wp-content/uploads/2013/12/TRRA_2013_final.pdf.

Flomenhoft, Gary. 2012. Applying the Alaska Model in a Resource-Poor State: The Example of Alaska. In *Exporting the Alaska Model: Adapting the Permanent Fund Dividend*, ed. Karl Widerquist and Michael W. Howard, Chapter 6. New York: Palgrave Macmillan.

Flomenhoft, Gary. 2017. Total Economic Rents of Australia as a Source for Basic Income. In *Financing Basic Income: Addressing the Cost Objection*, ed. Richard Pereira, 77–100. New York: Palgrave Macmillan.

Friedman, Milton. 1969. The Optimum Quantity of Money. In *The Optimum Quantity of Money and Other Essays*, Chapter 1. London: Macmillan.

Gaffney, Mason. 2009. The Hidden Taxable Capacity of Land: Enough and to Spare. *International Journal of Social Economics* 36 (4, March): 328–411.

George, Henry. [1885] 1901. Land and Taxation: A Conversation Between David Dudley Field and Henry George. In *The Complete Works of Henry George [Volume 8]: Our Land and Land Policy: Speeches, Lectures, and Miscellaneous Writings*, ed. Henry George Jr., 219–240. New York: Doubleday and McClure.

Goodman, Ellen P. 2004. Spectrum Rights in the Telecosm to Come. *San Diego Law Review* 41: 269–404.

Hallsmith, Gwendolyn, and Bernard Lietaer. 2011. *Creating Wealth: Growing Local Economies with Local Currencies*. Gabriola Island, BC: New Society Publishers.

Hannesson, Rögnvaldur. 2001. *Investing for Sustainability: The Management of Mineral Wealth*. New York: Springer Science & Business Media.

Hardin, Garrett. 1968. The Tragedy of the Commons. *Science* 162: 1243–1248.

Hardin, Garrett. 1991. The Tragedy of the Unmanaged Commons: Population and the Disguises of Providence. In *Commons Without Tragedy: Protecting the Environment from Over-Population: A New Approach*, ed. Robert V. Andelson, 162–185. London: Shepheard-Walwyn.

Hartwick, John M. 1977. Intergenerational Equity and the Investing of Rents from Exhaustible Resources. *American Economic Review* 67 (5, December): 972–974.

Hartzok, Alanna. 2012. Room for Improvement? Assessing the Strengths and Shortcomings of the Alaska Model in Advance of Export. In *Exporting the Alaska Model: Adapting the Permanent Fund Dividend*, ed. Karl Widerquist and Michael W. Howard, Chapter 4. New York: Palgrave Macmillan.

Hayes, Adam. 2020. "Economic Rent." *Investopedia*. https://www.investopedia.com/terms/e/economicrent.asp. Last updated September 29, 2020.

Hazlett, Thomas W. 1997. Physical Scarcity, Rent Seeking, and the First Amendment. *Columbia Law Review* 27 (4, May): 905–944.

Hazlett, Thomas W. 2001. *The Wireless Craze, the Unlimited Bandwidth Myth, the Spectrum Auction Faux Pas, and the Punchline to Ronal Coase's 'Big Joke': An Essay on Airwave Allocation Policy*. AEI-Brookings Joint Center for Regulatory Studies. Working Paper 1–2.

Heydorn, M. Oliver. 2014. *Social Credit Economics*. Ancaster, ON: CreateSpace.

Hickel, Jason. 2012. Constituting the Commons: Oil and Development in Postindependence South Sudan. *Exporting the Alaska Model: Adapting the Permanent Fund Dividend*, ed. Karl Widerquist and Michael W. Howard, Chapter 8. New York: Palgrave Macmillan.

Hockett, Robert, and Aaron James. 2020. *Money from Nothing: Or, Why We Should Stop Worrying About Debt and Learn to Love the Federal Reserve*. New York: Melville House.

Huber, Joseph. 2020. The Hemispheres of Finance: GDP and Non-GDP Finance. *Real-World Economics Review* 94 (9 December): 113–139.

Hudson, Michael. 2016. Rentier Capitalism—Veblen in the 21st Century (October 21). https://michael-hudson.com/2016/10/rentier-capitalism-veblen-in-the-21st-century/.

Hyde, Lewis. [1983] 2007. *The Gift: Creativity and the Artist in the Modern World*, 25th Anniversary Edition. New York: Vintage Books.

Internet Corporation for Assigned Names and Numbers (ICANN). 2009. *The End of Domain Tasting: Status Report on AGP Measures*. August 12. https://www.icann.org/en/system/files/files/agp-status-report-12aug09-en.pdf.

ICANN. 2012. Registrar Accreditation: History of the Shared Registry System. https://www.icann.org/resources/pages/history-2012-02-25-en. Accessed November 29, 2020.

International Telecommunication Union (ITU). n.d. Constitution. https://www.itu.int/council/pd/constitution.html. Accessed November 29, 2020.

Jackson, Andrew. 2013. *Sovereign Money: Paving the Way for a Sustainable Recovery.* Positive Money. https://positivemoney.org/2013/11/sovereign-money-paving-the-way-for-a-sustainable-recovery-new-report/.

Kahneman, Daniel, and Amos Tversky. 1979. "Prospect Theory: An Analysis of Decisions under Risk. *Econometrica* 47 (2, March): 263–291.

Khan, Mushtaq H. 2000. Rents, Efficiency and Growth. In *Rents, Rent-Seeking and Economic Development: Theory and Evidence in Asia*, ed. M.H. Khan and K.S. Jomo, Chapter 1. Cambridge, UK: Cambridge University Press.

Kimmerer, Robin Wall. 2013. *Braiding Sweetgrass: Indigenous Wisdom, Scientific Knowledge and the Teachings of Plants*. Minneapolis: Milkweed Editions.

Kruse, Elizabeth M. 2002. Property from the Sky: The Creation of Property Rights in the Radio Pectrum in the United States. University of Massachusetts Amherst PhD Dissertation.

Leopold, Aldo. [1949] 1989. *A Sand County Almanac, and Sketches Here and There*. Oxford: Oxford University Press.

Lerman, Allen H. 2018. Paying Dividends to American Residents from Carbon Fee Revenue. Citizens' Climate Education. May.

Levin, Harvey J. 1971. *The Invisible Resource: Use and Regulation of the Radio Spectrum*. Baltimore: Published for Resources for the Future, Inc. by Johns Hopkins University Press.

Lifschutz, Marissa. 2019. Top 10 Most Profitable US Industries. IBISWorld (June 6). https://www.ibisworld.com/industry-insider/analyst-insights/top-10-most-profitable-us-industries/.

Locke, John. [1690] 2017. *Two Treatises of Government*, ed. Peter Laslett. Cambridge, UK: Cambridge University Press.

Mackin, Chris. 2011. Employee Ownership: The Road to Shared Prosperity. *The Nation* (June 8). https://www.thenation.com/article/archive/employee-ownership-road-shared-prosperity/.

Mill, John Stuart. 1875. *Principles of Political Economy with Some of Their Applications to Social Philosophy*. London: Longmans.

Morrison, Rodney J. 1996. Sports Fans, Athletes' Salaries, and Economic Rent. *International Review for the Sociology of Sport* 31 (3, September 1): 257–270.

Ostrom, Elinor, Joanna Burger, Christopher B. Field, Richard B. Norgaard, and David Policansky. 1999. Revisiting the Commons: Local Lessons, Global Challenges. *Science* 284 (9 April 1999): 278–282.

Paine, Thomas. [1797] 1945. Agrarian Justice, in *Complete Writings of Thomas Paine*, vol. 1, ed. Philip Foner. New York: Citadel Press.

Paseur, E.C., Jr. 1987. Rent Seeking: Some Conceptual Problems and Implications. *The Review of Austrian Economics* 1 (1): 123–143.

Pope Francis. 2015. *Encyclical Letter* Laudato Si' *of The Holy Father Francis: On Care for Our Common Home*.

Positive Money. 2018. *Escaping Growth Dependency: Why Reforming Money Will Reduce the Need to Pursue Economic Growth at Any Cost to the Environment*. January. https://positivemoney.org/wp-content/uploads/2018/01/Escaping-Growth-Dependency-final_print.pdf.

Ranalli, Brent. 2015. M. Oliver Heydorn: Social Credit Economics. *Basic Income Studies* 10 (2): 281–283.

Ranalli, Brent. 2016a. Pin- and Pencil-Making in the Twenty-First Century. *Fortnightly Review* (30 April). https://fortnightlyreview.co.uk/2016/04/pin-making/.

Ranalli, Brent. 2016b. Adam Smith's Dilemma and the Algonquian Model of Political Virtue. *TELOSscope* (12 May). https://www.telospress.com/adam-smiths-dilemma-and-the-algonquian-model-of-political-virtue/.

Ranalli, Brent. 2016c. Fueling Value Change. A Review of Ian Morris's *Foragers, Farmers, and Fossil Fuels: How Human Values Evolve*. Great Transition Initiative (February). https://www.greattransition.org/images/GTI_publications/Ranalli-Fueling-Value-Change.pdf.

Ranalli, Brent, James D'Angelo, and David King. 2018. *The 1970s Sunshine Reforms and the Transformation of Congressional Lobbying*. The Congressional Research Institute. December. https://congressionalresearch.org/Ranalli2018SunshineReformsAndTransformationOfLobbying.pdf.

Ranalli, Brent. 2020. Thomas Paine's 'Neglected' Pamphlet: Agrarian Justice. *Journal for the Study of Radicalism* 14 (1): 167–190.

Rosston, Gregory L. 2014. Increasing the Efficiency of Spectrum Allocation. *Review of Industrial Organization* 45: 221–243.

Ryan, Patrick S. 2005. Wireless Communications and Computing at a Crossroads: New Paradigms and Their Impact on Theories Governing the Public's Right to Spectrum Access. *Journal on Telecommunications & High Technology Law* 3: 239–274.

Serbu, Jared. 2014. DoD, Industry Must Learn to Share Radio Spectrum as It Grows More Scarce. *Federal News Network* (February 2014). https://federalnewsnetwork.com/defense/2014/02/dod-industry-must-learn-to-share-radio-spectrum-as-it-grows-more-scarce/.

Shepherd, A. Ross. 1970. Economic Rent and the Industry Supply Curve. *Southern Economic Journal* 37 (2): 209–211. https://doi.org/10.2307/1056131.

Shepherd, William G. 1989. Capital Gains as Economic Rent. *Review of Social Economy* 47 (2, Summer): 155–172.

Smith, Adam. [1759] 1976. *The Theory of Moral Sentiments*. Indianapolis: Liberty Classics.

Smith, Adam. [1776] 1986. *The Wealth of Nations Books I–III*. London: Penguin Classics.

Smith, Noah. 2016. How Finance Took Over the Economy: Competition Doesn't Seem to Erode the Industry's Huge Profits. *Bloomberg Opinion* (April 20). https://www.bloomberg.com/opinion/articles/2016-04-20/how-finance-came-to-dominate-the-u-s-economy.

Solow, Robert M. 1974. Intergenerational Equity and Exhaustible Resources. *The Review of Economic Studies* 41 (5, December): 29–45.

Stiglitz, Joseph E. 2016. Joseph Stiglitz Says Standard Economics Is Wrong. Inequality and Unearned Income Kills the Economy. *Evonomics* (September 9). https://evonomics.com/joseph-stiglitz-inequality-unearned-income/.

Stiglitz, Joseph E. 2018. The American Economy Is Rigged: And What We Can Do About It. *Scientific American* (November 1). https://www.scientificamerican.com/article/the-american-economy-is-rigged/.

Tollison, Robert D. 1982. Rent Seeking: A Survey. *Kyklos* 35 (4): 575–602.

Wackernagel, Mathis, and Bert Beyers. 2019. *Ecological Footprint: Managing Our Biocapacity Budget*. Gabriola Island, BC: New Society Publishers.

Werbach, Kevin. 2002. *Open Spectrum: The New Wireless Paradigm*. New America Foundation Spectrum Policy Program, Spectrum Series Issue Brief #8 (October).

Wood, Mary Christina. 2013. *Nature's Trust: Environmental Law for a New Ecological Age*. Cambridge, UK: Cambridge University Press.

Yeung, Ying, and Stephen Howes. 2015. *Resources-to-Cash: A Cautionary Tale from Mongolia*. Australian National University, Development Policy Centre. August.

Index

A
absolute dominion (law of the biggest pump), 46
accountability
of central banks, 143
democratic versus fiduciary, 112, 150
of executive agencies to legislature, 111
in handling resource revenue, 41
money creation and, 150
taxation promotes, 41, 150
Adamites, 9, 11
agrarian law/*lex agraria*, 2, 11, 14, 17, 21, 23
agriculture, farming, 13–17, 24, 31, 64, 85, 106, 107, 124, 131
Alaska, 2, 21, 27, 32, 33, 35–38, 40, 41, 43–47, 49, 50, 60, 84, 103, 106, 108, 114, 115, 154, 155
North Slope, 2, 33
"Alaska, Inc.", 33, 34, 38
Alaska Permanent Fund (APF), 4, 27, 32–38, 40, 41, 43, 44, 46, 47, 85, 92, 103, 105, 155
Alaska Permanent Fund Corporation, 35
Albany, 20
Alberta, 74
Alexander the Great, 14
Allentown, 27
Amazon.com, 140
American Indians, Alaska Natives, 11, 12, 15, 38, 114, 152
American War of Independence/American Revolution, 1, 7, 17, 143
Anabaptists, 11
Anchorage, 114
Antarctica, 51
anti-competitive practices, 119, 123, 127–130
Aquinas, Thomas, 9–12, 16, 32, 114
Arctic Ocean, 33, 66
Arden, Delaware, 27

B. Ranalli, *Common Wealth Dividends*,
Exploring the Basic Income Guarantee,
https://doi.org/10.1007/978-3-030-72416-0

Arrhenius, Svante, 62
"Asian Tigers" (countries), 27
Athens, 13, 14
Atlantic Ocean, 20, 66
atmosphere, 1, 4, 59–65, 79, 84, 88, 91, 110, 113, 137, 138, 153, 156
auction, 68, 72, 80–82, 87, 89, 126, 136, 138, 139, 141, 153
ascending clock, 81
Australia, 27, 74, 76, 78, 85

B

Babeuf, François-Noël ("Gracchus"), 11, 16, 21
Baker–Shultz plan (climate policy). *See* Climate Leadership Council (CLC)
Baker III, James A., 70, 71
Baltimore, 20
banks, banking system, 141–144
Barnes, Peter, 1, 4, 5, 44, 47, 59–61, 68–70, 76, 84, 85, 89–91, 101, 108, 112, 114, 118, 129, 132–135, 153, 155, 156
basic income, basic income guarantee, 2–4, 8, 26, 61, 88, 92, 93, 151
"laziness" argument against, 3, 151
Basu, Rahul, 47, 48, 50, 51
benchmarking (climate policy), 64, 83
Bernanke, Ben, 145–147
Beyer, Don, 70, 71
"big men" (anthropology), 15
biodiversity, loss of, 58, 65. *See also* extinction, mass
blockchain, 93
Bluetooth, 138
Bolivia, 44
Bonaparte, Napoleon, 20
bonds (financial instruments), 142
Bone, John, 21
border adjustments (climate policy), 80–82, 149
Boyce, James, 71, 84–87, 108
"Bristol Bay, Inc.", 38, 39, 78
Bristol Bay Borough, 38, 39
British Columbia, 5, 40, 73, 75, 88
Climate Action Tax Credit, 75
broadcast spectrum, 131, 134–139
Brown, Gordon, 67
Burke, Edmund, 17, 19
Bush, George W., 47

C

California, 72, 74, 88, 126, 155
California Climate Credit, 72
Canada, 75, 87, 88
provincial Heritage Funds, 48
Cantwell, Maria, 70
cap-and-dividend, 60, 68, 70, 77, 93, 154
cap-and-permit, 5, 60, 72–74, 76, 78–80, 82–84, 87, 88, 91–93, 126, 149
cap-and-trade, 67–69, 78, 82
CapGlobalCarbon, 89, 90, 93
carbon dioxide (CO_2), 57, 59, 60, 62, 63, 65–67, 86
carbon dividend(s), 1, 2, 4, 62, 67–72, 76, 84–88, 93, 108, 114, 151
global, 88–93, 154
Carbon Limits and Energy for America's Renewal (CLEAR) Act, 70
carbon pricing, 5, 59, 66–69, 72, 73, 76, 78, 80, 84–89, 93, 107, 108, 126, 149, 154, 156
distribution effects (progressive, regressive), 61, 75, 86, 87
upstream versus midstream versus downstream approaches, 79, 80, 82, 83, 92

carbon tax, 5, 67–70, 72–76, 78–80, 82–84, 86, 88, 91, 93, 126, 149
celebrity pay, 128
cellular phone service, 134, 136, 139
central banks, central banking, 142–148
Chicago Plan, 142
children, 3, 19, 21, 25, 61, 70, 87, 88, 93, 104, 155
Cicero, 9
Citizens Broadband Radio Service (CBRS), 137
Citizens Climate Lobby (CCL), 69–71, 78, 88
Claeys, Gregory, 7–10, 116
Claim the Sky, 91
Clemons, Steven, 47
Climate Action Rebate Act, 70
climate change, global warming, 58, 60, 61, 65, 66, 68, 71, 76
  climate change adaptation, 66
  climate change mitigation, 4, 66–69, 71, 76, 77, 83, 84, 88, 90, 91, 108
Climate Leadership Council (CLC), 70, 71, 88
coal, 49, 61, 62, 67, 77
cognitive radio, 137, 138
Collins, Susan, 70
Common Heritage of Mankind (CHM), 50, 51
common law, 111, 115
common wealth dividends
  creating a political constituency, 37, 84, 106, 108
  eligibility for, 88, 155
  geographic scope of, 46, 88, 90–93, 153, 154
  pooling of, 152
ConocoPhillips, 70
conservation ethic, environmental ethic, 102, 114
consumer surplus, 121
contraction and convergence (climate policy), 83
Coons, Chris, 70
copper, 49
coral reefs, 65. *See also* Great Barrier Reef
Cork, 20
corruption (government), 40, 41, 43
Costanza, Robert, 90, 91, 108
counter-dominance (anthropology), 15
COVID-19 pandemic, 147
Credo Mobile, 59
cultural sensitivity, 152

D
Data Dividend Project (DDP), 127, 151
debt, 13, 22, 41, 42, 128, 142, 144, 146, 147
debt-slavery, 14
deep sea mining, 50
deflation, 142, 145, 146
deism, 17, 116
Denmark, 27, 73
desertification, 58
Deutch, Ted, 70
Diggers (English), 11
Directory (French regime), 20
domain names, 131, 139–141
Douglas, Major C.H., 147
Douthwaite, Richard, 89, 90
Dove, Patrick Edward, 23
Dublin, 20
Dunant, Henri, 90
Dutch disease, 42

E
Earth Atmospheric Trust, 90, 91
Earth Overshoot Day, 104

ecological footprint, 104
ecosystems, 51, 58, 103
ecosystem services, 4, 57, 58, 101, 103, 107, 112, 113, 119, 125, 126, 130
Edinburgh, 20
education, schools, 3, 19, 21, 25, 34, 39, 42–45, 77, 110, 113, 151, 152, 155
Ellerman, David, 116–118, 131
emissions trading scheme (ETS), 82
Employee Stock Ownership Plan (ESOP), 129
Energy Innovation and Carbon Dividend Act, 70
England, Britain, United Kingdom, 11, 14, 16, 17, 20, 26, 42, 62, 67, 89, 92, 112
entertainment (business sector), 120, 129
Eritrea, 89
Estonia, 73
European Union, Europe, 4, 13, 17, 26, 77, 88, 135, 154
Evans, George H., 22–24, 32, 38, 134
executive compensation, 120, 128, 129
extinction, mass, 103. *See also* biodiversity, loss of
ExxonMobil, 70

F

Facebook, 127
Fairhope, Alabama, 27
fairness doctrine, 135, 136
Feasta, 89, 90, 93, 152
Federal Communications Commission (FCC), 135–138
Federal Deposit Insurance Corporation (FDIC), 141
fee-and-dividend, 61, 68–70, 78, 86, 88
Feinstein, Dianne, 70
Fertile Crescent, 58
Filmer, Robert, 11, 114
finance (business sector), 16, 60, 119, 120, 128, 130, 141
financial crisis of 2008, 128, 144
Finland, 73
fishing, fisheries, 1, 38, 46, 51, 103, 106, 107, 109, 110, 112, 113, 122, 126, 148, 149, 154, 156
Flomenhoft, Gary, 46, 47, 101, 118, 120, 129, 132, 133, 135, 140
Foote, Eunice, 62
Ford, 70
forests, forestry, 32, 38, 46, 102, 104, 112, 126, 148, 149, 156
Forest Stewardship Council, 90
France, 7, 11, 17–21, 26, 45, 74, 108, 144
  French constitution, 17–20
  French National Convention, 17, 18
French Revolution, 1, 7, 17
Friedman, Milton, 144, 145
The Future We Need, 50, 51

G

Genesis (creation story), Eden, 8, 115
geoengineering, 66
George, Henry, 4, 23–27, 31, 32, 60, 125, 149, 156
  Progress and Poverty, 23–26, 60
Georgist versus Paineite approaches (to use of common wealth revenue), 4, 26, 40, 42, 44, 61, 149
Germany, 67
Ghana, 47
gifts, Nature as gift, 11, 32, 57, 60, 102, 114, 116

Girondins, 17
GM, 70
Goa, 50
Goa Foundation, 50
Goa Iron Ore Permanent Fund, 50
gold, 49, 147
Goldman Sachs, 70
Gracchus, Tiberius and Gaius (the Gracchi), 13, 14
Graeber, David, 13
grassroots advocacy, 45, 46, 69, 88
Great Barrier Reef, 107
Greece, 2, 13
greenhouse effect, 62, 63
greenhouse gases, 1, 4, 59–63, 66, 67, 72, 79
Greenland, 40
Grotius, Hugo, 9–12, 102, 114, 115
ground rent, 8, 23
groundwater, aquifer, 1, 45–47, 57–59, 103–106, 110, 126, 154, 156

H
Hammond, Jay, 1, 4, 33–41, 43, 44, 47, 48, 50, 61, 76, 78, 156
Hansen, James, 4, 61, 62, 67–69, 78, 87, 156
Hardin, Garret, 109
Harrisburg, 27
Hartwick's Rule, 105
Hawken, Paul, 90
healthcare (business sector), 119
Healthy Climate and Family Security Act, 70
helicopter money, 145, 146
Hockett, Robert, 143, 146
Homestead Law, 22
honeybees, 58
human genome, 51
hunter-gatherers, foraging societies, 2, 15, 16
Hussein, Saddam, 47
Hyde, Lewis, 102, 114
hyperinflation, 142, 143, 145

I
IBM, 70
Idaho, 131
India, 47, 50, 111
  Indian Supreme Court, 50
Industrial Revolution, 16, 58, 62, 64, 104
inflation, 7, 143, 145, 148
infrastructure, 12, 33, 34, 37, 42, 45, 66, 69, 70, 76, 77, 84, 87, 92, 105, 132, 150
Inglis, Bob, 70
innocent buyer problem, 148, 149
intellectual property protections, 108, 122, 132, 133, 141
intergenerational equity, 50. *See also* sustainability, sustainable resource management
Intergovernmental Panel on Climate Change (IPCC), 63, 64, 83
International Court for the Environment, 90
International Seabed Authority (ISA), 50, 51
International Space Station, 57
International Telecommunication Union (ITU), 134
Internet, 65, 81, 132, 136
Internet Corporation for Assigned Names and Numbers (ICANN), 139–141
Iran, 49, 155, 156
Iraq, 47
Ireland, 23, 89

J
Jacobins, Reign of Terror, 17, 18

James, Aaron, 143, 146
Japan, 146
Jefferson, Thomas, 21–23

K
Kenya, 92
Keynes, John Maynard, 144
Kimmerer, Robin Wall, 102
Kuwait, 44, 47
Kyoto Protocol, 66, 67, 72

L
labor theory of property (LTP), 5, 115–117, 120, 130, 132, 140, 150, 154
negative application of the LTP, negative LTP, 117, 118, 120, 132, 135, 139
labor theory of value (LTV), 116, 117
land, 1, 2, 4, 8–16, 21–25, 27, 31–33, 38, 44, 46, 57, 59, 60, 101, 102, 107, 110–114, 116–118, 125, 126, 130, 131, 133, 135, 137, 140, 141, 148, 149, 151–153, 155
land reform, 4, 13, 19, 22, 32
land taxation, (Georgist) Single Tax, 4, 23–27, 59, 113, 125, 126, 131, 132, 149, 151, 153
land values, contribution of social context to, 131
Larson, John, 69
Le Havre, 20
Leopold, Aldo, 102
Lévi-Strauss, Claude, 114
Liberia, 89
lobbying, 4, 22, 50, 69, 119, 125. *See also* grassroots advocacy
local currencies, 143
Locke, John, 10–12, 21, 24, 32, 116
London, 20, 23
loss-aversion, 105
lottery, 106, 136
Louis XVI, 16, 17
Luxembourg prison, 18, 20
Lycurgus, 13, 14

M
Macedon, 14
Madison, James, 18
Maine, 1, 15, 44–46, 59, 70, 154
Maine Water Dividend Trust, 44
Manhattan, 131
man-made sources of common wealth, 2, 5, 101, 118, 125, 130, 155
Mannabase, 93
Mars, 57
Marxist economics, 117
Masquerier, Lewis, 22
Massachusetts, 112
McCain, John, 68
medical research, 51, 58, 104
Medicare, 43
Merkel, Angela, 67
Mesopotamia, 14
methane, 62, 63
Microsoft, 70
military, 16, 20, 35, 42, 90, 134, 139, 155
Mill, John Stuart, 116, 117
mining, minerals, 32, 33, 38, 42–44, 46, 48–50, 63, 103, 110–113, 122, 126, 148, 152, 153, 156
monetary system, 142, 144
money creation (by spending, by lending), 108, 131, 141–148, 150
money supply, 142–147
Mongolia, 49, 152
monitoring, reporting, and verification (MRV), 83
monopoly, 11, 118–120, 122, 123, 127, 129, 151

monopsony, 119, 129
Monroe, James, 7, 18
Moon, 51
Morris, Gouverneur, 18
Müntzer, Thomas, 11

N
Naknek, Alaska, 38
National Land Reform Association, 22
National Trust for Places of Historic Interest or Natural Beauty (National Trust), 112, 113
natural capital, 103, 105, 106
natural gas, 44, 63, 72, 77, 79
natural monopoly, 123, 127, 140
natural resource rents, resource rents, 32, 44, 48, 119, 122, 126, 153
natural resources, 2, 4, 5, 31–33, 37, 40, 42, 44, 46, 48, 49, 57, 101, 103, 109, 111–116, 123, 125, 130, 135, 150, 153
neo-classical economics, 26
Nestlé, 45
Netherlands, 42, 91
network effect, 127, 151
Network Solutions Inc. (NSI), 139, 140
Neustrelitz, 20
New Harmony (township in Indiana), 21
New York City, 20, 22, 23, 27
New York (state), 14, 17
New Zealand, 27
Nigeria, 47, 103
non-renewable resources, exhaustible resources, 36, 43, 44, 48, 103–106, 109–111, 126, 150, 153
North America, 4, 11, 33, 137
Northern Ireland, 112
North Sea, 47
Norway, 44, 47, 73, 103
nuclear energy, 66, 77, 105

O
Obama, Barack, 68
O'Brien, James Bronterre, 23, 135
ocean, 50, 63, 65, 66, 110, 137, 138
offsets (climate policy), 69, 83
Ogilvie, William, 24
oil/petroleum, 1, 4, 27, 32–38, 40, 41, 43, 44, 47, 49, 62, 66, 76, 77, 79, 84, 103, 104, 114, 126, 155
oligopoly, 119, 128
Oregon, 44
Orr, David, 90
Ostrom, Elinor, 90, 109
outer space, 51
Owen, Robert, 21, 22

P
Pacific Ocean, 24
Pacific Power, 72
Paine, Thomas, 1, 4, 7, 8, 11–23, 25–27, 31–33, 42, 48, 61, 76, 84, 116, 118, 133, 149, 155, 156
The Age of Reason, 7, 18
Agrarian Justice, 7, 8, 11, 16, 19–22, 60, 116, 133
Common Sense, 7, 17
The Rights of Man, 7, 17, 19
Panetta, Jimmy, 70
Paris, 7, 16, 18, 20, 91
Paris (climate) agreement, COP21, 64, 72, 89, 91
Parkinson's Law, 39
peat, 104
Pennsylvania, 27
Penobscots, 15
pension (old age), 8, 19, 26, 44, 74, 76

Permanent Fund Dividend (PFD), 1, 2, 4, 27, 32, 33, 35–38, 40, 41, 43, 45, 60, 108
Perrier, 45
PG&E, 72
Philadelphia, 17, 20, 23
Philippines, 111
Phoenicia, 14
Pinchot, Gifford, 31
Pittsburgh, 27
plastics, 79
Plutarch, 13, 14
Poland Springs, 45
political instability, (political) revolution, 13, 14, 16
Portugal, 74
positive money, 143, 145, 150
poverty, 3, 12, 23, 24, 39, 45, 48, 49, 91, 92
Powell, Colin, 47
precautionary principle, 104
price elasticity, 84, 85
price floors and ceilings (carbon pricing), 79, 84
price signals, 58, 59, 77, 108
primogeniture, 23
Principles of Fair Mining, 50
producer surplus, 121, 122, 125, 126
property theory, 5, 114, 115, 120
  initial property rights, 116
Prudhoe Bay, 33, 38, 40
public domain, 132
public trust, public trust doctrine, 5, 38, 45, 46, 91, 110, 115, 130, 150, 154

Q

quantitative easing (QE), 144, 145
  QE for the people, 144

R

radio, 134–136, 139
radioastronomy, 135
rationing, 67, 89, 90, 126, 127
Reagan, Ronald, 135
rebound (climate policy), 77
Red Cross, International Committee of the, 90
Redefining Progress, 59, 60
referendum, 45, 46
Regional Greenhouse Gas Initiative (RGGI), 72, 73
regulation (government), 58, 69, 71, 77–79, 82, 83, 119, 123, 124, 127, 128, 133–138, 140
renewable energy, 84, 92, 105, 124
renewable resources, 58, 103, 104, 106, 107, 109, 110, 126, 135, 150
Renta Dignidad, 44
rent, economic rent, 5, 23, 24, 27, 48, 50, 118–130, 134, 140–142, 150, 153
  "bad" rents, 122–124, 127, 128, 130, 154
  "good" rents, 121–126, 130
  from positional advantage, 118, 123–125, 128–130
rent-seeking, 119, 125
resource curse, 4, 41–44, 87, 150
responsibility principle, 117. *See also* labor theory of property (LTP)
revenue recycling, 72–76, 86–88, 127, 128, 151
reverse auction, 137
Ricardo, David, 26
Rome, 2, 13, 14, 110, 115
Roosevelt, Theodore, 31
Rose, Dave, 32–38, 40
royalties, 38, 50, 111

S

San Francisco, 23, 24, 59
Santander, 70
satellite communication, 135
Saudi Arabia, 44, 47
Saunders, Marshall, 69
Schumpeterian rents, 122, 123
Scotland, 23, 24
seed capital (for youth coming of age), nest egg, 8, 26, 88, 155
septic system, 45, 58, 59, 154
severance tax, 38, 148
Shell, 70
Sherman County, Oregon, 44
Shultz, George P., 70, 71
silver, 42
Sky Trust, 4, 5, 59–61, 70, 87, 88
Smith, Adam, 26, 77, 117, 118, 125, 133, 134
social contract, 42
Social Credit, 147
social media, 127, 128, 130, 136
Social Security, 70, 71, 86, 153
software-defined radio, 137
solar power, 59, 76
Solon, 13, 14
South America, 42
South Sudan, 47
sovereign wealth fund (SWF), 44, 47, 92, 103, 106
Soviet Union, 89
Spain, 42, 43
Sparta, 13–15, 17, 21
species loss, 104. *See also* biodiversity, loss of
speculation, 22, 24, 25, 124, 125, 128–130, 136, 140, 141
Spence, Thomas, 11, 21
sports (business sector), professional athletes, 120, 129
Stevens, Ted, 47
stewardship, 102, 105, 109–111, 126
stolen goods, 149
stratospheric ozone, 57, 58
subsidies, 44, 49, 77, 80, 83, 85, 119, 123, 124, 128, 129, 138, 156
subsurface mineral rights, 38
supply and demand, 77, 78, 84, 106, 120, 125, 128, 137, 142, 149
sustainability, sustainable resource management, 36, 43, 49, 59, 89, 90, 101–104, 106, 107, 109, 111–115, 118, 149–151, 153
  political stability as sustainability, 12
  weak sustainability, 105
sustainable yield, 104, 106
Sweden, 62, 73
Switzerland, 5, 73, 75, 87, 88

T

tax-and-dividend, 68, 75, 76, 78, 86
taxation, tax rebates, tax reductions, 2, 3, 19, 22, 24, 38, 39, 42–44, 68, 70, 72, 73, 75, 78, 79, 84, 85, 87, 113, 119, 124, 128, 129, 146–150, 153, 156
taxi licenses, 128
technological development, 12, 58, 69, 70, 76, 77, 91, 93, 104, 108, 122, 128, 131, 132, 136–138
television, 40, 47, 134–139
Texas, 44–46
theism (God of the Old Testament/Yahweh), 102, 114, 116
third world nations/developing nations, 41, 43, 48, 83, 89, 92, 93
Tobin tax, 129
tragedy of the commons, 109, 123
transition fund, transition assistance (for decarbonization), 61, 70, 154
Trump, Donald, 71, 136

Trustees of Reservations, 112, 113
trusts (for managing assets), trustees, 2, 45, 60, 70, 88–90, 111–113, 115, 117, 150, 153, 154
Tyndall, John, 62

U
United Nations, 44, 92, 134
  United Nations Convention on the Law of the Sea (UNCLOS), 50
  United Nations Environmental Programme, 50
  United Nations Framework Convention on Climate Change (UNFCCC), 67
United States of America, 4, 5, 7, 16, 18, 20–23, 25–27, 38, 47, 60, 62, 67–69, 71–73, 78, 80, 86–88, 90, 111, 113, 119, 127, 129, 132, 135, 136, 139, 141–143, 145, 147, 153
  United States Notes, 142
  U.S. Congress, 5, 33, 47, 61, 62, 69, 71, 90, 145, 146
  U.S. Department of Commerce, 139, 140
  U.S. Federal Reserve (Fed), 70, 141, 142, 145, 146
  U.S. Forest Service, 31, 111
  U.S. Supreme Court, 35
  U.S. Treasury Department, 79, 80, 86, 142, 146
utilities (business sector), 72–74, 76, 88, 123, 126, 139, 140. *See also* natural monopoly

V
Van Hollen, Chris, 70, 71
Venezuela, 41, 47
Verisign, 139, 140
Vermont, 46–48
  Vermont Common Asset Trust, 47
Victoria, 128
Virginia, 23

W
Wales, 21, 112
Washington, D.C., 40, 69, 71, 72, 119
Washington, George, 20
Washington (state), 91
water vapor, 62–64
Western versus Eastern cultures, 152, 155
WiFi, 138
Wilfong, Jim, 44–46, 156
windfall profits tax, 129, 148
wind power, 44, 46
Wood, Mary Christina, 109, 111, 115
work ethic, 3, 25, 118
Working Assets, 59
workplace democracy, 117
World Bank, 40, 41, 44, 48, 72, 75, 87, 93
World Basic Income (WBI), 92, 93
World Resources Institute, 70
World Wildlife Federation, 70

Y
Yakut, 114
Yang, Andrew, 2, 88
Yellowstone National Park, 107
yellow vest movement (France), 108

Z
zero loss, 105. *See also* sustainability, sustainable resource management